Education, Globalization, and the State in the Age of Terrorism

D1550437

Interventions: Education, Philosophy & Culture
Michael A. Peters & Colin Lanskhear, Series Editors

After the Death of the Subject
   by Gert Biesta

Education, Globalization, and the State in the Age of Terrorism
   edited by Michael A. Peters

Democracy, Ethics, and Education: A Thin Communitarian Approach
   by Mark Olssen

Education, Globalization, and the State in the Age of Terrorism

edited by
Michael A. Peters

Paradigm Publishers
Boulder • London

All rights reserved. No part of this publication may be transmitted or reproduced in any media or form, including electronic, mechanical, photocopy, recording, or informational storage and retrieval systems, without the express written consent of the publisher.

Copyright © 2005 by Paradigm Publishers

Published in the United States by Paradigm Publishers, 3360 Mitchell Lane, Suite C, Boulder, Colorado 80301 USA.

Paradigm Publishers is the trade name of Birkenkamp & Company, LLC, Dean Birkenkamp, President and Publisher.

Library of Congress Cataloging-in-Publication Data has been applied for.

Printed and bound in the United States of America on acid-free paper that meets the standards of the American National Standard for Permanence of Paper for Printed Library Materials.

Designed and Typeset by Straight Creek Bookmakers.

09 08 07 06 05 04
5 4 3 2 1
ISBN 1–59451–072–5 (cloth)
ISBN 1–59451–073–3 (paper)

For the many thousands of Iraqi children—those would-be citizens to come—who were killed, maimed, orphaned, and traumatized by the U.S.-U.K.–led war against Iraq.

Contents

CONTENTS

Preface

The geopolitical consequences of empire, of past administrative division and colonial policies, are always hard to predict and even harder to deal with. "Blowback" is also a reality that must be contemplated as an inevitable accompaniment to contemporary political decisions that involve regime change. Arguably, the extremist Islamic terrorist attacks on civil society in the West—most recently in Madrid—have their origin not only in the formation of extremist Islamic terrorist networks in the last twenty years, but also perhaps more profoundly in British and U.S. intervention and ongoing struggle for control of oil stakes in the Middle East, notably Iraq and Saudi Arabia, dating back at least to the 1920s. Some scholars like Samuel Huntington argue that we face a "clash of civilizations," which, if true, would emphasize an even greater historical legacy of Christian-Islamic relations now centuries old. Britain, while an architect of the military campaign against Saddam Hussein's regime and a willing partner of the U.S.-defined "war against terror," has largely escaped the terrorist ravages and attacks against civil society on their own soil in a way that other countries have not.

In the United Kingdom, where I live currently, various well-placed authorities, including Sir John Stevens, the Commissioner of Police, and Eliza Manningham-Buller, Director General of the Security Service, inform us that this immunity is unlikely to last and that it is only a matter of time before terrorists strike soft targets in London or some other British city. Stevens stated, "Since September 11 (2001), there have been 520 arrests, half have been charged with an offense and there are 90 about to go through to court" (http://www.theage.com.au/articles/2004/03/16/1079199233826.html, last accessed 21 January 2004). Manningham-

Buller is reported as saying: "I see no prospect of a significant reduction in the threat posed to the UK and its interests from international terrorism over the next five years, and I fear for a considerable number of years thereafter" (quoted in the Government discussion paper *Counter-Terrorism Powers*, see below).

Britain has begun in earnest to prepare itself for the eventuality of a terrorist strike which is regarded as inevitable. In early April 2004, Home Secretary David Blunkett appointed a minister, Hazel Blears, to take responsibility for domestic security and counter-terrorism, previously a portfolio shared with Immigration. Following the events of 11 September, the U.K. enhanced its existing anti-terrorism legislation, updating the Terrorism Act 2000 (http://www.hmso.gov.uk/acts/acts2000/20000011.htm) with the passage of the Anti-Terrorism, Crime and Security Act, 2001 (http://www.hmso.gov.uk/acts/acts2001/20010024.htm). The new act spells out provision for the forfeiture of terrorist property, freezing orders, disclosure of information, new powers of immigration and asylum, especially deportation. It also clarified the meaning of racial hatred and its relation to religion, included amendments to the Biological Weapons Act 1974 and the Chemical Weapons Act 1996 under Part 6, "Weapons of Mass Destruction," and introduced legislation for the security of pathogens and toxins, the nuclear industry and aviation. Perhaps most controversially, it granted police new powers of identification, stop, search and seizure, and addressed questions of data retention, bribery and corruption. The 2000 Act still remains the main piece of legislation. It outlaws certain terrorist groups and makes it illegal for them to operate in the U.K. (a process known as proscription), and specifically extends this proscription regime to include international terrorist groups, like al-Qaeda. It also gives police enhanced powers to investigate terrorism, including wider stop and search powers, and the power to detain suspects after arrest for up to seven days, and creates new criminal offences. Between 11 September 2001 and 31 January 2004, 544 individuals were arrested under the Terrorism Act 2000. Of those, 98 were charged with offenses under the Terrorism Act (see Table 2 of *Counter-Terrorism Powers* [see below]).

These legislative measures have taken place alongside tightened security abroad after the devastating attack on the British

Embassy in Istanbul in November 2003 and renewed efforts to coordinate anti-terrorism, rescue and civil emergency forces within British cities. A full account of British counterterrorism can be gathered from the Home Office at http://www.homeoffice.gov.uk (last accessed 21 April 2004), especially the discussion paper entitled *Counter-Terrorism Powers* (February 2004). The paper discusses the critical balance in a democracy between security and rights. It states: "The challenge, therefore, is how to retain long held and hard won freedoms and protections from the arbitrary use of power or wrongful conviction, whilst ensuring that democracy and the rule of law itself are not used as a cover by those who seek its overthrow." Yet at the same time the report goes against the recommendation of Lord Newton in seeking a derogation from the European Convention on Human Rights. Critics, including Lord Newton, who reviewed the new legislation, have argued that the new laws erode and impinge upon liberties crucial to the concept of a democracy. Significantly, although terrorism is recognized by authorities as a long-term problem, no coordinated educative response to the problem has been contemplated.

Despite the introduction of these legislative and emergency measures, and as predicted, in late March 2004 eight terror suspects in and around London—all Muslims of Pakistani descent—were arrested and held for questioning under new terror laws. The eight suspects are thought to have been planning a massive car bombing using ammonium nitrate, an easily available chemical used as agricultural fertilizer. Further, in April 2004 the metropolitan police in Greater Manchester and West Midlands arrested and questioned ten people of North African and Kurdish descent who are reported as being involved in a planned terrorist attack on British civil society, but refused to comment on media reports that the arrests thwarted a suicide attack on targets including the Manchester United soccer stadium.

Muslim youths, politicized in some mosques by radical clerics and actively recruited by older foreign provocateurs, are turning to jihad and threatening to take new religious wars into the streets of Britain. The *Times* recently carried a story headed "The Battle for Young Minds" (30 March 2003), pointing out that young unemployed male Muslims in Luton—a city that has experienced strong racial tensions going back well before the Iraq war—are the disaffected from which new Islamic extremists are created. Unemployment amongst young Muslim men in this area is reported to run at 22 percent, four times the national average. The *Times* thus provided an "ecological" explanation of violence, in part due to high poverty levels, structural unemployment and poor youth facilities. It also pictured the struggle against Islamic extremism as a battle for the minds of these young Muslims, understanding the issue principally as an *educational* struggle for a moral outlook and worldview that is distinctively British and Muslim. The problem is that young Muslims are finding it harder to maintain both identities, especially in increasingly hostile communities where there is a growing sense of unease and alienation. The arrests of the eight terror suspects is one more event that has helped to shape a culture of surveillance, suspicion, fear and vigilance where Muslims youth are more likely to be influenced by extremist imams. Some Muslim leaders have blamed Blair's war on Iraq for the growing alienation. Dr Ghayasuddin Siddiqui, leader of the Muslim Parliament of Great Britain suggested that the Blair government was using the scare of Islamic fundamentalism as a way of justifying the war. In addition, Iqbal Sacranie, the secretary general of the Muslim Council of Britain, asserted that some sections of the media actively promoted Islamophobic propaganda.

In a culture of suspicion, the risk is that youth of the United Kingdom's two-million Muslim community will increasingly experience tensions in their identity as Muslims and British subjects, sacrificing the latter for the former, especially in locations where the objective socio-economic conditions, such as high unemployment, encourage this process of identity splitting (although poverty may be only one factor and not a determining one). The situation, while not identical, is similar in the U.S., although I would not pretend to speak on the behalf of either young Muslims or any other group. The answer in part is an educative strategy that encourages a greater understanding of Western-Islamic relations in all its facets but that also affirms both parts of the couplet "British Muslim" or "American Muslim" and attempts to reinvent new cultural ways of enhancing this historical conjunction. The present West/Islam confrontation or some sections of both—conservative Christian West/radical Islam—is a simmering cauldron that has historic roots and now has become a determinant of modernity, its resolution or accommodation absolutely vital to world peace, security and development. The present crisis will not be resolved easily or within a generation. It will require dialogue across differences and will not ever be satisfactorily resolved through force or terrorism; rather, it is more likely to reach a settlement through dialogue at the level of theology and philosophy, or so I would like to believe.

I would like to thank all my contributors, scholars of international reputation engaged politically and educationally with enormously difficult issues, from the U.S., U.K., and N.Z. All of us believe that education has a crucial role to play in both understanding the present difficulties and also in contributing to a fair and constructive emergence from these dark times. I would also like to thank Dean Birkenkamp, Michael Peirce and Dianne Ewing at Paradigm Publishers, who so expertly expedited the publication of this collection and had the courage to entertain the publication of such a work.

Michael A. Peters
University of Glasgow

Acknowledgments

I would like to thank the contributors to this volume who responded at short notice to prioritize this project. They are scholars of international reputation engaged politically and educationally with enormously difficult issues from the United States, the United Kingdom, and New Zealand. All of us believe that education has a crucial role to play in both understanding the present difficulties and also in contributing to a fair and constructive emergence from these dark times.

I would also like to thank my colleagues Harry Blee, Bob Davis, Alan Britton, Jacqui Doogan of The Global Citizenship Project at the University of Glasgow, Scotland, for the opportunity to participate in the seminar program where I first presented ideas of "globalization as war" (chapter 8) and "education in an age of terrorism" (the introduction). My ideas and political views have undergone a profound transformation as a result of my involvement in this project. Finally, I would like to acknowledge and thank Dean Birkenkamp, Michael Peirce, and Dianne Ewing of Paradigm Publishing for their support and editorial guidance.

Education in the Age of Terrorism

Michael A. Peters

The authority that controlled the universal economy, if it were in American hands, would irresistibly tend to control education and training also. It might set up, as was one in the American zone in Germany, a cultural department, with ideological and political propaganda. The philanthropic passion for service would prompt social, if not legal intervention in the traditional life of all other nations, not only by selling there innumerable American products, but by recommending, if not imposing, American ways of living and thinking.
—*George Santayana*, Dominations and Powers: Reflections on Liberty, Society and Government *(Clifton: Augustus M. Kelly, 1972, p. 91)*

[T]he most egregious globalization has been the exploitation and abuse of children in war, pornography, poverty, and sex tourism. Children have been soldiers and victims in the

1

raging ethnic and religious wars; children are the majority of the global cohort that suffers poverty, disease and starvation. Children are our terrorists-to-be because they are so obviously not our citizens to come.

Benjamin R. Barber, Jihad vs. McWorld: Terrorism's Challenge to Democracy *(London: Corgi, 2003, p. xxvii)*

1. There Are Many Ways to Be Modern

There has been a spate of books following September 11 and the wars on Afghanistan and Iraq that seek to uncover the real motives behind attacks and counterattacks both by and on the West. Some of these works seek to inquire into the deeper historical causes and reasons why the tenor of post-Cold War politics has degenerated from the advertised safe global world we were promised—after the "end of ideology"—in the "new world order." We were told by the likes of Francis Fukuyama that with liberalism in the ascendancy, after the collapse of communism all that was left to do was the "tidying up" of a few local skirmishes. Geoffrey Robertson (2000, 473), the noted English QC and specialist in international law, begins the last chapter—"Terrorism: 11 September and Beyond"—of his book *Crimes Against Humanity: The Struggle for Global Justice* with the following comment: "On 10 September it might have been said with some confidence that the third age of human rights, that epoch in which basic humanitarian norms will achieve some level of enforcement, was underway." He indicates how 42 states had ratified the Rome Statute, the International Criminal Court had finally been established, Milošević was in the docks, East Timor was busy nation-building, old enmities had settled down, and the world looked as though it was making progress on the advancement of civil and political rights. Then, he suggests "out of the blue" came the September 11 attacks. Western intelligence did not see it coming. And yet al-Qaeda had attacked an Aden hotel in 1992 and al-Qaeda had made the bomb that demolished the New York World Trade Center in 1993. Al-Qaeda links were traced to killing American soldiers in Mogadishu and in Saudi Arabia in 1995–6.[1]

Some writers have sought to provide the inside story on al-Qaeda, or the Bush "neo-cons," while others have focused on larger issues separating the Islamic world from the West, and still others have probed behind contemporary events to discuss pivotal historical trends and emerging events. Let me take three prominent examples that are representative of the literature I describe.[2] Benjamin R. Barber's *Jihad vs McWorld*, originally published in 1995, explains the confrontation between two worlds as a struggle that has put into question the "seemingly ineluctable march" of a secularized, free-market, commercialized and materialist McWorld "into a complacent postmodernity" (2003, xi). His major argument is that the modern response to the clash between Jihad and McWorld—a trope echoing Samuel Huntington's "clash of civilizations"—cannot be simply military but "must entail a commitment to democracy and justice even when they are in tension with the commitment to cultural expansionism and global markets" (xi-xii). Democracy is the instrument, Barber argues, by which we can avoid the choice between "a sterile cultural monism (McWorld) and a raging cultural fundamentalism (Jihad)" (xiii).

In one sense I think Barber is right. The fundamental challenge for the West and for Western education is in promoting a form of political education that highlights and takes into account the quotation from Barber with which I have begun this introduction: "Children are our terrorists-to-be because they are so obviously not our citizens to come." But this would have to be a form of political education that is not based on the logic of *conversion* or crass assimilation to American or Western values but to an as-yet unformulated ethos of a world civic space and concept of world citizenship. Such a vision may not be based on a simple projection of Kant's "perpetual peace," although it might invoke a kind of cosmopolitanism that can still be shaped through participation, dialogue, and exchange of world cultures.

In a world split between Jihad and McWorld the question of education in its two dominant political forms—multiculturalism and citizenship education—can no longer be viewed simply as "therapies" of the modern state designed to enhance the workings of a pluralistic political culture. More radically, education must actively reach beyond the confines of the modern state and the project of nation-building to establish an orientation to the Other in cultural and political terms as a basis of a new internationalism and world civic culture. The question is what forms "democratic education" should take in this context and whether education can help steer a course between mutually unacceptable alternatives. Certainly, the promise of Western education in the longer term is more to do with renouncing its ethnocentrism in order to debate with other cultural and educational traditions philosophical and theological questions concerning religious faith and its role in the political order and in the process of modernization. The Western academy must promote Islamic studies and Arabic languages and engage with Islamic scholars on a broad range of topics. Ultimately, in this intergenerational struggle, philosophy and theology are more powerful tools of mutual transformation than bombs, missiles, and military force.

Not so differently, John Gray (2003, 1–2), in *Al Qaeda and What It Means to Be Modern,* explains that al-Qaeda is a "by-product of globalisation" whose most distinctive feature is the "projection of a privatised form of organised violence worldwide" and whose closest models are not medieval assassins but "the revolutionary anarchists of late-nineteenth century Europe." He makes the Baudrillardian point that the attack on the World Trade Center did more than kill thousands of civilians.[3] The spectacular event also "destroyed the West's ruling myth" that modernity is "a single condition, everywhere the same and always benign." He elaborates:

> As societies become more modern, so they become more alike. At the same time they become better. Being modern means realising our values—the values of the Enlightenment, as we like to think of them (1).

Gray very firmly demonstrates that revolutionary terror is "a modern invention" and that al-Qaeda is also modern (I would say postmodern). He also neatly demonstrates that "[t]here are many ways of being modern, some of them monstrous," and he tracks three modern projects—Positivism, Communism, and Nazism. All three projects defined themselves as modern and as the basis of universal civilization. He continues: "It came to be that only American-style 'democratic capitalism' is truly modern, and that it is destined to spread everywhere. As it does, a universal civilization will come into being, and history will come to an end"

(3). Yet radical Islam, insofar as it is represented in al-Qaeda, is also modern, although the West likes to depict it as a medieval relic. While it is anti-Western, it is shaped as much by Western ideology as it is by Islamic traditions. Gray argues, "Like Marxists and neo-liberals, radical Islamists see history as a prelude to a new world. All are convinced they can remake the human condition. If there is a uniquely modern myth, this is it." And he concludes his argument with the idea that part of the modern myth is that science—read also education in its broadest sense—enables humanity to "take charge of its destiny; but 'humanity' is itself a myth, a dusty remnant of religious faith" (4).

I am largely in sympathy with Gray's argument. His little book serves as a moralizing tale (in the best polemical sense) that not only details "the original modernisers" (Saint-Simon, Comte, etc.) but also provides "[a] very short history of the global free market" (Chapter 4) and an analysis of both "[g]eopolitics and the limits of growth" and "Pax Americana?" before emphasizing "Why we still do not know what it means to be modern" (Chapter 8). He correctly points out that the word itself only appeared at the end of the sixteenth century to become gradually associated with the idea of novelty and the new, finally coming to convey the Enlightenment view of a deliberate break with the past—that the future would be different from the past. He thrusts home the point of his argument:

> Western societies are ruled by the myth that, as the rest of the world absorbs science and becomes modern, it is bound to become secular, enlightened and peaceful—as contrary to all evidence, they imagine themselves to be (118).

He adds a further paradox: "Al Qaeda destroyed this myth; and yet it continues to be believed" (118).

What disheartens me a little with Gray's analysis is that he does not capitalize on his argument. Perhaps within the space of a little book there is not the space to do so. Perhaps he wanted to end on a provocative note, without suggesting a way forward. Gray's argument certainly should sensitize us to the fact that American-style "democratic capitalism" is itself, after all, only another way of being modern and, thus, also a modernist ideology of the future.

From Gray's perspective Barber needs to convince us that democracy can be uncoupled from American capitalism, that the influence of the multinationals does not structure extranational political space in its own interests, and that there is room, therefore, for the project of a world civic culture and political education appropriate to its needs. Barber needs also to address this question as a future possibility: How possible is Barber's scenario and can the Western powers ever really divorce themselves from their national self-interest that has structured their approach to foreign policy in the Middle East since the turn of the last century?

There are many possible responses to Gray's argument that depend not only on a greater awareness of historiography and philosophy of history—modes of consciousness based on models of conceiving historical time—but also on the *actual* history of the ancient Mediterranean together with its first encounters between East and West (see, for example, Braudel 2001) and the analysis of forms of cultural diffusion upon which the Greek ideal is based. These methods of analysis need to be put side by side with both the philosophical investigation of European humanism and its contemporary expression in the new European constitution with its charter of fundamental human rights. What is the promise of Europe? Does Europe offer a distinct way forward or an alternative moral and political vision of globalization? Is there a form of humanism that is sufficiently self-reflexive and open to cultural development to serve as a platform both for cosmopolitical institutions and a project of political education?[4]

In the last work I am going to cite, two of the world's leading philosophers—Habermas and Derrida—normally antagonistic, stand side by side for the first time. In *Philosophy in a Time of Terror,* Giovanna Borradori (2003) conducts dialogues with Habermas and Derrida as well as providing an essay in each case analyzing their work in relation to terrorism—both reconstructing and deconstructing terror. Borradori sets up two models of public participation, political activism symbolized by Bertrand Russell, and social critique symbolized by Hannah Arendt. Borradori works hard to find the similarities between Habermas and Derrida: they are both more like Arendt than Russell; they are "post-Holocaust philosophers" who display a commitment to "human laws and institutions as they evolve through time" (13). Borradori writes that they share an understanding of the experience of history as trauma: "Both of them have encountered and embraced philosophy in the context of the traumas of twentieth-century European history: colonialism, totalitarianism, and the Holocaust. Their contributions to the subject of 9/11 and global terrorism follow in the same vein" (8–9). In a newly globalized world, both share an allegiance to the Enlightenment, even if they differ over the understanding of "tolerance" and its relevance to democratic society. Where Habermas attributes universal value to tolerance, along with republican institutions and democratic participation, Derrida suggests that its roots in the Christian concept of charity, defeats the possibility of its universalization and its use in secular contexts. For Habermas, religious intolerance—a fundamentalism of the *modern* age—constitutes a defensive reaction against modernism and its uprooting of traditional forms of life. The violence of terrorism that springs from fundamentalism Habermas understands as a form of communicative pathology that follows from the spiral of mistrust that leads to a breakdown of communication. Thus, only reason, understood as transparent and non-manipulative communication, can possibly cure or overcome the problems of terrorism—a symptom of modernization. For Derrida, by contrast, terrorism is a symptom of an autoimmune disorder where defensive mechanisms designed to protect the system end up by "suiciding" and turning the system against itself. The biological paradigm of autoimmunity and its breakdown takes many forms—the breakdown of communication is clearly only one form (albeit a highly significant one in a media-saturated society). Its cure is both painful and time-consuming.

My brief response to this dialogue is to see in it some hope. I would want to explore with Habermas the congruence of forms of political education with his notion of communicative reason, not necessarily construed simply as a democratic conversation "among friends" or even considering democracy as the method of inquiry. Broadly, what are the hopes for communication reason as the telos for a conversation among adversaries? Derrida's response provides us with a biohistorical analysis based on three moments comprising the "Cold War," the "end of the Cold War," and the "balance of terror." His analysis of terrorism in terms of the breakdown of autoimmunity draws attention to the system as a whole and the structural oppression built into current processes of globalization. Perhaps we can conceive of political education as a cure to the breakdown of autoimmunity—a form of education that educates world citizens for a kind of cosmopolitanism without the presupposition of state sovereignty, that is, a form of democracy-to-come based on global social justice. Certainly, such a vision might imply a form of human rights education, although its pedagogy would need to be consistent with the ideals it espouses.

Derrida and Habermas provide us with useful analyses that extend aspects of Barber's and Gray's theses. They elaborate the historical context within which terrorism should be understood—in part, as a symptom of the modernization process in its new phase of globalization. They thereby draw our attention to the structural oppressions built into this process—not only its historical dimensions but also its future projections. Whether the violence of terrorism should be understood as pathology of communication or autoimmune disease, both Derrida and Habermas provide some historical reminders of the structural conditions of global justice that must prevail if world democracy is to have a chance. Realistically, they inform us that the project of world democracy will be neither easy nor quick.

We need to inquire into the history and structure of violence and terror as violence. Is it as it has always been? Are there new conditions for the spawning of terror that have come about with the advent of globalization?

2. Postmodern Terror in a Globalized World

Just as the state form itself is changing, so too are forms of war, resistance, and terrorism. As the postmodern European system of states based on transparency, mutual surveillance, and economic interdependency (Cooper 2000) evolves and moves toward its final constitutional form, so too new forms of terrorism have developed that are different from its predominantly modern form.[5] The postmodern European state system operates according to a new logic and it is unimaginable that member states would attack each other. By contrast, when confronted with premodern zones of anarchy—weak states intimidated by mafia bosses, drug lords or terrorists—Cooper (2000) argues, the modern or postmodern state must intervene.[6] The world now confronts postmodern forms of terrorism that have invented new rules to play an old game (Laqueur 1996).[7]

Postmodern terrorists are both less ideological than their 1960s and '70s counterparts and yet more committed on grounds of religious and ethnic grievances.[8] While Marxist-Leninist militant groups survive, the initiative has passed from the left to the extreme, fundamentalist right. Terrorism, whether domestic or international—and increasingly in a borderless world the line is harder to draw—tends to be neither left nor right but rather ethnic and separatist. Postmodern terrorism seemingly has no limits, no inside or outside; it is transnational, truly global, highly mobile, and cellular. It makes use of new global technologies in communication and information exchange; cells are "intelligent networks," able to conduct surveillance and decode and hack into official systems and databases. Cyberterrorism is a reality as airport controllers have discovered to their dismay.[9] Postmodern terrorism is also telegenic: It is aware that wars and terrorism must use the media in all its forms to shape the subjectivities of the viewing public. Militarily, postmodern terrorism avails itself of the latest developments in light weaponry and at the same time poses a threat to state nuclear arsenals and supplies. It can also be small-scale yet "high-tech," especially in the new area of biotechnology and its application in biological warfare. It bases itself on the principle of asymmetry, turning back upon itself the sophisticated technological systems of the postindustrial West—not only the weaponization of civilian aviation as in the case of September 11, but also the weaponization of all facilities, including water supplies, gas stations, transport systems, and the like. Postmodern terrorism is sensitive to its business and funding sources, often in cahoots with global crime, especially the powerful drug lords and cartels. Of all the changes in the nature of terrorism, perhaps the most important is that in recent decades many militant organizations have developed political as well as military arms, encouraging a division of labor that provides education and social services and engages in the normal activities of business and politics while a dissociated military arm carries out terrorism (Laqueur 1996). Above all, postmodern terrorism has many faces: School boy friends with a grudge against their classmates; the Christian fundamentalist who bombs abortion clinics; the computer hacker next door; and transnational, state-sponsored terrorism. Terrorism is on the rise in both advanced societies and in the stateless "zones of anarchy." In this environment we no longer have the "peace education" that developed out of the Peace Corps and propaganda of the Cold War but "education for war" or "education for empire"—an accent on the preparedness and training for terrorist attacks, a perpetual civil vigil and emphasis on "homeland security," a veritable rush of information, analysis, courses, reports, and Internet resources centering on "strategic education."[10]

In contrast to the view of political education—at once pluralist, internationalist, and aimed at world democracy—that I have been exploring in the first section of the paper by reference to Barber, Gray, Habermas, and Derrida, we might also distinguish an opposing notion of "education for war" that conceives of education as a form of counterterrorism. Education as counterterrorism is essentially content- and ideologically driven, oriented toward civil readiness or preparedness against the possibility of attack, and based on a defensive mentality. In exploring the differences between these two broad conceptions of education we need to focus on the structure of political violence, its representation and definition, and the best possible educational response to it.

In the remainder of this paper I examine the "war on terrorism," focusing on "Operation Enduring Freedom," and analyze definitions of patterns of global terror by reference to the U.S. State Department's (2003) *Patterns of Global Terrorism, 2002* and the United Nations' *Report of the Policy Working Group on the United Nations and Terrorism*, which provide contrasting accounts of "terrorism" and educational responses to it. On the one hand, the U.S. response can be seen as a variant of "education for war," whereas the U.N. response typifies a working practical example of political education focused on the U.N. ideology of human rights.

3. The War on Terrorism: "Operation Enduring Freedom"

After the 11 September 2001 attacks on the World Trade Center and the Pentagon, the United States military entered into a war against global terrorism. President Bush declared a War on Terrorism. This war was unlike any other that the United States had engaged in; it was not declared against a specific state (cf., War on Drugs); it was fought on both domestic and foreign soil; and it required massive coordination of resources—military, financial, and political. The military response to the 11 September 2001 terrorist attacks on the United States was called Operation Enduring Freedom. President Bush addressed a joint session of Congress on 20 September to announce a "war on terror." He demanded of the Taliban leadership in Afghanistan that it turn over all the leaders of the al-Qaeda terrorist group based in that country, close every terrorist training camp there, hand over all terrorists to appropriate authorities, and give the United States full access to terrorist training camps. He added:

> The terrorists practice a fringe form of Islamic extremism that has been rejected by Muslim scholars and the vast majority of Muslim clerics—a fringe movement that perverts the peaceful teachings of Islam. The terrorists' directive commands them to kill Christians and Jews, to kill all Americans, and make no distinctions among military and civilians, including women and children. (http://www.globalsecurity.org/military/library/news/2001/09/mil-010920-usia01.htm)

Bush was careful in this speech to distinguish between Muslims and the terrorists. The speech itself is structured around a series of questions: "Americans are asking . . . Who attacked our country? . . . Why do they hate us? . . . How will we fight and win this war? . . . What is expected of us?" Bush's analysis of the second question is interesting in that he suggests "They hate our freedoms—our freedom of religion, our freedom of speech, our freedom to vote and assemble and disagree with each other." In this response Bush's speechwriters tend to simplify, to propagandize, to jingoize, and to overlook the growing anti-Americanism that has intensified since 9/11, which is not limited to the terrorist organizations he names.

Bush also announced a different coordinated kind of war that is unprecedented in America's history, and which is ongoing and integrates military strategy with a range of other measures, including new provisions for homeland security. On 7 October 2001,

Bush announced that the U.S. military had launched strikes against al-Qaeda terrorist camps and Taliban military installations in Afghanistan. In the 7 October speech he spelled out the objectives of Operation Enduring Freedom:

> This military action is a part of our campaign against terrorism, another front in a war that has already been joined through diplomacy, intelligence, the freezing of financial assets and the arrests of known terrorists by law enforcement agents in 38 countries. Given the nature and reach of our enemies, we will win this conflict by the patient accumulation of successes, by meeting a series of challenges with determination and will and purpose. (http://www.globalsecurity.org/military/library/news/2001/10/mil-011007–usia01.htm

Campaign objectives were laid out by the British government also, in terms of a set of immediate objectives focused on the capture of Osama bin Laden and other al-Qaeda leaders, the prevention of further attacks by al-Qaeda, and the removal of Mullah Omar and the Taliban regime. Wider goals included the end of terrorism, the deterrence of state sponsorship of terrorism, and the reintegration of Afghanistan into the international community.

Compare the U.K. public discussion paper *The Strategic Defence Review: A New Chapter* (http://www.mod.uk/issues/sdr/new_chapter/pubdisppr.htm). In this document the Ministry of Defence commented upon "Tackling the Basis of Terrorism," indicating that politics, religion, and ideology might generate terrorism but equally may produce the sets of values that lead to the rejection of terrorism. The discussion paper then considers the contribution that conflict, failures of good governance and social justice, and economic factors might make in causing terrorism, while making clear that such understanding never amounts to a justification for resorting to terrorism. The document continues:

> Whilst the causes of terrorism can be found in a mixture of social, political and economic factors, the key seems to lie in gaining specific understanding of the particular political conditions within which particular groups emerge and operate. In taking short-term action against the symptoms of terrorism, we need to minimize the risk of contributing, in the long-term, to its causes.

The events that transpired following the attack against al-Qaeda and the Taliban regime in Afghanistan, leading up to the war against Iraq, have indicated for some commentators a risky unilateralism by the United States-United Kingdom, which has in some instances resulted in the curtailing of liberties at home and the suspension of the international rule of law and human rights. Some scholars have argued that the risks of blowback and reprisal are greater now than before and that the U.S.-U.K. war against Iraq signally failed to develop a global coalition against terrorism. Moreover, given that most of the new "international terrorist" groups named by the United States are Islamic, the fraternization with Israel and the dominance of pro-Israel elements advising the White House has imperiled and prevented the necessary dialogue with Arab nations (Kellner 2002). Indeed, Sardar and Davies (2002, 7) argue "a more careful and imaginative approach to US foreign policy is essential if worldwide anti-American feeling is not to spiral out of control." They note that the events of 9/11 "have spawned innumerable courses and classroom initiatives at all levels of the US education system" and write:

> It is one of our central arguments that at the heart of relation between America and the rest of the world stands a problem of knowledge. In precise terms, we call it the problem of 'knowledgeable ignorance': knowing people, ideas, civilizations, religions, histories as something they are not, and could not possibly be, and maintaining these ideas even when the means exist to know differently. Knowledgeable ignorance is a term applied to the Western view of Islam and Muslims in particular. It refers to more than general negative attitudes and ideas; it defines the way in which such attitudes are built into an approach to knowledge, a body of study and expertise called Orientalism (12).

4. Definitions and Patterns of Terrorism: U.S. vs. U.N.

Definitions of terrorism are notoriously difficult to draft, and the lack of agreement on a definition of terrorism has been a major obstacle to meaningful international countermeasures. Current definitions of terrorism fail to capture the magnitude of the problem worldwide and tend to falter around differences of political ideology: one state's "terrorist" is another state's "freedom fighter." Witness the status of Nelson Mandela and the African National Congress before, during, and after apartheid. U.N. Member States still have not agreed upon a definition. The League of Nations Convention in 1937 came up with the following definition: "All criminal acts directed against a State and intended or calculated to create a state of terror in the minds of particular persons or a group of persons or the general public." A.P. Schmid, a terrorist expert, in 1992 suggested in a report for the then U.N. Crime Branch that terrorism might be best defined in terms of a peacetime equivalent of "war crime," incorporating deliberate attacks on civilians, hostage taking, and the killing of prisoners. The U.S. State Department uses the definition contained in Title 22 of the United States Code (Section 2656f[d]):

> The term "terrorism" means premeditated, politically motivated violence perpetrated against noncombatant targets by subnational groups or clandestine agents, usually intended to influence an audience. The term "international terrorism" means terrorism involving citizens or the territory of more than one country. The term "terrorist group" means any group practicing, or that has significant subgroups that practice, international terrorism.[11]

The U.N., by contrast, has refrained from adopting any single comprehensive definition. It defines terrorism in terms less equivocal than the United States:

> Terrorism is, in most cases, essentially a political act. It is meant to inflict dramatic and deadly injury on civilians and to create an atmosphere of fear, generally for a political or ideological (whether secular or religious) purpose. Terrorism is a criminal act, but it is more than mere criminality. To overcome the problem of terrorism it is necessary to understand its political nature as well as its basic criminality and psychology (5).

The U.S. definition does not seem to allow for the possibility that terror may be a state activity—not simply "state-sponsored"—whereas the U.N. definition is more open, acknowledging the difficulties of self-serving and semantic-ideological dimensions of legal classification, especially in international law.

Organized political violence increasingly is aimed at civilians and civil spaces, yet it has become increasingly difficult to distinguish combatants from victims.[12] One question concerns international terrorism and how the existing international political order should respond to violence instigated by nonstate actors. Some scholars argue that the international system of nation-states now pervasively modeled on Western democracies should be strengthened. Warfare then should be regulated by international convention. Others argue that Western nation-states, which foster decentralized warfare by perpetrating inequalities among nations, are the real problem. For some, terrorism threatens an ideal political order in which war is only fought according to rules agreed upon among states ("just war" theory). As nonstate actors, terrorists operate outside the rule of law and, unlike state armies, deliberately attack civilian populations and facilities (Hoffman 1998). Yet this analysis seems to exempt Western powers, as the originators of the international rules of war, from self-examination and precludes the possibility that they could sponsor or perpetrate political violence themselves. It also ignores the critique of Western militarism, the growth of the arms industry as part of the military-research-industrial complex, the indirect forms of warfare waged on the underdeveloped world, and the way in which militarism is and always has been a daily part of the social and institutional fabric of the Western way of life.[13]

The representation of political violence as *terrorism*—its narrativization and its embodiment as a discourse—reifies it, cutting it off from other forms of violent behavior, and often disguises or prevents examination of claims to political legitimacy.[14] In particular, the representation of terrorism by globalized media and in official discourse can reduce the complexities and ignore the ethnic and gender differences of organized violence.

Patterns of Global Terrorism, 2002—U.S. Department of State (2003)

Ambassador Cofer Black, Coordinator for Counterterrorism, indicates that the war on terrorism has five fronts: diplomatic, intelligence, law enforcement, financial, and military. He reports on the four principles of U.S. counterterrorism strategy: make no concessions to terrorists and strike no deals; bring terrorists to justice for their claims; isolate and apply pressure on states that sponsor terrorism to force them to change their behavior;[15] bolster the counterterrorist capabilities of those countries that work with the United States and require assistance.

The U.S. State Department report provides an overview of all major regions of the world and state-sponsored terrorism. In some ways the appendices are more informative, although statistical analysis on an annual basis is easily distorted through the cataclysmic event. Appendix A provides a chronology of significant terrorist incidents for 2002. Of 134 incidents including some 33 different countries, India scores highest with 67 incidents followed by West Bank and Israel (15), and Pakistan (9). Appendix B, which provides background on designated foreign terrorist organizations, lists a total of 36 organizations, of which 22 are Islamic and 14 non-Islamic. Many of the non-Islamic organizations are classified as Marxist-Leninist or Maoist and were established during the 1960s and 1970s. The vast majority of the named Islamic organizations were established in the 1980s and '90s, although there are some Islamic groups (Marxist/religious) that date from the 1970s or earlier. What the data reveal is the new waves of Islamic terrorist organizations set up in the last couple of decades.[16] These named terrorist groups make up a much larger group of some 250 terrorist groups and entities designated by the U.S.

Report of the Policy Working Group on the U.N. and Terrorism

The U.N. places a great deal of importance on understanding terrorism and on an educative response to it. The *Report of the Policy Working Group* places great emphasis on a tripartite strategy of *dissuasion* of disaffected groups, *denial* of the means to carry out terrorism, and *sustaining* broad-based international cooperation in the struggle against terrorism. Dissuasion is based upon norm-setting, human rights, and communication—clearly an educative set of functions. The Working Group recognizes that terrorism often thrives where human rights are violated and where there is lack of hope for social justice; therefore, the promotion of human rights (and the ideology of the U.N.) becomes the basic response. Denial of opportunity for the commission of acts of terrorism, together with more systematic international counterterrorism co-operation, defines the approach of the U.N. that is based on the U.N.'s comparative advantage. The Working Group also set up eight subgroups to address specific issues, including international legal instruments, human rights, weapons of mass destruction (WMD), counterterrorism, media and communications, and the use of ideology to justify terrorism. The U.N. report does recognize that transnational networks are a relatively new phenomenon and that the spillover effects of terrorism, including cross-border violence, make it difficult to draw sharp distinctions between domestic and international terrorism. The U.N. is also more forthright than the U.S. State Department in acknowledging "terror has been adopted by rules at various times as an instrument of control." This means "the rubric of counter-terrorism can be used to justify acts in support of political agendas, such as the consolidation of political power, elimination of dissent and/or suppression of resistance to military occupation." Perhaps most importantly in these times, the U.N. recognizes "Labelling opponents or adversaries as terrorists offers a time-tested technique to delegitimize and demonize them" (p. 5).

The U.N. report provides a set of 31 recommendations under dissuasion (international legal instruments and nonlegal norm-setting), denial (counterterrorism committee, disarmament, and preventive measures), and cooperation (non-U.N. multinational initiatives and coordination of U.N. system). Importantly, the U.N. emphasizes the premise that counterterrorism must be firmly grounded in international law and that terrorists ought to be tried before the International Criminal Court. The U.N. stresses a universalism based on human rights ideology framed within the international rule of law, which places it in some tension with U.S. solutions that tend to be less constrained by the international rule of law and more Ameri-centric. The U.N. also places great stress on information-enhancement and a strong role for education as revealed through its emphasis on human rights and nonlegal norm setting. Recommendations 8 and 9 refer to information enhancement, while recommendation 10 focuses on dissemination of the work of the U.N. agencies that relate to terror, including UNESCO's role in relation to "educational initiatives, such as curricula reform, that aim to increase understanding, encourage tolerance and respect for human dignity, while reducing mutual distrust between communities in conflict." Recommendation 10 reads:

> Elements of the United Nations system which address the issue of education should meet to determine how best to mount a coherent worldwide program to assist countries in which educational systems need support or that are under control of groups advocating terror.

And Recommendation 11 provides a kind of guide to curricula:

> Continue emphasizing the importance to the fight against terrorism of existing United Nations work in the area of human rights, democratic capacity-building, and social and economic justice.

5. Postscript

The world has changed since 9/11. There is a greater awareness of the vulnerability of global civil society, increasingly articulated in cybernetic terms. If there is one thing that commentators seem to agree upon, it is that we are dealing with or experiencing a new phenomenon. Paul Gilbert (2003) entitles his book *New Terror, New Wars* and he contrasts conditions, conduct, roles, and identities of the Falklands conflict of 1982 with the so-called "War on Terror." Walter Laquer (1996) also acknowledged well before the terrorist event we refer to as 9/11 that terrorism itself had changed:

> Society has also become vulnerable to a new kind of terrorism, in which the destructive power of both the individual terrorist and terrorism as a tactic are infinitely greater. Earlier terrorists could kill kings or high officials, but others only too eager to inherit their mantle quickly stepped in. The advanced societies of today are more dependent every day on the electronic storage, retrieval, analysis, and transmission of information. Defense, the police, banking, trade, transportation, scientific work, and a large percentage of the government's and the private sector's transactions are on-line. That exposes enormous vital areas of national life to mischief or sabotage by any computer hacker, and concerted sabotage could render a country unable to function. Hence the growing speculation about infoterrorism and cyberwarfare.

There are also different responses to what I have called "postmodern terror." We can in terms of the above discussion, for instance, identify two contrasting responses: the one typified by the U.S. State Department, which I call "defensive modernism." By this I mean that the newly created, massively funded Department of Homeland Security is designed to turn the U.S. into "fortress America," supplemented by a national defense and security strategy aimed at "regime change." This response is accompanied by what I have called "education for war." The second response is a more considered form of political education, based on "dissuasion, denial, and cooperation." It is less willing to declare a "war on terrorism" and seeks to provide an alternative rights-based program.

If there is agreement among commentators, it is that new terrorism and new wars are, as Gilbert (2003, 10) puts it, "essentially, manifestations of the politics of identity," which presupposes that "one enters life as a person with a particular collective identity." Reinhard Schulze (2002, xiii) makes a similar point in relation to his study of the Islamic world when he argues that "[a]t the end of the 1980s, the great ideological narratives had ostensibly spun their tales, fizzled out," and "social utopias went out of fashion." He suggests that "globalization re-created 'culture' as an effective and powerful concept of its own in order to newly determine hierarchies on a global level," and as a response classical Islamism "turned increasingly into a kind of ethical conservatism, based on the assumption that ethical values should be safeguarded in the face of globalization." If this is so, or if something very like it is the case, then the question of understanding and responding to terrorism must begin with an appreciation of globalization and the politics of identity. A critical question in this regard, for instance, is whether British or American Muslims can sustain both aspects of their identities—Britishness and Americanness, on the one hand, and being a Muslim, on the other—without sacrificing or accommodating one to the other. Increasingly, it seems that young British and American Muslims are finding it harder to identify as British or American as the war on terrorism unfolds and they come to perceive what they take to be injustices and, under greater state surveillance and scrutiny, come to experience forms of alienation from mainstream society. The philosophy of terrorism and war must also recognize this changed context in order to answer questions concerning both whether terrorism is ever morally justified and whether war is a morally justified response to it. Both philosophical questions, considered within the context of international justice, must now come to terms with the *cultural* nature of religions and moral traditions and the possibilities for radical cross-cultural dialogue, reflection, and discussion. These are essentially educational and pedagogical questions.

The Organization of This Book

It is clear that education already plays an important role in challenging, combating, and providing tools for understanding terrorism in its different forms, whether as counterterrorism or as a form of human rights education. Of course these two dominant conceptions do not exhaust the possibilities or the promise of education in relation to terrorism, globalization, and empire. Just as education has played a significant role in the process of nation-building, crucial to new nation-states, so education also plays a strong role in both the process of empire, of globalization and of resistance to global forces, and of terrorism, especially where it is linked to emergent statehood.

In the opening chapter, Douglas Kellner argues that critical educators need to understand the conflicts and contradictions of globalization and the terrors it inflicts in order to develop appropriate pedagogies that can maintain relevance in the present age. He links the terror attacks of September 11 to dimensions of globalization and provides a critical theory of globalization, before suggesting pedagogical initiatives for the democratic reconstruction of education after 9/11. As Kellner explains in his first footnote, the chapter is part of a much broader project and view on globalization, new technologies, and their role within education. He provides a flavor of his project in concluding:

> [I]n opposition to the globalization of corporate and state capitalism, I would advocate an oppositional democratic, pedagogical, and cosmopolitan globalization, which supports individuals and groups using information and multimedia technologies to create a

more multicultural, egalitarian, democratic, and ecological globalization.

And he develops an account of postmodern pedagogy, which
draws on the concept of *multiple literacies*—at once cultural, social, and ecological—as a basis for the empowerment of students
and citizens, as well as the use of emergent technologies to create
a better society and to enhance democratic participation.

In chapter 2, Tom Steele and Richard Taylor draw on the inspiration of Plato and Aristotle to argue that "civic education is central to republican and democratic government not simply to inform the populace of its duties but to imagine and reinvent those
radical utopias that are necessary for *eudaemonia* or the good life
of all." They focus on the concept of citizenship, which is necessary in their eyes for a healthy democracy to function in the context of globalization, and, in turn, they consider its classical forms
and historical origins, the role of the nation-state and the international rule of law in the light of globalization, and, finally, the
prospects for global citizenship in relation to cultural difference
and pluralism. They conclude by tackling the thorny question of
whether Western notions of democratic citizenship can accommodate the religious and ethnic forms of government and embrace cultural difference while promoting universal human rights.

In "Globalization, Family Terrorism and Feminism Post-9/11"
(chapter 3), Rhonda Hammer argues for a critical feminist theoretical perspective on globalization, which enables an understanding of
the patriarchal nature of terrorism and the appreciation of both local
and global analyses of "family terrorism." It is an approach that draws
on theories of colonization to emphasize the importance of social
relations and the role of alienation in the practices of terrorism. It is
also an approach that grounds itself in the familial relations of the
domestic sphere and public domain in "the globalized world of neoliberal capitalism" and employs a transformative agenda of social
justice that attempts to realize difference and solidarity. For Hammer this transformative perspective is "cognizant of the hierarchical
natures of a multiplicity of patriarchal relations," including

pathological families, overt and blatant segregated communities, governments and businesses, nation states, nationalized

organizations, fundamentalist religious ideologies, and, especially contemporary forms of militarism which, many argue, are provoking genocidal terrorist policies directed, primarily, at women, children, and the elderly.

In chapter 4, Tina Besley discusses how some sections of youth in the United Kingdom constructed their own identities through their participation in a series of antiwar protests and the use of new media technologies in citizenship education projects. Her chapter makes use of Foucault's "technologies of the self" and his rehabilitation of the classical Greek concept of *parrhesia* (normally rendered as "free speech") as the means to understand and analyze how youth constitute themselves in response to globalization, the mass media, information technology, and consumer society. Besley, thus, demonstrates that the question of youth self-constitution does not necessarily focus solely on questions of style and lifestyle in the narcissistic consumerist sense. She explores the way in which youth in the United Kingdom have become politically radicalized in response to the war against Iraq and she examines the way in which much of the information, communication, and organization for youth anti-war protests took place outside the classroom. She puts up a powerful argument "that teachers now need to pay attention to the ways that youth construct themselves in a globalized postmodern world in relation to the Other, and in response to threats to the security of their world."

In the chapter "Globalization, the Third Way and Education Post–9/11: Building Democratic Citizenship" (chapter 5), Mark Olssen suggests that terrorism "forces a new consideration of the themes of democracy, community and individual rights" that must entail a new understanding of citizenship and the role of education in its creation. Olssen is worried that terrorism has altered the terms of the contract between the state and the individual and between collective interests and individual rights, imperiling traditional rights and liberties. A new postliberal political settlement involves neo-liberal policies in the economic sphere and the erosion of traditional liberties in the political sphere, including increased surveillance and data gathering on citizens. It is in this new context that Olssen reassesses the role of education and the possibilities for rebuilding democratic citizenship.

In chapter 6, Henry Giroux talks of "democracy under siege" in a "culture of permanent war," dedicated to combating terrorism. In this situation and under the influence of the right, the U.S. state has reneged on its social welfare functions and social democratic responsibilities, substituting the principle of security that has licensed a greater militarization and an accompanying shift privileging property rights over human rights. Giroux's fierce criticisms are directed at the Bush administration. He writes:

> Bush's permanent war strategy, discourse of anti-terrorism, and rhetoric of moral absolutes promote democracy neither abroad nor at home, and their alleged value can best be understood in the hard currency of human suffering that children all over the globe are increasingly forced to pay.

In "Education and War: Primary Constituents of the Contemporary World System" (chapter 7), Cliff Falk investigates the relationships among education, war, and subjectivity. Falk argues that an overview of these connections allows us to see the ways in which education is a function of war. He maintains that "post World War II expansion of the educational system and knowledge production was more a function of war than of general cultural and economic development." In this view, the martial intrusion into the school and university is a result of the operation of the military/capitalist complex, which in large part determines budgets and funding of knowledge production in the universities and subject formation in the schools. He quotes the French theorist Paul Virilio to good effect: "All of us are already civilian soldiers without knowing it. And some of us know it. The great stroke of luck for the military class's terrorism is that no one recognizes it. People don't recognize the militarized part of their identity, of their consciousness." In a radical thesis Falk plots the growing privatization, militarization, and marketization of education.

Finally, in chapter 8, entitled "War as Globalization: The 'Education' of the Iraqi People," Michael Peters investigates the following assertions:

> that war and globalization go hand in hand; that contemporary globalization *is* a form of war (and war may be a form of globalization); that militarization and war are integral parts of the neo-liberal

agenda; and that there are inextricable links between the US military-industrial complex, the free market, and world order.

The chapter examines these claims within the context of the war against Iraq. It begins with "a civilizational analysis" of globalization, following (although not adopting) Huntington's thesis, and proceeds to contextualize the U.S. National Security Strategy and the neoconservative influence in the White House. The chapter concludes by examining the role of education in understanding the relationship between war and globalization.

The authors of these essays share certain characteristics: They all operate on the assumption that the world has changed since September 11, although exactly *how* is still a matter for argument and investigation. They agree also that the change can be seen as a change not merely in U.S. or U.K. foreign policy or in terms of the "war against terrorism," but that it involves a change in world political economy and worldview necessitating new theories and analyses that engage in a grounded way with the new set of relations that has been engendered between the state and the citizen, between the "West" and the rest, or more particularly, the Muslim world. They agree that there is a set of deeper relationships between education, war, and globalization that must be fathomed simultaneously at a historical, political, economic, and social level; and they agree that the possibility for democracy in the new order actively requires a rethinking of education both in its traditional tasks and in its new global media environment in order to sustain the practice and promise of democracy. These essays, then, are offered up as a first engagement and theorization of the issues, and not the last word.

References

Barber, B.R. (2003) *Jihad vs. McWorld: Terrorism's Challenge to Democracy.* London: Corgi.

Baudrillard, J. (2002) *The Spirit of Terrorism and the Requiem for the Twin Towers,* translated by C. Turner. London & New York: Verso.

Braudel, F. (2002) *The Mediterranean in the Ancient World.* London: Penguin.

Chomsky, N. (2001) *9–11.* New York: Seven Stories Press.

Cooper, R. (2000) *The Postmodern State and the World Order.* London: Demos, The Foreign Policy Centre.

———. (2003) *The Breaking of Nations: Order and Chaos in the Twenty-First Century.* London: Atlantic Books.

Derrida, J. (1982) "The Ends of Man." In *Margins of Philosophy,* translated by A. Bass. Chicago: University of Chicago Press.

Friedman, T. L. (2002) *Longitude and Attitudes: Exploring the World After September 11.* New York: Farrar, Strauss & Giroux.

Gilbert, P. (2003) *New Terror, New Wars.* Edinburgh: Edinburgh University Press.

Gray, J. (2003) *Al Qaeda and What It Means to Be Modern.* London: Faber & Faber.

Gunaratna, R. (2002) *Inside Al Qaeda: Global Network of Terror.* London & New York: Granta.

Halliday, F. (2002) *Two Hours that Shook the World: September 11th, 2001, Causes and Consequences.* London: Saqui Books.

Hoffman, B. (1998) *Inside Terrorism.* New York: Columbia University Press.

Joas, H. (2003) *War and Modernity,* translated by R. Livingstone. Cambridge: Polity Press.

Kagan, R. (2003) *Of Passion and Power: America and Europe in the New World Order.* New York: Alfred A. Knopf.

Kellner, D. (2003) *From 9/11 to Terror War: The Dangers of the Bush Legacy.* Lanham & Oxford: Rowman & Littlefield.

Laqueur, W. (1996) "Postmodern Terrorism: New Rules for an Old Game." *Foreign Affairs,* September/October. Accessed 20 October, 2003: http://www.fas.org/irp/news/1996/pomo-terror.htm.

———. (2003) *No End to War: Terrorism in the Twenty-First Century.* New York: Continuum.

Peters, M.A. (2003a) "Between Empires: Rethinking Identity and Citizenship in the Context of Globalisation." Plenary address to *Between Empires: Communication, Globalisation and Identity,* School of Communication Studies and the Centre for Communication Research, Auckland University of Technology, 13–15 February 2003 and published in *New Zealand Sociology* 18(2), 135–157.

———. (2003b) "The Postmodern State, Security and World Order." A version of this paper was originally given as an invited public lecture given at Beijing Normal University, China, Thursday 10 October, 2002 and published in *Globalization* 2(2), http://globalization.icaap.org/currentissue.html.

———. (2003c) "Deconstructing 'the West'? Competing Visions of New World Order," *Globalization,* 2(3), http://globalization. icaap.org/currentissue.html.

Robertson, G. (2000) *Crimes Against Humanity: The Struggle For Global Justice.* London: Penguin.

Ruthven, M. (2002) *A Fury for God: The Islamist Attack on America.* London & New York: Granta.

Sardar and Davies (2002) *Why People Hate America.* London: Pluto Press.

Schulze, R. (2002) *A Modern History of the Islamic World.* London & New York: I.B. Tauris.

Sterba, J. P. (2003) (ed.) *Terrorism and International Justice.* New York & Oxford: Oxford University Press.

Turshen, M., and Twagiramariya, C. (1998) (Eds.) *What Women Do in Wartime: Gender and Conflict in Africa.* London: Zed Books.

United Nations, the (2003) *Report of the Policy Working Group on the United Nations and Terrorism.* Accessed 20 October 2003: http://www.un.org/terrorism/.

U.S. Department of State (2003) *Patterns of Global Terrorism.* Accessed, 20 October 2003: http://www.usis.usemb.se/terror/rpt2002/index.html.

Wardlaw, G. *Political Terrorism: Theory, Tactics, and Countermeasures,* Second Edition. Cambridge: Cambridge University Press.

Ziauddin, S. (2003) *Islam, Postmodernism And Other Futures: A Ziauddin Sardar Reader,* edited by S. Inayatullah and G. Boxwell. London: Pluto Press.

Zulaika, J., and Douglass, W.A. (1996) *Terror and Taboo: The Follies, Fables and Faces of Terrorism.* New York: Routledge.

Notes

1. I think Robertson's historical view is an exaggeration to say the least. It tends to buy in too easily to neoliberal and neoconservative views of history that assert America as the true inheritor of the Enlightenment and the pinnacle of its development in terms of human rights culture. In historical terms, of course, the U.S.'s position as the sole superpower—as Empire (see Hardt and Negri, 2001)—in the mere decade or so since 1989 is a drop in the ocean of empiric time. On the question of citizenship "between Empires," see Peters (2003a).

2. See also Chomsky (2002), Gunaratna (2002), Ruthven (2002), Friedman (2002), Halliday (2002).

3. Baudrillard (2002, 41) in *The Spirit of Terrorism,* an otherwise limited analysis, makes the same point as Gray: "The September 11 attacks also concern architecture, since what was destroyed was one of the most prestigious buildings, together with a whole (Western) value-system and a

world order." He builds on aspects of his thesis that emphasize *the specular* (my word), which indicates something new. As he writes: "We have to face facts, and accept that a new terrorism has come into being, a new form of action which plays the game, and lays hold of the rules of the game, solely with the aim of disrupting it. Not only do these people not play fair, since they put their own deaths into play—to which there is no possible response ('they are cowards')—but they have taken over all the weapons of the dominant power. Money and stock market speculation, computer technology and aeronautics, spectacle and the media networks—they have assimilated everything of modernity and globalism, without changing their goal, which is to destroy that power" 19). This is important also for my analysis. Baudrillard adds: "Suicidal terrorism was a terrorism of the poor. This is a terrorism of the rich" and he clarifies the emphasis on the specular, thus: "Among the other weapons of the system which they turned round against it, the terrorists exploited the 'real time' of images, their instantaneous worldwide transmission, just as they exploited stock-market speculation, electronic information and air traffic" (27).

4. After Heidegger's "Letter on Humanism," it is difficult to overlook how every humanism has been grounded in metaphysics. After Derrida (1982) it is difficult to hold on to "the unity of man"—an anthropological idea connecting the Renaissance with the Enlightenment.

5. Terrorism had been a political instrument in many ancient societies. Examples of terrorism can be found in ancient Israel, twelfth-century Islam, and fourteenth-century India. Theories of the means for achieving a more just society through the tactical use of political murder occurred in Western Europe well before the French Revolution. Modern terrorism emerged out of these earlier traditions in the nineteenth century and coalesced into its contemporary structure and ideology.

6. See also Cooper (2003) and, in response to Cooper, Peters (2003b). On the broader question of the divergence in strategic cultures between the United States and European Union see Kagan (2002) and Peters (2003c).

7. John Gray (2003) in an otherwise admirable book classifies al-Qaeda as *modern*, rather than postmodern. I do not think he would have too many objections to my use of the concept of postmodern applied to al-Qaeda in the present context, as his purpose, in part, is to disabuse us of the notion that al-Qaeda is a throwback to medieval times. He is prepared to entertain the epithet "postmodern" applied to the new Europe by Robert Cooper. As I have mentioned, Gray lampoons the prevailing idea in Western societies that "modernity is a single condition." He focuses on the rise of neoliberalism and the geopolitics accompanying the "global free market" in order to spell out the metamorphosis of war and

prospects for *Pax Americana*. As he argues: "In the volatile mix of geopolitical calculation and messianic enthusiasm that is presently shaping
America's foreign policy, it is not American *realpolitik* that the world most
resents. It is American universalism" (100). See also Ziauddin (2003)

8. Islamist terrorism has little or nothing to do with economics, according to one analysis of the social background of Hizbullah militants
in Lebanon. After also examining the income and education of Palestinian suicide bombers and Israelis implicated in civilian assassinations and
attacks, a recent study concluded that the connection between poverty,
education, and terrorism is indirect and probably quite weak. This indicates perhaps the lack of relevance of class analysis in understanding
Islamism.

9. The Dartmouth Interactive Media Lab makes the following comment: "Acts of cyberterrorism, such as the 'Love Bug' virus and loss of
air traffic control at Worcester Airport, have gained widespread media
attention. Fortunately, no fatalities resulted from these incidents; the
possibility of more serious attacks, however, is very real. A Socratic Dialogue, composed of panelists from such varying fields as law enforcement, emergency services, private industry, and information security,
was conducted with the purpose of illuminating some of the more pressing issues regarding cyberterrorism and providing insight into possible
solutions. Imagine the following:

As the passengers of Blue Skies Flight 2002 head toward a major sport-
ing event in Metropolis, the pilot comes on the public address system
with some news: the air traffic control computers at Metropolis International Airport have just gone down. The news is frustrating, both for the
passengers and for the city's 'first responders'—police, fire, Emergency
Medical Systems (EMS)—who have been planning and preparing for
the big day, but no one is especially concerned; after all, the air traffic
control computer crash is certainly no more than a fluke, an accident
which no doubt will be repaired soon . . . " (http://iml.dartmouth.edu/
ists/intro.html).

10. For a comprehensive collection of materials see "Terrorism: The
Threat and Post 9/11 Trends," compiled by Air University Library (http:/
/www.au.af.mil/au/aul/bibs/terror/sep11.htm). For a selection of education material see, for instance, "Public education materials to help kids
cope with terrorism" (http://www.apa.org/practice/ptindex.html);
"Dealing with War and Terrorism in the Classroom" (http://
www.educationworld.com/a_curr/profdev051.shtml); "Teaching Guide
on International Terrorism: Definitions, Causes and Responses" (http:/
/www.usip.org/ed/edmaterials/terrorism.html). "Teaching Resource
for High School and College Classrooms Using the SSRC's 'After Sep-

tember 11'" (http://www.ssrc.org/sept11/essays/teaching_resource/tr_intro.htm).

On preparation and training see, for instance, "Counter-Terrorist Preparedness and Training" (http://www.sais-jhu.edu/cse/); "Preparing for The Worst: Why Schools Need Terrorism Plans" (http://www.educationworld.com/a_admin/admin300.shtml). For "strategic education" see, for instance, "Center for Strategic Education (Johns Hopkins University)" (http://www.sais-jhu.edu/cse/).

11. The term "noncombatant" is meant to include not only civilians but also those military personnel who are unarmed or off duty.

12. Eliza Manningham-Buller, the head of Britain's domestic intelligence service MI5, told a conference in London (Tuesday, 17 June 2003) that a terror attack on a major Western city using chemical, biological, radiological, or nuclear (CBRN) technology is "only a matter of time." Violent extremists were becoming more sophisticated in developing such nonconventional threats thanks to help from "renegade scientists." "We are faced with the realistic possibility of some form of unconventional attack. That could include a CBRN attack," she is reported as saying. "Sadly, given the widespread proliferation of the technical knowledge to construct these weapons, it will only be a matter of time before a crude version of a CBRN attack is launched at a major Western city," she added. Such blunt words in public from a senior secret service official are rare.

13. That the Western way of life is "war saturated" has surprisingly received little attention. There is no sociology of war, but see Hans Joas' (2003) *War and Modernity* where he examines ideologies of war, the relation between war and violence, and the dream of a modernity without war.

14. I am reminded of a scene from the movie *Bowling for Columbine* in which Mike Moore is interviewing the manager of the local missile plant, who is standing in front of a gigantic missile. When Moore asks whether he (i.e., the manager) can see any connection between the events of the Columbine school massacre and his own plant's production of missiles, the manager looks completely perplexed. The level of youth violence reached epidemic proportions in the United States during the decade 1983–93, peaking in 1993, indicating since the highpoint a decline in arrests records, victimization data, and hospital emergency room records, as the report of the Surgeon General (the first on youth violence) make clear, see http://www.surgeongeneral.gov/library/youthviolence/summary.htm.

Of the 104,000 arrests of people under 18 for serious violent crime, 1,400 were for homicides. For every youth arrested in any given year in the later 1990s "at least ten were engaged in some form of violent behaviour that could have seriously injured or killed another person."

The Surgeon General's report adopts a developmental perspective focusing on a public health approach rather than examining the political economy of a war-saturated *socius*.

15. Seven states have been designated state sponsors of terrorism: Cuba, Iran, Iraq, Libya, North Korea, Sudan, and Syria.

16. The list of most wanted terrorists are all Islamic, see http://www.fbi.gov/mostwant/terrorists/fugitives.htm.

Chapter One

The Conflicts of Globalization and Restructuring of Education

Douglas Kellner

The September 11 terrorist attacks have generated a wealth of theoretical reflection as well as regressive political responses by the
Bush administration and other governments (Kellner 2003b). The
9/11 attacks and subsequent Bush administration military response have dramatized once again the centrality of globalization in contemporary experience and the need for adequate
conceptualizations and responses to it for critical theory and pedagogy to maintain their relevance in the present age. In this article,
I want to argue that critical educators need to comprehend the
conflicts of globalization, terrorism, and the prospects and obstacles to democratization in order to develop pedagogies adequate to the challenges of the present age. Accordingly, I begin
with some comments on how the September 11 terror attacks call
attention to key aspects of globalization, and I then provide a critical theory of globalization, after which I suggest some pedagogi-

cal initiatives to aid in the democratic reconstruction of education after 9/11.[1]

September 11 and Globalization

The terrorist acts on the United States on September 11 and the subsequent Terror War throughout the world dramatically disclose the downside of globalization and the ways that global flows of technology, goods, information, ideologies, and people can have destructive as well as productive effects.[2] The disclosure of powerful anti-Western terrorist networks shows that globalization divides the world just as it unifies, that it produces enemies as it incorporates participants. The events reveal explosive contradictions and conflicts at the heart of globalization and that the technologies of information, communication, and transportation that facilitate globalization can also be used to undermine and attack it, and to generate instruments of destruction as well as production.

The experience of September 11 points to the objective ambiguity of globalization, that positive and negative sides are interconnected, that the institutions of the open society unlock the possibilities of destruction and violence, as well as destruction of and violence against democracy, free trade, and cultural and social exchange. Once again, the interconnection and interdependency of the networked world was dramatically demonstrated as terrorists from the Middle East brought local grievances from their region to attack key symbols of U.S. military power and the very infrastructure of Wall Street. Some see terrorism as an expression of "the dark side of globalization," while I would conceive it as part of the objective ambiguity of globalization that simultaneously creates friends and enemies, wealth and poverty, and growing divisions between the "haves" and "have nots." Yet the downturn in the global economy, intensification of local and global political conflicts, repression of human rights and civil liberties, and general increase in fear and anxiety have certainly undermined the naïve optimism of globophiles who perceived globalization as a purely positive instrument of progress and well-being.

The use of powerful technologies as weapons of destruction also discloses current asymmetries of power and emergent forms of terrorism and war, as the new millennium exploded into dangerous conflicts and military interventions. As technologies of mass destruction become more available and dispersed, perilous instabilities have emerged that have elicited policing measures to stem the flow of movements of people and goods across borders and internally. In particular, the U.S.A. Patriot Act has led to repressive measures that are replacing the spaces of the open and free information society with new forms of surveillance, policing, and restrictions of civil liberties, thus significantly undermining U.S. democracy (see Kellner 2003b).

Ultimately, however, the abhorrent terror acts by the bin Laden network and the violent military response by the Bush administration may be an anomalous paroxysm whereby a highly regressive premodern Islamic fundamentalism has clashed with an old-fashioned patriarchal and unilateralist Wild West militarism. It could be that such forms of terrorism, militarism, and state repression will be superseded by more rational forms of politics that globalize and criminalize terrorism, and that do not sacrifice the benefits of the open society and economy in the name of security. Yet the events of September 11 may open a new era of Terror War that will lead to the kind of apocalyptic futurist world depicted by cyberpunk fiction (see Kellner 2003b).

In any case, the events of September 11 have promoted a fury of reflection, theoretical debates, and political conflicts and upheavals that put the complex dynamics of globalization at the center of contemporary theory and politics. To those skeptical of the centrality of globalization to contemporary experience, it is now clear that we are living in a global world that is highly interconnected and vulnerable to passions and crises that can cross borders and can affect anyone or any region at any time. The events of September 11 and their aftermath also provide a test case to evaluate various theories of globalization in the contemporary era. In addition, they highlight some of the contradictions of globalization and the need to develop a highly complex and dialectical model to capture its conflicts, ambiguities, and contradictory effects.

Consequently, I argue that in order to properly theorize globalization one needs to conceptualize several sets of contradictions generated by globalization's combination of technological revolution and restructuring of capital, which, in turn, generate tensions between capitalism and democracy, and "haves" and "have nots." Within the world economy, globalization involves the proliferation of the logic of capital, but also the spread of democracy in information, finance, investing, and the diffusion of technology (see Friedman, 1999 and Hardt and Negri, 2000). Globalization is thus a contradictory amalgam of capitalism and democracy, in which the logic of capital and the market system enter ever more arenas of global life, even as democracy spreads and more political regions and spaces of everyday life are being contested by democratic demands and forces. But the overall process is contradictory. Sometimes globalizing forces promote democracy and sometimes they inhibit it; thus, either equating capitalism and democracy, or simply opposing them, are problematical.

The processes of globalization are highly turbulent and have generated intense conflicts throughout the world. Benjamin Barber (1996) describes the strife between McWorld and Jihad, contrasting the homogenizing, commercialized, Americanized tendencies of the global economy and culture with anti-modernizing Jihadist movements that affirm traditional cultures and are resistant to aspects of neoliberal globalization. Thomas Friedman (1999) makes a more benign distinction between what he calls the "Lexus" and the "Olive Tree." The former is a symbol of modernization, of affluence and luxury, and of Westernized consumption, contrasted with the Olive Tree that is a symbol of roots, tradition, place, and stable community. Barber (1996), however, is too negative toward McWorld and Jihad, failing to adequately describe the democratic and progressive forces within both. Although Barber recognizes a dialectic of McWorld and Jihad, he opposes both to democracy, failing to perceive how they generate their own democratic forces and tendencies, as well as opposing and undermining democratization. Within Western democracies, for instance, there is, not just top-down homogenization and corporate domination, but also globalization-from-below and oppositional social movements that desire alternatives to capitalist globalization. Thus, it is not only traditionalist, non-Western forces of Jihad that oppose McWorld. Likewise, Jihad has its democratizing forces, as well as the reactionary Islamic fundamentalists who are now the most demonized elements of the contemporary era, as I discuss below. Jihad, like McWorld, has its contradictions and its potential for democratization, as well as elements of domination and destruction.[3]

Friedman, by contrast, is too uncritical of globalization, caught up in his own Lexus, high-consumption life-style, failing to perceive the depth of the oppressive features of globalization and the breadth and extent of resistance and opposition to it. In particular, he fails to articulate the contradictions between capitalism and democracy, and the ways that globalization and its economic logic undermine democracy as well as encourage it. Likewise, he does not grasp the virulence of the premodern and Jihadist tendencies that he blithely identifies with the Olive tree, and the reasons why globalization and the West are so strongly resisted in many parts of the world.

Hence, it is important to present globalization as a strange amalgam of both homogenizing forces of sameness and uniformity, *and* heterogeneity, difference, and hybridity, as well as a contradictory mixture of democratizing and anti-democratizing tendencies. On one hand, globalization unfolds a process of standardization in which a globalized mass culture circulates the globe creating sameness and homogeneity everywhere. But globalized culture makes possible unique appropriations and developments all over the world, thus proliferating hybrids, difference, and heterogeneity.[4] Every local context involves its own appropriation and reworking of global products and signifiers, thus proliferating difference, otherness, diversity, and variety (Luke and Luke 2000). Grasping that globalization embodies these contradictory tendencies at once, that it can be both a force of homogenization and heterogeneity, is crucial to articulating the contradictions of globalization and avoiding one-sided and reductive conceptions.

My intention is to present globalization as conflictual, and contradictory and open to resistance and democratic intervention and transformation, and not just as a monolithic juggernaut of progress or domination as in many other discourses. This goal is advanced by distinguishing between "globalization from below" and "globalization from above" of corporate capitalism and the capitalist state, a distinction that should help us to get a better sense of how globalization does or does not promote democratization. "Globalization from below" refers to the ways in which marginalized individuals and social movements and critical pedagogues resist globalization and/or use its institutions and instruments to further democratization and social justice.

Yet, one needs to avoid binary normative articulations, since globalization from below can have highly conservative and destructive effects, as well as positive ones, while globalization from above can help produce global solutions to problems like terrorism or the environment. Moreover, on one hand, as Michael Peters argues (in chapter 8 of this book), globalization itself is a kind of war, and much militarism has been expansive and globalizing in many historical situations. On the other hand, antiwar and peace movements are also increasingly global; hence globalization is marked by tensions and contradictions.

Thus, while on one level globalization significantly increases the supremacy of big corporations and big government, it can also give power to groups and individuals that were previously left out of the democratic dialogue and terrain of political struggle. Such potentially positive effects of globalization include increased access to education for individuals excluded from sharing culture and knowledge and the possibility for oppositional individuals and groups to participate in global culture and politics through gaining access to global communication and media networks and to circulate local struggles and oppositional ideas through these media. The role of information technologies in social movements, political struggle, and everyday life forces social movements and critical theorists to reconsider their political strategies and goals and democratic theory to appraise how new technologies do and do not promote democratization (Kellner 1995b, 1997 and 1999b; Best and Kellner 2001; Kahn and Kellner 2003).

In their book *Empire,* Hardt and Negri (2000) present contradictions within globalization in terms of an imperializing logic of "Empire" and an assortment of struggles by the multitude, creating a contradictory and tension-filled situation. As in my conception, Hardt and Negri present globalization as a complex process that involves a multidimensional mixture of expansions of the global economy and capitalist market system, information technologies and media, expanded judicial and legal modes of governance, and emergent modes of power, sovereignty, and resistance.[5] Combining poststructuralism with "autonomous Marxism," Hardt and Negri stress political openings and possibilities of struggle within Empire in an optimistic and buoyant text that envisages progressive democratization and self-valorization in the turbulent process of the restructuring of capital.

Many theorists, by contrast, have argued that one of the trends of globalization is depoliticization of publics, the decline of the nation-state, and the end of traditional politics (Boggs 2000). While I would agree that globalization is promoted by tremendously powerful economic forces and that it often undermines democratic movements and decision-making, one should also note that there are openings and possibilities for a globalization from below that inflects globalization for positive and progressive ends, and that globalization can thus help promote as well as destabilize democracy.[6] Globalization involves both a disorganization and reorganization of capitalism, a turbulent structuring process, which creates openings for progressive social change and intervention as well as highly destructive transformative effects. On the positive ledger, in a more fluid and open economic and political system, oppositional forces can gain concessions, win victories, and effect progressive changes. During the 1970s, new social movements, new nongovernmental organizations (NGOs), and new forms of struggle and solidarity emerged that have been expanding to the present day (Hardt and Negri 2000; Burbach 2001; Best and Kellner 2001; and Foran 2003).

The anticorporate globalization of the 1990s emerged as a form of globalization from below, but so too did al-Qaeda and various global terror networks, which intensified their attacks and helped generate an era of Terror War. This made it difficult simply to affirm globalization from below while denigrating globalization from above, as clearly terrorism was an emergent and dangerous form of globalization from below that was a threat to peace, security, and democracy. Moreover, in the face of Bush administration unilateralism and militarism, multilateral approaches to the problems of terrorism called for global alliances and responses to a wide range of global problems (see Kellner 2003b and Barber 2003), thus demanding a progressive and cosmopolitan globalization to deal with contemporary challenges.

Moreover, the present conjuncture is marked by a conflict between growing centralization and organization of power and wealth in the hands of the few, contrasted with opposing processes exhibiting a fragmentation of power that is more plural, multiple, and open to contestation. As the following analysis will suggest, both tendencies are observable, and it is up to individuals and groups to find openings for progressive political intervention, social transformation, and the democratization of education that pursue positive values such as democracy, human rights, literacy, equality, ecological preservation and restoration, and social justice, while fighting poverty, ignorance, terror, and injustice. Thus, rather than just denouncing globalization, or engaging in celebration and legitimation, a critical theory of globalization reproaches those aspects that are oppressive, while seizing upon opportunities to fight domination and exploitation and to promote democratization, justice, and a forward looking reconstruction of the polity, society and culture.

Against capitalist globalization from above, there has been a significant eruption of forces and subcultures of resistance that have attempted to preserve specific forms of culture and society against globalization and homogenization, and to create alternative forces of society and culture, thus exhibiting resistance and globalization from below. Most dramatically, peasant and guerrilla movements in Latin America, labor unions, students, and environmentalists throughout the world, and a variety of other groups and movements have resisted capitalist globalization and attacks on previous rights and benefits.[7] Several dozen people's organizations from around the world have protested World Trade Organization (WTO) policies, and a backlash against globalization is visible everywhere. Politicians who once championed trade agreements like GATT and NAFTA are now often quiet about these arrangements; for example, at the 1996 annual Davos World Economic Forum its founder and managing director published a warning entitled: "Start Taking the Backlash Against Globalization Seriously." Reports surfaced that major representatives of the capitalist system expressed fear that capitalism was getting too mean and predatory, that it needs a kinder and gentler state to ensure order and harmony, and that the welfare state may make a comeback (see the article in *New York Times*, Feb. 7, 1996, A15).[8]

One should take such reports with the proverbial grain of salt, but they express fissures and openings in the system for critical discourse and intervention.

Indeed, by 1999, the theme of the annual Davos conference was making globalization work for poor countries and minimizing the differences between the "haves" and "have nots." The growing divisions between rich and poor were worrying some globalizers, as were the wave of crises in Asian, Latin American, and other "developing countries." In James Flanigan's report in the *Los Angeles Times* (Feb. 19, 1999), the "main theme" is to "spread the wealth. In a world frightened by glaring imbalances and the weakness of economies from Indonesia to Russia, the talk is no longer of a new world economy getting stronger but of ways to 'keep the engine going.'" In particular, the globalizers were attempting to keep economies growing in the more developed countries and capital flowing to developing nations. U.S. Vice President Al Gore called on all countries to spur economic growth, and he proposed a new U.S.-led initiative to eliminate the debt burdens of developing countries. South African President Nelson Mandela asked: "Is globalization only for the powerful? Does it offer nothing to the men, women and children who are ravaged by the violence of poverty?"

As the new millennium opened, there was no clear answer to Mandela's question. In the 2000s, there have been ritual proclamations of the need to make globalization work for the developing nations at all major meetings of global institutions like the WTO or G-8 convenings. For instance, at the September 2003 WTO meeting in Cancun, organizers claimed that its goal was to fashion a new trade agreement that would reduce poverty and boost development in poorer nations. But critics pointed out that in the past years the richer nations of the United States, Japan, and Europe continued to enforce trade tariffs and provide subsidies for national producers of goods such as agriculture, while forcing poorer nations to open their markets to "free trade," thus bankrupting agricultural sectors in these countries that could not compete. Significantly, the September 2003 WTO trade talks in Cancun collapsed as leaders of the developing world concurred with protestors and blocked expansion of a "free trade zone" that would mainly benefit the United States and overdeveloped countries.

Likewise, in Miami in November 2003, the "Free-Trade Summit" collapsed without an agreement as the police violently suppressed protestors.[9]

Moreover, major economists like Joseph Stiglitz (2002), as well as anti-corporate globalization protestors and critics, argued that the developing countries were not adequately benefiting under current corporate globalization policies and that divisions between the rich and poor nations were growing. Under these conditions, critics of globalization were calling for radically new policies that would help the developing countries, regulate the rich and over-developed countries, and provide more power to working people and local groups.

The Global Movement Against Capitalist Globalization

With the global economic recession and the Terror War erupting in 2001, the situation of many developing countries has worsened. As part of the backlash against globalization in recent years, a wide range of theorists have argued that the proliferation of difference and the shift to more local discourses and practices best define the contemporary scene. In this view, theory and politics should shift from the level of globalization (and its accompanying often totalizing and macro dimensions) in order to focus on the local, the specific, the particular, the heterogeneous, and the micro level of everyday experience. An array of theories associated with poststructuralism, postmodernism, feminism and multiculturalism focus on difference, otherness, marginality, the personal, the particular, and the concrete, in contrast to more general theory and politics that aim at more global or universal conditions.[10] Likewise, a broad spectrum of subcultures of resistance have focused their attention on the local level, organizing struggles around identity issues such as gender, race, sexual preference, or youth subculture (see Kahn and Kellner 2003).

It can be argued that such dichotomies as those between the global and the local express contradictions and tensions between crucial constitutive forces on the present scene. It may be a mistake to focus on one side of the global/local polarity in favor of exclusive concern with the other side (Cvetkovitch and Kellner

1997). Hence, an important challenge for a critical theory of globalization is to think through the relationships between the global and the local by observing how global forces influence and even structure an increasing number of local situations. This requires analysis as well of how local forces mediate the global, inflecting global forces to diverse ends and conditions, and producing unique configurations of the local and the global as the matrix for thought and action in today's world (see Luke and Luke 2000).

Globalization is thus necessarily complex and challenging to both critical theories and radical democratic politics. But many people these days operate with binary concepts of the global and the local, and promote one or the other side of the equation as the solution to the world's problems. For globalists, globalization is the solution, while underdevelopment, backwardness, and provincialism are the problems. For localists, globalization is the problem and localization is the solution. But politics is frequently contextual and pragmatic, and whether global or local solutions are most fitting depends on the conditions in the distinctive context that one is addressing and the specific solutions and policies being proposed.[11]

For instance, the Internet can be used to promote capitalist globalization or struggles against it. One of the more instructive examples of the use of the Internet to foster movements against the excesses of corporate capitalism occurred in the protests in Seattle and throughout the world against the WTO meeting in December 1999. Behind these actions was a global protest movement using the Internet to organize resistance to the WTO and capitalist globalization, while championing democratization. Many Web sites contained anti-WTO material and numerous mailing lists used the Internet to distribute critical material and to organize the protest. The result was the mobilization of caravans from throughout the United States to take protestors to Seattle, many of whom had never met before and were Internet recruits. There were also significant numbers of international participants in Seattle, which exhibited labor, environmentalist, feminist, anti-capitalist, animal rights, anarchist, and other protests against aspects of globalization while forming new alliances and solidarities for future struggles. In addition, protests occurred throughout the world, and a proliferation of anti-WTO material against the extremely secret group spread throughout the Internet.[12]

Furthermore, the Internet provided critical coverage of the event, documentation of the various groups' protests, and debate over the WTO and globalization. Whereas the mainstream media presented the protests as "anti-trade," featured the incidents of anarchist violence against property, and minimized police violence against demonstrators, the Internet provided pictures, eyewitness accounts and reports of police brutality and the generally peaceful and nonviolent nature of the protests. Mainstream media framed the protests negatively and privileged suspect spokespersons like Patrick Buchanan, an extreme right wing and authoritarian critic of globalization; the Internet provided multiple representations of the demonstrations, advanced reflective discussion of the WTO and globalization, and presented a diversity of critical perspectives.

Initially, the incipient antiglobalization movement was precisely that—an *anti*globalization movement. The movement itself, however, became increasingly global, linking a diversity of movements into global solidarity networks and using the Internet and instruments of globalization to advance its struggles. Moreover, many opponents of capitalist globalization recognized the need for a global movement to have a positive vision and be for such things as social justice, a democratized globalization, equality, labor, civil liberties and human rights, and a sustainable environmentalism. Accordingly, the anticapitalist and pro-social-justice-and-democracy globalization movements began advocating common values and visions.

In particular, the movement against capitalist globalization used the Internet to organize mass demonstrations and to disseminate information to the world concerning the policies of the institutions of capitalist globalization. The events made clear that protestors were not against globalization per se, but were against neoliberal and capitalist globalization, opposing specific policies and institutions that produce intensified exploitation of labor, environmental devastation, growing divisions among the social classes, and the undermining of democracy. The emerging anticorporate globalization movements are contesting the neoliberal model of market capitalism that extols maximum profit with zero accountability and have made clear the need for democratization, regulation, rules, and globalization in the interests of people, not just profit.

The movements against capitalist globalization have thus placed the issues of global justice, human rights, and environmental destruction squarely in the center of important political concerns of our time. Hence, whereas the mainstream media had failed to vigorously debate or even report on globalization until the eruption of a vigorous antiglobalization movement, and rarely, if ever, critically discussed the activities of the WTO, World Bank, and IMF, there is now a widely circulating critical discourse and controversy over these institutions. Stung by criticisms, representatives of the World Bank, in particular, are pledging reform, and pressures are mounting concerning proper and improper roles for the major global institutions, highlighting their limitations and deficiencies and the need for reforms like debt relief for overburdened developing countries to solve some of their fiscal and social problems.

Against capital's globalization-from-above, cyberactivists and a multitude of groups have thus been attempting to carry out globalization-from-below, developing networks of solidarity and propagating oppositional ideas and movements throughout the planet. To the capitalist international of transnational corporate-led globalization, a Fifth International—to use Waterman's phrase (1992)—of computer-mediated activism is emerging, that is qualitatively different from the party-based socialist and communist internationals. Such networking links labor, feminist, ecological, peace, and other anticapitalist groups, providing the basis for a new politics of alliance and solidarity to overcome the limitations of postmodern identity politics (see Dyer-Witheford 1999; Hardt and Negri 2000; Burbach 2001; and Best and Kellner 2001).

Of course, right wing and reactionary forces can and have used the Internet to promote their political agendas as well. In a short time, one can easily access an exotic witch's brew of Web sites maintained by the Ku Klux Klan and myriad neo-Nazi assemblages, including the Aryan Nation and various militia groups. Internet discussion lists also disperse these views, and right wing extremists are aggressively active in many computer forums, as well as radio programs and stations, public access television programs, fax campaigns, video and even rock music productions. These organizations are hardly harmless, having carried out terrorism of various sorts extending from church burnings to the bombings of public buildings. Adopting quasi-Leninist discourse and tactics for ultraright causes, these groups have been successful in recruiting working-class members devastated by the developments of global capitalism, which has resulted in widespread unemployment for traditional forms of industrial, agricultural, and unskilled labor. Moreover, extremist Web sites have influenced alienated middle-class youth as well (a 1999 HBO documentary on *Hate on the Internet* provides a disturbing number of examples of how extremist Web sites influenced disaffected youth to commit hate crimes).

A recent twist in the saga of technopolitics, in fact, seems to be that allegedly "terrorist" groups are now increasingly using the Internet and Web sites to promote their causes. An article in the *Los Angeles Times* (Feb. 8, 2001, A1 and A14) reports that groups like Hamas use their Web site to post reports of acts of terror against Israel, rather than calling newspapers or broadcasting outlets. A wide range of groups labeled as "terrorist" reportedly use e-mail, list-serves, and Web sites to further their struggles, including Hezbollah and Hamas, the Maoist group Shining Path in Peru, and a variety of other groups in Asia and elsewhere. The Tamil Tigers, for instance, a liberation movement in Sri Lanka, offer position papers, daily news, and free e-mail service. According to the *Los Angeles Times* story cited above, experts are still unclear "whether the ability to communicate online worldwide is prompting an increase or a decrease in terrorist acts."

There have been widespread discussions of how the bin Laden al-Qaeda network used the Internet to plan the September 11 terrorist attacks on the United States, how the group members communicated with each other, got funds, and purchased airline tickets via the Internet, and used flight simulations to practice their hijacking (see Kellner 2003a). In the contemporary era, the Internet can thus be used for a diversity of political projects and goals ranging from education to business, to political organization and debate, to terrorism.

Moreover, different political groups are engaging in cyberwar as an adjunct of their political battles. Israeli hackers have repeatedly attacked the Web sites of Hamas and Hezbollah, while pro-Palestine hackers have reportedly placed militant demands and slogans on the Web sites of Israel's army, foreign ministry, and parliament. Likewise, Pakistani and Indian computer hackers have waged similar cyberbattles against the opposing nation's Web sites in the bloody struggle over Kashmir, while rebel forces in the Philippines taunt government troops with cell-phone calls and messages and attack government Web sites.

The examples in this section suggest how technopolitics makes possible a refiguring of politics, a refocusing of politics on everyday life and the use of the tools and techniques of new computer and communication technology to expand the field and domain of politics. In this conjuncture, the ideas of Guy Debord and the Situationist International are especially relevant with their stress on the construction of situations, the use of technology, media of communication, and cultural forms to promote a revolution of everyday life, and to increase the realm of freedom, community, and empowerment.[13] To some extent, the new technologies are revolutionary; they do constitute a revolution of everyday life, but they also promote and disseminate the capitalist consumer society and involve new modes of fetishism, enslavement, and domination, yet to be clearly perceived and theorized.

The Internet and emerging forms of technopolitics also point to the connection between politics and pedagogy. Paulo Freire has long argued that all pedagogy is political and politics contains a pedagogical dimension (which could be manipulative or emancipatory). Critical educators need to devise strategies to use the Internet and information and communication technologies to enhance education and to produce more active democratic and global citizens.

The Internet is thus a contested terrain, used by Left, Right, and Center to promote their own agendas and interests. The political battles of the future may well be fought in the streets, factories, parliaments, and other sites of past struggle, but politics is already mediated by broadcast, computer, and information technologies and will increasingly be so in the future. Those interested in the politics and culture of the future should, therefore, be clear on the important role of the new public spheres and intervene accordingly, while critical pedagogues have the responsibility of teaching students the skills that will enable them to participate in the politics and struggles of the present and future.

Contradictions of Globalization and Challenges for Democratization

And so, to paraphrase Foucault, wherever there is globalization from above, globalization as the imposition of capitalist logic, there can be resistance and struggle. The possibilities of globalization from below result from transnational alliances between groups fighting for better wages and working conditions, social and political justice, environmental protection, and more democracy and freedom worldwide. In addition, a renewed emphasis on local and grass-roots movements has put dominant economic forces on the defensive globally and in their own backyard. Often, the broadcasting media or the Internet have called attention to oppressive and destructive corporate policies on the local level, putting national and even transnational pressure upon major corporations for reform. Moreover, proliferating media and the Internet make possible a greater circulation of struggles and the possibilities of new alliances and solidarities that can connect resistant forces who oppose capitalist and corporate-state elite forms of globalization from above (Dyer-Witheford 1999).

In a certain sense, the development of globalization replicates the history of the United States and other Western societies. In most so-called capitalist democracies, tension between capitalism and democracy has been a defining feature of the conflicts of the past 200 years. In analyzing the development of education in the United States, Bowles and Gintis (1986), Aronowitz and Giroux (1993), and others have analyzed the conflicts between corporate logic and democracy in schooling; Robert McChesney (1996 and 1999), myself (Kellner 1990, 1992, 2001, and 2003a), and others have articulated the contradictions between capitalism and democracy in the media and public sphere. Joel Cohen and Joel Rogers (1983) argue that contradictions between capitalism and democracy are defining features of the U.S. polity and history, while Benjamin Barber (1996) argues that in the current international situation tensions between capitalism and democracy are a major feature of global conflicts and tensions.

Searching for emancipatory hopes, Hardt and Negri (2000) have stressed the openings and possibilities for democratic transformative struggle within globalization, or what they call "Empire."

I am arguing that similar arguments can be made in which globalization is not conceived merely as the triumph of capitalism and democracy working together as it was in the classical theories of Milton Friedman or, more recently, in Francis Fukuyama and Thomas Friedman. Nor should globalization be depicted solely as the triumph of capital as in many despairing antiglobalization theories. Rather, one should see that globalization unleashes conflicts between capitalism and democracy. In its restructuring processes this creates new openings for struggle, resistance, and democratic transformation.

The model of Marx and Engels as deployed in the "Communist Manifesto" could also be usefully employed to analyze the contradictions of contemporary globalization (Marx and Engels 1978, 469ff). From the historical materialist optic, capitalism was interpreted as the most progressive force in history for Marx and Engels, destroying a backward feudalism, authoritarian patriarchy, and backwardness and provincialism in favor of a market society, global cosmopolitanism, and constant revolutionizing of the forces of production. Yet, in Marxist theory, so too was capitalism presented as a major disaster for the human race, condemning a large part to alienated labor and regions of the world to colonialist exploitation, and generating conflicts between classes and nations, the consequences of which the contemporary era continues to suffer.

Marx deployed a similar dialectical and historical model in his later analyses of imperialism, arguing, for instance, in his writings on British imperialism in India, that British colonialism was a great productive and progressive force in India at the same time it was highly destructive (Marx and Engels 1978, 653ff). A similar dialectical and critical model can be used today that articulates the progressive elements of globalization in conjunction with its more oppressive features, deploying the categories of negation and critique, while sublating (*Aufhebung*) the positive features. Moreover, a dialectical and transdisciplinary model is necessary to capture the complexity and multidimensionality of globalization today that brings together in theorizing globalization, the economy, technology, polity, society, and culture, articulating the interplay of these elements and avoiding any form of determinism or reductivism.

Theorizing globalization dialectically and critically requires that we analyze both continuities and discontinuities with the past, specifying what is a continuation of past histories and what is new and original in the present moment. To elucidate the latter, I believe that the discourse of the postmodern is useful in dramatizing changes and novelties of the mode of globalization. The concept of postmodern can signal that which is fresh and original, calling attention to topics and phenomena that require novel theorization and intense critical thought and inquiry. Hence, although Manual Castells has the most detailed analysis of information and communication technologies and the rise of what he calls a networked society, by refusing to link his analyses with the problematic of the postmodern, he cuts himself off from theoretical resources that enable theorists to articulate the novelties of the present that are unique and different from previous modes of social organization.[14]

Consequently, although there is admittedly some mystification in the discourse of the postmodern, it emphatically signals shifts and ruptures in our era, as well as novelties and originalities, and dramatizes the mutations in culture, subjectivities, and theory which Castells and other critics of globalization or the information society gloss over. The discourse of the postmodern in relation to analysis of contemporary culture and society is just jargon, however, unless it is rooted in analysis of the global restructuring of capitalism and dissection of the scientific-technological revolution that is part and parcel of it.[15]

As I have argued in this study, the term "globalization" is often used as a code word that stands for a large diversity of issues and problems and that serves as a front for a variety of theoretical and political positions. While it can function as a legitimating ideology to cover over and sanitize ugly realities, a critical globalization theory can inflect the discourse to point precisely at these deplorable phenomena and can elucidate a series of contemporary problems and conflicts. In view of the different concepts and functions of globalization discourse, it is important to note that the concept of globalization is a theoretical construct that varies according to the assumptions and commitments of the theorist in question. Seeing the term "globalization" as a construct helps rob it of its force of nature, as a sign of an inexorable triumph of market forces and the hegemony of capital, or, as the extreme right fears, of a rapidly encroaching world government. While the term can both describe and legitimate capitalist transnationalism and supranational government institutions, a critical theory of globalization does not buy into ideological valorizations and affirms difference, resistance, and democratic self-determination against forms of global domination and subordination.

Globalization should thus be seen as a contested terrain with opposing forces attempting to use its institutions, technologies, media, and forms for their own purposes. A critical theory of globalization should be normative, specifying positive values and potentials of globalization such as human rights, rights for labor, women, children, and oppressed groups; ecological protection and enhancement of the environment; and the promotion of democracy and social justice. Yet it should also critique negative aspects to globalization which strengthen elite economic and political forces over and against the underlying population, and specify in detail bad aspects of globalization such as destructive IMF policies; unfair policies within the WTO; and environmental, human rights and labor abuse throughout the world. Thus, a dialectic of globalization seeks both positive potential while criticizing negative and destructive aspects. Other beneficial openings include the opportunity for greater democratization, increased education and health care, and new opportunities within the global economy that open entry to members of races, regions, and classes previously excluded from mainstream economics, politics and culture within the modern corporate order.

Globalization and the Reconstruction of Education

Consequently, critical educators need to develop transformative educational strategies to counter the oppressive forces and effects of globalization in order to empower individuals to understand and act effectively in a globalized world and to struggle for social justice. This requires teaching important skills such as media and computer literacy, as well as helping to empower students and citizens to deploy information and communication technologies for progressive purposes (Kellner 1998 and 2002; Kahn and Kellner

2003). Globalization and information and communication technologies are dominant forces of the future and it is up to critical educators and activists to illuminate their nature and effects, to demonstrate the threats to democracy and freedom and to seize opportunities for progressive education and democratization.

The project of transforming education will take different forms in different contexts. In the postindustrial or "overdeveloped" countries, individuals need to be empowered to work and act in a high-tech information economy, and thus should learn skills of media and computer literacy in order to survive in the novel social environment. Traditional skills of knowledge and critique should also be fostered, so that students can name the system, describe and grasp the changes occurring in it as well as the defining features of the evolving global order, and can learn to engage in critical and oppositional practice in the interests of democratization and progressive transformation. This requires gaining vision of how life can be, of alternatives to the present order, and of the necessity of struggle and organization to realize progressive goals. Languages of knowledge and critique must thus be supplemented by the discourse of hope and praxis.

In much of the world, the struggle for daily existence is paramount, and meeting unmet human and social needs is a high priority. Yet, everywhere, education can provide the competencies and skills to improve one's life, to create a better society and a more civilized and developed world. Moreover, as the entire world becomes a global and networked society, gaining the multiple literacies necessary to use a range of technologies becomes important the world over as media and cyberculture become more ubiquitous and the global economy requires people with ever more sophisticated technical skills.

It is interesting that one of the godfathers of critical pedagogy, Paulo Freire, was positive toward media and technologies, seeing them as potential tools for empowering citizens, as well as instruments of domination in the hands of ruling elites. Freire wrote that "Technical and scientific training need not be inimical to humanistic education as long as science and technology in the revolutionary society are at the service of permanent liberation, of humanization" (1972, 157).[16] Many critical pedagogues, however, are technophobes, seeing new technologies solely as instruments of domination. In a world inexorably undergoing processes of globalization and technological transformation, one cannot, however, in good conscience advocate a policy of clean hands and purity, distancing oneself from technology and globalization, but must intervene in the processes of economic and technological revolution, attempting to deflect these forces for progressive ends and developing critical and oppositional pedagogies to advance the project of human liberation and well-being.

A critical theory of technology maintains that there is utopian potential in the information and communication technologies, as well as the possibility for increased domination and the hegemony of capital. While the first generation of computers were large mainframe systems controlled by big government and big business, later generations of "personal computers" and networks created a more decentralized situation in which ever more individuals own their own computers and use them for their own projects and goals. A coming generation of wireless communication could enable areas of the world that do not even have electricity to participate in the communication and information revolution of the emergent global era. This would require, of course, something like a Marshall Plan for the developing world that would necessitate help with disseminating technologies that would address problems of world hunger, disease, illiteracy, and poverty.

In relation to education, the spread and distribution of information and communication technology signifies the possibility of openings of opportunities for research and interaction not previously open to students who did not have the privilege of access to major research libraries or institutions. The Internet opens more information and knowledge to more people than any previous technology and institution in history, despite its many problems and limitations. Moreover, the Internet enables individuals to participate in discussions, to circulate their ideas and work and to access material that was previously closed off to many excluded groups and individuals.

A progressive reconstruction of education that is done in the interests of democratization would demand access to emergent technologies for all, helping to overcome the so-called digital divide and divisions of the "haves" and "have nots" (see Kellner

2002). Expanding democratic and multicultural reconstruction of education forces educators and citizens to confront the challenge of the digital divide, in which there are divisions between information and technology "haves" and "have nots," just as there are class, gender, and race divisions in every sphere of existing of societies and cultures. Although the latest surveys of the digital divide indicate that the key indicators are class and education and not race and gender, nonetheless, making computers a significant force of democratization in education and society will require significant investment and programs to assure that everyone receives the training, literacies, and tools necessary to properly function in a hi-tech global economy and culture.[17]

As a response to globalization and technological revolution, transformations in pedagogy must be as radical as the technological transformations that are taking place. Education should be reconstructed in the light of the importance of citizenship and participation, thus linking, à la Dewey, education and democracy. A public pedagogy involves teaching citizens what is going on in their and other democratic and nondemocratic societies, threats to democracy, and the demands of citizenship. Training individuals for citizenship involves education in rhetoric, public speaking, and the fundamentals of reading and writing. It also requires cultivating critical tolerance in a multicultural society that affirms respect and tolerance for all, while being critical of social institutions and groups that themselves promote fundamentalism and assault tolerance, or that use terrorism, militarism, and violence to promote their ends.

Tolerance should be linked with cultural cosmopolitanism that affirms the value of world culture and multicultures and that is not chauvinistic and noncritical toward one's own culture and society. While democratic patriotism can help cultivate respect for the positive features of a culture or society and help create solidarities in times of trouble, a blind nationalistic patriotism can lead to submission to aggressive and nondemocratic policies and practices of political manipulation.

Critical citizenship thus involves cultivating abilities to read and critique the text of one's own and other cultures, including political and media discourses, television programming, popular music, advertising, and other cultural forms. Thus a public pedagogy articulates with critical cultural studies that together require progressive educators to rethink the concepts of literacy and the very nature of education in any hi-tech and rapidly evolving society. Literacy must be expanded to develop novel forms of cultural and technological literacy, for at the same time that the world is undergoing technological revolution, important demographic and sociopolitical changes are occurring in the United States and elsewhere. Emigration patterns have brought an explosion of diverse peoples into the United States in recent decades, and the country is now more racially and ethnically diverse, more multicultural, than ever before. This creates the challenge of providing people from diverse races, classes, and backgrounds with the competencies and tools to enable them to succeed and participate in an ever more complex and changing world.

In my previous work, I have delineated the *multiple literacies* necessary to utilize information and communication technologies, including an expanded role for media literacy, computer and information literacies, and multimedia literacies that provide literacy in reading, researching, and producing in the evolving multimedia world (see Kellner 1998, 2000, and 2002). But radically reconstructing education requires a wide range of other literacies often neglected in the current organization of schooling. Since a multicultural society is the context of education for many in the contemporary moment, innovative forms of social interaction and cultural awareness are needed that appreciate differences, multiplicity, and diversity. Therefore, an expanded *cultural literacy* is needed, one that appreciates the cultural heritage, histories, and contributions of a diversity of groups. Whereas one can agree with E.D. Hirsch (1987) that we need to be literate in our shared cultural heritage, we also need to become culturally literate in cultures that have been hitherto invisible, as Anthony Appiah, Henry Louis Gates, and their colleagues have been arguing in their proposals for a multicultural education (1998).

Social literacy should also be taught throughout the educational systems, ranging from a focus on how to relate and get along with a variety of individuals, how to negotiate differences, how to resolve conflicts, and how to communicate and socially interact in a diversity of situations. Social literacy involves ethical training in values and norms, delineating proper and improper individual and social values (which may well be different in various regions and countries). It also requires knowledge of contemporary societies, and thus overlaps with social and natural science training. In fact, in the light of the significant role of science and technology in the contemporary world, threats to the environment, and the need to preserve and enhance the natural as well as social and cultural worlds, it is scandalous how illiterate some overdeveloped societies, like the United States, are concerning science, nature and even peoples' own bodies. An *ecoliteracy* should thus appropriately teach competency in interpreting and interacting with our natural environment, ranging from our own body to natural habitats, like forests, oceans, lakes, and deserts.

The challenge for education today is thus to develop multiple literacies to empower students and citizens to use emergent technologies to enhance their lives and to create a better culture and society based on respect for multicultural differences and aiming at fuller democratic participation of individuals and groups largely excluded from wealth and power in the previous modern society. A positive postmodernity would thus involve creation of a more egalitarian and democratic society in which more individuals and groups were empowered to participate. A great danger facing us, of course, is that globalization and emergent technologies will increase the current inequalities based on class, gender, and racial divisions. So far, privileged groups have had more direct and immediate access to new technologies. It is therefore a challenge of education today to provide access to multiple technologies, and to the literacies needed for competence, to excluded or oppressed individuals and groups in order to overcome some of the divisions and inequalities that have plagued contemporary societies during the entire modern age.

Radical educators must attempt to connect the phenomenon of evolving technologies and the technological revolution and the multicultural explosion and drama of conflicting ethnicities, classes, genders, religions, and so on, so that differences can create diversity, tolerance, and an enhanced and strengthened democracy and society, and not increasing conflict, intolerance, division, and violence. It is not just a question of talking about media literacy, computer literacy, or other multiple literacies from a technological viewpoint, but thinking together emergent technologies and multiculturalism, with technological and social transformation. Thus, a challenge for critical educators is to discover how multiple technologies and literacies can serve the interests of multiculturalism, making teachers, students and citizens aware of how the proliferating technologies are transforming everything from education to work to war, the challenges involved, the multiple literacies needed, and the opportunities for educational reform and social reconstruction.

To be sure, legitimate concerns have been raised in regard to the possibilities that emergent technologies will increase the regnant inequalities in relation to privileged class, gender, and racial groupings. As is well known, the original computer culture was largely a white, male, middle to upper class "geek," or "nerd," culture that tended to exclude women, people of color, and members of classes without access to computer technologies. As multiple technologies become a more central aspect of schooling, work, and everyday life, however, more and more women and members of groups previously excluded from computer culture are now becoming participants as they gain access to computers and multimedia technologies in schools, in the workplace, and at home. Of course, the question of access to multiple technologies becomes increasingly important as work, education, and every other aspect of social life is undergoing transformation, making multiple literacies essential to work, cultural, educational, and political exigencies of the future. If the previously disadvantaged and marginalized groups will not gain access to the emerging technologies, class, gender, race, and other divisions will exponentially grow, creating ever more virulent divisions and the prospects of social upheaval and turbulence.

Yet there are aspects of the forms of literacy being spawned by information technologies and multimedia culture that are potentially democratizing and empowering for individuals and groups previously on the bottom end of prevailing configurations of class, gender, and racial power. The increased informality, closeness to speech patterns, and spontaneity of e-mail composition and participation in chat rooms and computer-mediated communications and forums provide access to individuals and groups whose literacies and modes of writing were deemed inferior or deficient from more standard classical print-media perspectives. Indeed,

the openness of many forums of computer-mediated communication, the possibility of ever more individuals able to produce
their own Web sites, and access to volumes of information previously limited to those who had access to elite libraries potentially
democratize education, cultural production, and participation in
cultural and political dialogue and movements.

Thus, issues of access and exclusion in relation to multiple technologies and literacies are crucial to realizing the promises of democracy. Yet there are potential threats in the mushrooming of
seductive technologies of information, communication, and entertainment. There is the danger that youth will become totally
immersed in an alluring world of hi-tech experience and lose its
social connectedness and ability to interpersonally communicate
and relate concretely to other people. Informal modes of computer communication can create private languages and subcultures, and disadvantage participants in broader cultural communication and participation.

Statistics suggest that more and more sectors of youth are able
to access cyberspace and that college students with Internet accounts are spending as much as four hours a day in the novel
realm of technological experience.[18] Increasingly, the media have
been generating a moral panic concerning allegedly growing dangers in cyberspace with lurid stories of young boys and girls lured
into dangerous sex or running away from home, endless accounts
of how pornography on the Internet is proliferating, and the pub-
licizing of calls for increasing control, censorship, and surveillance
of communication—usually by politicians or others who are computer illiterate. The solution, however, is not to ban access to those
technologies but to teach students and citizens how to use them
so that they can be employed for productive and creative, rather
than problematical, ends.

To be sure, there are dangers in cyberspace as well as elsewhere,
but the threats to adolescents are significantly higher through the
danger of family violence and abuse than seduction by strangers
on the Internet. And while there is a flourishing trade in pornography on the Internet, this material has become increasingly available in a variety of venues from the local video shop to the newspaper stand. So it seems unfair to demonize the Internet. Attempts
at Internet censorship are part of the attack on youth, which would

circumscribe their rights to obtain entertainment and information and create their own subcultures.[19] Consequently, devices like the V-chip that would exclude sex and violence on television, or block computer access to objectionable material, are more an expression of adult hysteria and moral panic than responses to genuine dangers to youth, which certainly exist, but much more strikingly in the real world than in the sphere of hyperreality.

Throughout this century, there has been a demonization of new media and forms of media culture, ranging from comic books to film to popular music to television and now to the Internet. As Jenkins (1997) argues, this demonization is supported by an assumption of the innocence of childhood, that children are merely passive receptacles, easily seduced by cultural images, and in need of protection from nefarious and harmful cultural content. But as he also contends (1997, 30f), the myth of "childhood innocence" strips children of active agency, of being capable of any thoughts of their own, and of having the ability to decode and process media materials themselves. Of course, children need media education. They need to be involved in an active learning process concerning their culture. But censorship and vilification of media does not help young people become active critics, and participants in their culture.

Accordingly, Jon Katz (1996) has argued for children's "cyber-rights," asserting that our youth's access to Internet cyberculture and media culture in general is necessary for their participation in the larger culture and their own education and development. Mastery of the culture can be the difference between economic success and hardship, between social connectedness or isolation. The Internet, in particular, allows participation in many dimensions of social and cultural life, as well as the cultivation of those technical skills that can help children in later life.

Therefore, it is necessary to divest ourselves of myths of childhood innocence and the passivity of children's media consumption, positing instead the possibility of active and creative use of media material in which media education is seen as part of youth's self-development and constitution. Accordingly, Henry Jenkins proposes

a new kind of radical media education based on the assumption that children are active participants within popular culture rather than passive victims. We need to help our children become more critically reflective about the media they use and the popular culture they embrace, yet we can only achieve this by recognizing and respecting their existing investments, skills, and knowledge as media users. In the end, our goals must be not to protect our children but to empower them. (Jenkins 1997, 31).

Rather than demonizing and rejecting out of hand all new technologies, we should criticize their misuse, but also see how they can be used constructively and positively. In studying the kaleidoscopic array of discourses which characterize the evolving technologies, I am rather bemused by the extent to whether they expose either a technophilic discourse which presents new technologies as salvation, claiming that they will solve crucial contemporary problems, or they embody a technophobic discourse that sees technology as damnation, demonizing it as the major source of present day problems. It appears that similarly one-sided and contrasting discourses greeted the introduction of other new technologies this century, often hysterically. It is indeed curious that whenever an innovative technology is introduced a polarized response emerges in relation to its novelty and differences from previous technologies. New technologies seem to attract both advocates and champions and critics and detractors. This was historically the case with mass media, and now computers.

Film, for instance, was celebrated by early theorists as providing a marvelous documentary depiction of reality. Siegfried Krakauer published a book on film as the "redemption of reality," and it was described early on as an innovative art form, as well as providing novel modes of mass education and entertainment. Likewise, it was soon demonized for promoting sexual promiscuity, juvenile delinquency, and crime, violence, and copious other forms of immorality and evil. Its demonization led in the United States to a Production Code that rigorously regulated the content of Hollywood films from 1934 until the 1950s and 1960s— no open mouthed kissing was permitted, crime could not pay, drug use or attacks on religion could not be portrayed, and a censorship office rigorously surveyed all films to make sure that no subversive or illicit content emerged.

Similar extreme hopes and fears were projected onto radio, television, and now computers. It appears whenever there are new technologies; people project all sorts of fantasies, fears, hopes and dreams onto them. This is now happening with computers and multimedia technologies. It is indeed striking that the literature on computer and information technologies is either highly celebratory and technophilic, or sharply derogatory and technophobic. A critical theory of technology, however, and critical pedagogy, should avoid either demonizing or deifying emergent technologies and should instead develop pedagogies that will help teachers, students, and citizens use technology to enhance education and life, and to criticize the limitations and false promises made on behalf of ever proliferating technologies.

Certainly there is no doubt that the cyberspace of computer worlds contains as much banality and stupidity as real life. One can waste much time in useless activity. But compared to the bleak and violent urban worlds portrayed in rap music and youth films like *Kids* (1995) and *Elephant* (2003), the technological worlds are havens of information, entertainment, interaction, and connection, where youth can gain valuable skills, knowledge, and power necessary to survive the postmodern adventure. Youth can create alternative, more multiple and flexible selves in cyberspace as well as their own subcultures and communities. Indeed, it is exciting to cruise the Internet and to discover how many interesting Web sites young people and others have established, often containing valuable educational and political material. There is, of course, the danger that corporate and commercial interests will come to colonize the Internet, but it is likely that there will continue to be spaces where individuals can empower themselves and create their own communities and identities. A main challenge for youth (and others) is to learn to use the Internet for positive cultural and political projects, rather than just entertainment and passive consumption (see Best and Kellner 2001 and Kahn and Kellner 2003).

Reflecting on the growing social significance of computers and information technologies makes it clear that it is of essential importance for youth today to gain various kinds of literacy to empower themselves for the emerging cybersociety (this is true of teachers and adults as well). To survive in a postmodern world, individuals of all ages need to gain skills of media and computer literacy to enable ourselves to negotiate the overload of media images and spectacles. We all need to learn technological skills to use media and computer technologies to subsist in the hi-tech economy and to form our own cultures and communities. Youth, especially, need street smarts and survival skills to cope with the drugs, violence, and uncertainty in today's predatory culture (McLaren 1995), as well as new forms of multiple literacy.

It is therefore extremely important for the future of democracy to make sure that youth of all classes, races, genders, and regions gain access to information and multimedia technology. This requires receiving training in media and computer literacy skills in order to provide the opportunities to enter the high-tech job market and to fully participate in the society of the future, so as to prevent an exacerbation of class, gender, and race inequalities. And while multiple forms of new literacies will be necessary, traditional print literacy skills are all the more important in a cyberage of word-processing, information gathering, and Internet communication. Moreover, multiple literacy involves training in philosophy, ethics, value thinking, and the humanities, which is necessary today more then ever. In fact, *how* the Internet and emergent technologies will be used depends on the overall education of youth and the skills and interests they bring to the technologies, which can be used to access educational and valuable cultural and political material, or pornography and the banal wares of cybershopping malls.

Thus, the concept of multiple literacies and the postmodern pedagogy that I envisage maintains that it is not a question of either/or—e.g., either print literacy or multimedia literacy, either the classical curriculum or a new hi-tech curriculum—but it is rather a question of both/and that preserves the best from classical education, that enhances emphasis on print literacy, but that also develops multiple literacies to engage the emergent technologies. Obviously, cyberlife is just one dimension of experience, and one still needs to learn to interact in the "real world" of school, jobs, relationships, politics, and community. Youth—indeed all of us!—need to negotiate many dimensions of social reality and to gain a multiplicity of forms of literacy and skills that will enable individuals to create identities, relationships, and communities that will nurture and develop the full spectrum of their potentialities and satisfy a wide array of needs. Contemporary lives are more multidimensional than ever, so part of the postmodern adventure is learning to live in a variety of social spaces and to adapt to intense change and transformation (Best and Kellner 2001). Education, too, must meet these challenges and both utilize new technologies to improve education and devise pedagogical strategies in which technologies can be deployed to create a more democratic and egalitarian multicultural society.

In the light of the neoliberal projects to dismantle the Welfare State, colonize the public sphere, and control globalization, it is up to citizens, activists, and educators to create alternative public spheres, politics, and pedagogies. In these spaces, that could include progressive classrooms, students and citizens could learn to use information and multimedia technologies to discuss what kinds of society people today want and to oppose the society against which people resist and struggle. This involves, minimally, demands for more education, health care, welfare and benefits from the state, and the struggle to create a more democratic and egalitarian society. But one cannot expect that generous corporations and a beneficent state are going to make available to citizens the bounties and benefits of the globalized information economy. Rather, it is up to individuals and groups to promote democratization and progressive social change.

Thus, in opposition to the globalization of corporate and state capitalism, I would advocate an oppositional democratic, pedagogical, and cosmopolitan globalization, which supports individuals and groups using information and multimedia technologies to create a more multicultural, egalitarian, democratic, and ecological globalization. Of course, the emergent technologies might exacerbate existing inequalities in the current class, gender, race, and regional configurations of power and give dominant corporate forces powerful tools to advance their interests. In this situation, it is up to people of good will to devise strategies to use technologies to promote democratization and social justice. For as the proliferating technologies become ever more central to everyday life, developing an oppositional technopolitics in alternative public spheres and pedagogical sites will become increasingly important. Changes in the economy, politics, and social life demand a constant rethinking of politics and social change in the light of globalization and the technological revolution, requiring critical and oppositional thinking as a response to ever-changing historical conditions.

References

Appiah, A.A., and Gates, H. L. (1999) *Africana: The Encyclopedia of the African and African American Experience.* New York: BasicCivitas.

Aronowitz, S., and Giroux, H. (1993) *Education Still Under Siege.* Westport, CT: Bergin & Garvey.

Barber, Benjamin (1996) *Jihad vs. McWorld.* New York: Ballantine Books.

———. (2003) *Fear's Empire. War, Terrorism, and Democracy.* New York: Norton.

Best, S., and Kellner, D. (1991) *Postmodern Theory: Critical Interrogations,* London and New York: MacMillan and Guilford.

———. (1997) *The Postmodern Turn.* London and New York: Routledge and Guilford Press.

———. (2001) *The Postmodern Adventure.* London and New York: Routledge and Guilford Press.

———. (2003) "Contemporary Youth and the Postmodern Adventure," *The Review of Education/Pedagogy/Cultural Studies.* 25(2) (April-June), 75–93.

Boggs, C. (2000) *The End of Politics.* New York: Guilford Press.

Bowles, S., and Gintis, H. (1986): *On Democracy.* New York: Basic Books.

Burbach, R. (2001) *Globalization and Postmodern Politics. From Zapatistas to Hi-tech Robber Barons.* London: Pluto Press.

Castells, M. (1996) *The Rise of the Network Society.* Oxford: Blackwell.

Cohen, J., and Rogers, J. (1983) *On Democracy.* New York: Penguin.

Cvetkovich, A., and Kellner, D. (1997) *Articulating the Global and the Local. Globalization and Cultural Studies.* Boulder, CO: Westview.

Dewey, John (1997 [1916]) *Democracy and Education.* New York: Free Press.

Dyer-Witheford, N. (1999) *Cyber-Marx. Cycles and Circuits of Struggle in Hi-technology Capitalism.* Urbana and Chicago: University of Illinois Press.

Foran, J. (ed.) (2002) *The Future of Revolutions. Rethinking Radical Change in the Age of Globalization.* London: Zed Books.

Friedman, T. (1999) *The Lexus and the Olive Tree.* New York: Farrar Straus Giroux.

Fukuyama, F. (1992) *The End of History and the Last Man.* New York: The Free Press.

Giroux, H. (1996) *Fugitive Cultures: Race, Violence, and Youth.* New York: Routledge.

———. (2000) *Stealing Innocence. Youth, Corporate Power, and the Politics of Culture.* New York: Saint Martin's.

———. (2003a) "Neoliberalism's War Against Youth: Where are Children in the Debate About Politics?" (forthcoming).

———. (2003b) *The Abandoned Generation. Democracy Beyond the Culture of Fear.* New York: Palgrave Macmillan.

Hardt, M., and Negri, A. (2000) *Empire,* Cambridge, MA: Harvard University Press.

Harvey, D. (1989) *The Condition of Postmodernity,* Cambridge: Blackwell.

Hirsch, E.D. (1988) *Cultural Literacy: What Every American Needs to Know.* New York: Vintage.

Jenkins, H. (1997) "Empowering Children in the Digital Age: Towards a Radical Media Pedagogy," *Radical Teacher,* 50, (Spring), 30–36.

Kahn, R., and Kellner, D. (2003) "Internet Subcultures and Oppositional Politics," in D. Muggleton (ed.), *The Post-subcultures Reader.* London: Berg.

Kellner, D. (1995a) *Media Culture.* London and New York: Routledge.

———. (1995b) "Intellectuals and New Technologies," *Media, Culture, and Society,* 17, 201–217.

———. (1997) "Intellectuals, the New Public Spheres, and Technopolitics," *New Political Science,* 41–42 (Fall), 169–188.

———. (1998) "Multiple Literacies and Critical Pedagogy in a Multicultural Society," *Educational Theory,* 48(1), 103–122.

———. (1999a) "Theorizing McDonaldization: A Multiperspectivist Approach," in B. Smart (ed.), *Resisting McDonaldization.* London: Sage Publications, 186–206.

———. (1999b) "Globalization from Below? Toward a Radical Democratic Technopolitics," *Angelaki,* 4(2), 101–113.

———. (2000) "New Technologies/New Literacies: Reconstructing education for the new millennium," *Teaching Education,* 11(3), 245–265.

———. (2002) "Technological Revolution, Multiple Literacies, and the Restructuring of Education," in I. Snyder (ed.), *Silicon Literacies.* London and New York: Routledge, 154–169.

———. (2003a) *Media Spectacle.* London and New York: Routledge.

———. (2003b) *From September 11 to Terror War: The Dangers of the Bush Legacy.* Lanham, MD: Rowman and Littlefield.

———. (2003c) "Postmodern Military and Permanent War," in C. Boggs (ed.), *Masters of War. Militarism and Blowback in the Era of the American Empire.* New York and London: Routledge, 229–244.

Lash, S. (1990) *The Sociology of Postmodernism.* New York and London: Routledge.

Luke, A., and Luke, C. (2000) "A Situated Perspective on Cultural Globalization," in N. Burbules and C. Torres (eds.), *Globalization and Education*. London and New York: Routledge, 275–298.

Males, Mike (1996) *The Scapegoat Generation*. Boston: Common Courage
Press.

Mander, J., and Goldsmith, E. (1996) *The Case Against the Global Economy*,
San Francisco: Sierra Club Books.

Marx, K., and Engels, F. (1978) *The Marx-Engels Reader*, second edition,
R. Tucker (ed.). New York: Norton.

McChesney, Robert (1997) *Corporate Media and the Threat to Democracy*.
New York: Seven Stories Press.

———. (2000) *Rich Media, Poor Democracy*. New York: The New Press.

McLaren, Peter (1995) *Critical Pedagogy and Predatory Culture*. New York:
Routledge.

Moody, K. (1988) *An Injury to One*, London: Verso.

———. (1997) "Towards an International Social-Movement Unionism,"
New Left Review, 225, 52–72.

Peters, M. (2004) "War as Globalization: The 'Education' of the Iraqi
People," M. Peters (ed.), in *Education, Globalization, and the State in
the Age of Terrorism*. Boulder, CO: Paradigm.

Ritzer, G. (1993, revised edition 1996). *The McDonaldization of Society*.
Thousand Oaks, CA: Pine Forge Press.

Stiglitz, J. (2002) *Globalization and Its Discontents*. New York: Norton.

Waterman, P. (1992) "International Labour Communication by Computer:
The Fifth International?" *Working Paper Series* 129 (The Hague: Institute of Social Studies).

Watson, J. (ed.) (1998): *Golden Arches East: McDonald's in East Asia*. Palo
Alto, CA: Stanford University Press.

Notes

1. This study is part of a larger theoretical project. For my perspectives on globalization and new technologies which inform this study,
see Best and Kellner (2001) and Kellner (2002). For my perspectives on
education, new technology, and new literacies that I expand upon in
this study, see Kellner (1998, 2000, 2002, and 2003a). On 9/11 and the
subsequent Terror War, see Kellner (2003b and 2003c).

2. By "Terror War," I refer both to Islamicist terrorism and to the Bush
administration's "war against terrorism" and its doctrine of preemptive
and unilateral strikes against any state or organization presumed to har-
bor or support terrorism, or in order to eliminate "weapons of mass destruction" that could be used against the United States. The right wing of

the Bush administration seeks to promote Terror War as the defining struggle of the era, coded as an apocalyptic battle between good and evil, as do al-Qaeda and other terrorist Jihadist groups. For my theorizing of war and militarism in the contemporary era, see Kellner 2003b and 2003c.

3. Barber's recent *Fear's Empire* (2003) sharply criticizes the Bush administration policy of "preemptive strikes" and "preventive wars" as a unilateralist militarism, destructive of international law, treaties, alliances, and the multilateral approach necessary to deal with global problems like terrorism, a critique that I would agree with (see Kellner 2003b). I also am in accord with Barber's position that both bin Laden's terrorism and Bush militarism promote a politics of fear that is counter to building a strong democracy. Hence, while I find Barber's general categorical explication of globalization problematically dualistic and his categories of McWorld and Jihad too homogenizing and totalizing, I am in general agreement with his criticism of Bush administration policy.

4. For example, as Ritzer argues (1993 and 1996), McDonald's imposes not only a similar cuisine all over the world, but circulates processes of what he calls "McDonaldization" that involve a production/consumption model of efficiency, technological rationality, calculability, predictability, and control. Yet as Watson et al. (1997) argue, McDonald's has various cultural meanings in diverse local contexts, as well as different products, organization, and effects. Yet the latter goes too far toward stressing heterogeneity, downplaying the cultural power of McDonald's as a force of a homogenizing globalization and Western corporate logic and system; see Kellner 1999a and 2003a.

5. While I find Hardt and Negri's *Empire* (2000) to be an impressive and productive text, I am not sure, however, what is gained by using the word "Empire" rather than the concepts of global capital and political economy. While Hardt and Negri combine categories of Marxism and critical social theory with poststructuralist discourse derived from Foucault and Deleuze and Guatarri, they frequently favor the latter, often mystifying and obscuring the object of analysis. I am also not as confident as Hardt and Negri that the "multitude" replaces traditional concepts of the working class and other modern political subjects, movements, and actors, and find the emphasis on nomads, "New Barbarians," and the poor as replacement categories problematical. Nor am I clear on exactly what forms their poststructuralist politics would take. The same problem is evident, I believe, in an earlier decade's provocative and post-Marxist text by Laclau and Mouffe (1985), who valorized new social movements, radical democracy, and a postsocialist politics without providing many concrete examples of struggle or political alternatives in the present conjuncture.

6. I am thus trying to mediate in this paper between those who claim that globalization simply undermines democracy and those who claim

that globalization promotes democratization like Friedman (1999). I should also note that in distinguishing between globalization from above and globalization from below, I do not want to say that one is good and the other is bad in relation to democracy. As Friedman shows (1999), capitalist corporations and global forces might very well promote democratization in many arenas of the world, and globalization from below might promote special interests or reactionary goals, so I am criticizing theorizing globalization in binary terms as primarily "good" or "bad." While critics of globalization simply see it as the reproduction of capitalism, its champions, like Friedman, do not perceive how in many instances globalization undercuts democracy. Likewise, Friedman does not engage the role of new social movements, dissident groups, or the "have nots" in promoting democratization. Nor do concerns for social justice, equality, and participatory democracy play a role in his book.

7. On resistance to globalization by labor, see Moody (1988 and 1997); on resistance by environmentalists and other social movements, see the studies in Mander and Goldsmith (1996) and Burbach (2001), while I provide examples below from several domains.

8. Friedman (1999, 267f) notes that George Soros was the star of Davos in 1995, when the triumph of global capital was being celebrated, but that the next year Russian Communist Party leader Gennadi A. Zyuganov was a major media focus when unrestrained globalization was being questioned—though Friedman does not point out that this was a result of a growing recognition that divisions between "haves" and "have nots" were becoming too scandalous and that predatory capitalism was becoming too brutal and ferocious.

9. On the Cancun meetings, see Chris Kraul, "WTO Meeting Finds Protests Inside and Out," *Los Angeles Times* (Sept. 11, 2003, A3); Patricia Hewitt, "Making trade fairer," *The Guardian* (Sept. 12, 2003); and Naomi Klein, "Activists must follow the money," *The Guardian*, (Sept. 12, 2003). On the collapse of the so-called "Free-Trade Summit," see Carol J. Williams and Hohn-Thor Dahlberg, "Free-Trade Summit Ends Without Pact," *Los Angeles Times* (Nov. 21, 2003). On the growing division between rich and poor, see Benjamin M. Friedman, "Globalization: Stiglitz's Case," *The New York Review of Books* (Aug. 15, 2002) and George Monbiot, "The worst of times," *The Guardian* (Sept. 12, 2003).

10. Such positions are associated with the postmodern theories of Foucault, Lyotard, and Rorty, and have been taken up by a wide range of feminists, multiculturalists, and others. On these theorists and postmodern politics, see Best and Kellner (1991, 1997, and 2001), and the valorization and critique of postmodern politics in Hardt and Negri (2000) and Burbach (2001).

11. In a report on the 2002 World Social Forum event in Porto Alegre, Michael Hardt suggests that protestors divided into antiglobalization groups that promoted national sovereignty as a bulwark against globalization and local groups connected into networks affirming an alternative democratic globalization. See "Today's Bandung?" *New Left Review* 14 (Mar.-Apr. 2002, 112–118). Not all countries or regions that oppose specific forms of globalization should be labeled "antiglobalization." Moreover, one might also delineate a category of localists who simply focus on local problems and issues and do not engage globalization. There is accordingly a growing complexity of positions on globalization and alternative political strategies.

12. As a December 1 abcnews.com story titled "Networked Protests" put it:

> [D]isparate groups from the Direct Action Network to the AFL-CIO to various environmental and human rights groups have organized rallies and protests online, allowing for a global reach that would have been unthinkable just five years ago.
>
> As early as March, activists were hitting the news groups and list-serves—strings of e-mail messages people use as a kind of long-term chat—to organize protests and rallies.
>
> In addition, while the organizers demanded that the protesters agree not to engage in violent action, there was one Web site that urged WTO protesters to help tie up the WTO's Web servers, and another group produced an anti-WTO Web site that replicated the look of the official site (see RTMark's Web site, http://gatt.org; the same group had produced a replica of George W. Bush's site with satirical and critical material, winning the wrath of the Bush campaign). For compelling accounts of the anti-WTO demonstrations in Seattle and an acute analysis of the issues involved, see Paul Hawkens, "What Really Happened at the Battle of Seattle," (http://www.purefood.org/Corp/PaulHawken.cfm), and Naomi Klein, "Were the DC and Seattle Protests Unfocused, or Are Critics Missing the Point?" (www.shell.ihug.co.nz/~stu/fair).

13. On the importance of the ideas of Debord and the Situationist International to make sense of the present conjuncture, see Best and Kellner (1997, Chapter 3), and on the new forms of the interactive technological society and Debordian critique, see Best and Kellner (2001) and Kellner (2003a).

14. Castells (1996, 26f) claims that Harvey (1989) and Lash (1990) say about as much about the postmodern as needs to be said. With due respect to their excellent work, I believe that no two theorists or books exhaust the problematic of the postmodern, which involves mutations

in theory, culture, society, politics, science, philosophy, and almost every other domain of experience, and is thus inexhaustible (Best and Kellner 1997 and 2001). Yet one should be careful in using postmodern discourse to avoid the mystifying elements, a point made in the books just noted, as well as Hardt and Negri (2000).

15. See Best and Kellner (1997 and 2001).

16. Freire also stated that "It is not the media themselves which I criticize, but the way they are used" (1972, 136). Moreover, he argued for the importance of teaching media literacy to empower individuals against manipulation and oppression, and using the most appropriate media to help teach the subject matter in question (114–116).

17. The "digital divide" has emerged as the buzzword for perceived divisions between information technology haves and have nots in the current economy and society. A U.S. Department of Commerce report released in July 1999 claimed that the digital divide in relation to race is dramatically escalating, and the Clinton administration and media picked up on this theme (see the report "Americans in the Information Age: Falling Through the Net" at http://www.ntia.doc.gov/ntiahome/digitaldivide/). A critique of the data involved in the report emerged, however, claiming that it was outdated; more recent studies by Stanford University, Cheskin Research, ACNielson, and the Forester Institute claim that education and class are more significant factors than race in constructing the divide (see http:cyberatlas.internet.com/big-picture/demographics for a collection of reports and statistics on the divide). In any case, it is clear that there is a gaping division between information technology haves and have nots, that this is a major challenge to developing an egalitarian and democratic society, and that something needs to be done about the problem. My contribution involves the argument that empowering the have nots requires the dissemination of new literacies and thus empowering groups and individuals previously excluded from economic opportunities and socio-political participation; see Kellner (2002).

18. *Wired* magazine is a good source for statistics and data concerning growing computer and Internet use among all sectors of youth and documents the vicissitudes of cyberculture. Studies of Internet addiction, however, raise concerns about negative implications of excessive usage. The *Chronicle of Higher Education* has reported that "Students are unusually vulnerable to Internet addiction according to a new quarterly journal called *Cyberpsychology and Behavior*" (Feb. 6. 1998, A25). The study indicated that students from 18–22 are especially at risk and pointed to a correlation between high Internet use and a dropout rate that more than doubled among heavy users. Accordingly, the University of Washington has limited the amount of Internet time available to students, to cut

down on overuse, and several other colleges have set up support groups for Internet addiction. But such studies do not record the benefits of heavy Internet use or indicate potentially higher productive uses than, say, watching television, drinking, or engaging in traditional forms of collegiate socializing.

19. On the attack on youth in contemporary society and culture, see Giroux (1996, 2002, 2003a and 2003b); Males (1996); and Best and Kellner (2003).

Chapter Two

Citizenship and Global Chaos

Education, Culture, and Revolution

Tom Steele and Richard Taylor

Introduction

The overall aim of this chapter is to consider the concept of citizenship as a necessary function of a healthy and integrative democracy in the context of globalization and the rise to supremacy of a single, militant, hyperpower—the United States. It takes its lead from the classical insistence of Plato and Aristotle that civic education is central to republican and democratic government, not simply to inform the populace of its duties, but to imagine and reinvent those radical utopias that are necessary for *eudaemonia,* or the good life of all.

The chapter is in three parts. The first considers the classical forms and historical origins of citizenship. It then surveys the moments of citizenship discourse formation in the modern period from the Renaissance to the present day. We note the reinvention of the *polis* in the Renaissance city-states, the citizenship of the French Revolution, the repressive conceptions of citizenship under authoritarian systems, and the tension between individual and collective rights in Western liberal democracies. We also consider the seminal argument for citizenship education put forward by Karl Mannheim during World War II.

The second focuses on the role of the nation-state and the international rule of law in the light of globalization. Using the analyses of Habermas and others, it considers the function of *ethnos* in relation to *demos* in the formation of modern nation-states and the exceptionalism of the United States. It considers the relationship of liberal citizenship to republican citizenship and the negative and positive freedoms determined by these forms.

The final part of the chapter examines the prospects for global citizenship in relation to cultural difference and pluralism. Martha Nussbaum's classical defense of liberal humanist education in pursuit of global citizenship and her notion of cultural rationalism have offered a way of valuing pluralism without surrendering to absolute cultural relativism. Then, in the light of Hardt and Negri's book *Empire* (2000) and Bacevich's book (2002) on American strategic power, we consider the problem of global citizenship in the light of American exceptionalism. This section argues that a new popular civic education has to be reinvented to understand the new realities of global flows of migrant workers, technological communications, and militant American culture capitalism. The chapter concludes by asking whether Western notions of democratic citizenship can accommodate the religious and ethnic forms of government that have arisen against "the West" under the influence of Islam and protecting universal human rights while embracing cultural difference.

1. Forms of Citizenship

Our argument assumes six related positions: (a) that citizenship in contemporary developed societies is a key element of a democratic polity; (b) that citizenship is, however, a highly generalized term, meaning different things to different people (for example,

Le Pen's ultranationalistic version, Blunkett's limited tolerance of hospitality to foreigners, Charter 88 constitutionalism, and the Social Democracy in Scandinavia); (c) that citizenship can only play its part in the development of a democratic polity if it is construed within a transnational, global context; the identification of citizenship with the nation-state is increasingly anachronistic and exclusionary; (d) that all perspectives on citizenship are *culturally relative*, limited to place and time, but have a rational core—our perspective is one deriving from the secular legacy of the Enlightenment but modified and revalued to acknowledge the extreme importance of multicultural sensitivity and a realization that Western liberalism, and more particularly neoliberalism linked to late capitalism, has been dominant ideologically as well as materially; (e) that, nevertheless, and however sensitive to other perspectives one must be, there are certain inherent conflicts of perception over citizenship, as over all else where certain issues and moral positions have to be asserted (e.g., over the rights and social roles of women; over the equal treatment of all ethnic and religious groups; over freedom of expression for divergent, counter-cultural views; and so on); (f) that education for citizenship must engage with the "complexity of community" in contemporary societies to engender such development in civil society.

Since the 1980s, the Left has largely embraced citizenship as a beneficial and progressive concept in most developed societies. However, even in the recent past, citizenship has been regarded suspiciously by the Left: "Citizenship was seen as a part of the problem rather than a solution to the injustices of capitalism"(Faulks 2000, 2). Citizenship was held to be imbued with capitalist values: it legitimated private property and thus inequality and "class rule," and hid this inequality behind a rhetoric of spurious legal entitlement to equal treatment under the law. However, with the demise of Soviet Communism, and the decline of socialism as a mobilizing ideology and political project, there has been a realization, in the light of Foucaldian concepts of power, that not all inequality is *economic*. Feminists, for example, have found citizenship a useful concept for conceptualizing women's oppression. This is in large part because it contests the idea of passive belonging: "A key determining characteristic of citizenship and what differentiates it from . . . mere subjecthood, is an ethic of participation" (Faulks 2000, 4). Citizenship, in modern guise, is therefore incompatible with domination. But citizenship is not only about rights, it is also about obligations. In that sense, it carries strong resonances of Lockean social contract.

Historical Forms of Citizenship

In David Held's characterization, Aristotelian concepts of citizenship were essentially "developmental republicanism," whilst Machiavelli's perspective was of a "protective republicanism" (Held 1996). This is illuminating but needs further contextualization. In Athens, citizenship was the privilege of a small minority: Democracy and citizenship were the domains of a small, organic, but above all exclusive, inner circle. Within this inner circle all was highly progressive, but principal among those excluded were women, slaves, and indeed the whole underclass infrastructure. Citizens, as an *elite*, therefore ran their own affairs both as legislators and executors and defended themselves; there was a strong emphasis upon military obligation, and a pride in defending the existence and the values of the polis against the (inferior) "other." Aristotle argued, in the classic formulation, that to take no part in running the community is to be either a beast or a God. In order to be truly human one had to be a citizen (with obvious implications for women and slaves). The collective of the polis, and the obligations and duties that membership entailed, therefore took precedence over any private or individual morality. In fact, there was no question of "private morality"—everything was vested in the polis (Jordan 1989).

Roman concepts of citizenship were in many ways more inclusive, but at the same time much more centralist, and were seen as an agency of social control by an increasingly authoritarian state. This was especially true in the imperial period. As Faulks notes, this is analogous in many ways to the European Union: "Citizenship became detached from an ethic of participation and was increasingly a thin and legalistic concept with the largely instrumental motive of undermining sources of discontent" (Faulks 2000, 19). In essence, therefore, citizenship in Rome degenerated into one of the key means for the ruling class or elite of maintaining power.

With the demise of the Roman Empire and subsequent rise of medieval Christendom in Europe, republican citizenship declined in importance. The pursuit of honor and civic virtue through citizenship was replaced largely by Christian notions of obedience and salvation (already signaled in Constantine's choice of Christianity as the imperial religion). The Church, rather than the political community, became the focal point for collective loyalty and for the moral baseline. As Anderson notes, "the most important institutional effect of the religious change was the social promotion of a large number of 'service Christians', who had made their administrative careers by loyalty to the new faith, to the ranks of the enlarged 'clarissimate' of the 4th century" (Anderson 1974a, 91). The hold of the Catholic Church over political life was not broken until the French defeat of the papacy in the fifteenth century, which allowed the northern Italian cities to develop in a remarkable way. The Italian Renaissance was driven by an intense desire to dispel the darkness of the Middle Ages and, in Petrarch's words, to "walk back into the pure radiance of the past" (quoted in Anderson 1974b, 149). Italian city-states such as Florence and Venice attempted "the deliberate revival and imitation" of the civic and cultural life of classical civilization (Anderson 1974b, 149).

In seventeenth-century Britain, however, the materialist philosopher Hobbes was notably "anticitizenship." The individual had no rights, except self-preservation, and even that was subject to the will of the sovereign. Hobbes saw the aim of the social system as being the maintenance of stability and continuity through strong state control. But, in our context, he can be seen as a halfway house to Locke's (and subsequently Rousseau's) contractualism. Hobbes did believe in a contract, however one-sided, between the individual and the State, and he did believe in the equality of "ordinary men" to the effect that, despite individual differences of character and ability, it was remarkable how narrow these differences were.

Contrary to Aristotelian assumptions of organic social solidarity, Locke built a rights (law-based) theory of citizenship involving a social (legal) contract between the State and the individual citizen, which became the theoretical legitimation of the liberal conception of the capitalist state and the infrastructure that underpins it. It attempted to achieve a balance between economic freedom (inequality) and a "civilized" concern for rights and justice. Locke also assumed that a modern educational system would mold the right kind of human vehicle (from the "empty vessels" of the classroom) for the system. It was the French Revolution of 1789 that first fused legal citizenship with the nation-state. However, since then, conceptions of citizenship have been largely "subordinate to market principles and the intentions of political and economic elites" (Faulks 2000, 10).

In modern, contemporary societies, it has become clear that citizenship cannot be explained simply in terms of the hegemonic subordination of the lower classes to the ideas and values of the dominant class. This is only part of the explanation. Other dimensions include: (a) the effect of social movements; (b) the role of ideology—as Faulks notes, "The universalism of liberalism provided citizenship with an egalitarian potential that excluded groups could draw upon creatively"(Faulks 2000, 26); (c) economic factors. The needs of the market economy determine how citizenship can be and is articulated. There is ongoing debate over whether citizenship is therefore inherently opposed to or supportive of capitalism. "Social rights" can be held to be a concession granted to workers because of trade union power and the need to keep the working class incorporated into the economic and sociopolitical system, but they are also an effect of liberal thought. The 1980s and '90s saw capital undermine the economic and cultural power of organized labor, but at a cost—uncontrollable alienation of large sections of the disaffected population from all forms of cultural and economic "inclusion"; (d) an undertaking of the fractured complexity of the liberal state is essential to an understanding of citizenship in modernity/late capitalism. "There is a contradiction . . . at the heart of the modernist project: the tension between the State as an exclusionary community and citizenship as a universal status" (Faulks 2000, 30).

Citizenship Education in Britain

In Britain the issue of citizenship education figured poignantly in the twentieth century, particularly during the latter stages of global warfare. At the end of World War One and in the wake of the Soviet Revolution, the Ministry of Reconstruction under Lloyd

George urgently considered how citizenship education might be extended to an increasingly restless working class. The final report of the Ministry's Adult Education Committee, the famous *1919 Report* was seen as a blueprint for "a free and fully participatory democracy" (quoted in Fieldhouse et al. 1996, 47). Its enormous influence, according to Fieldhouse, "lay in its emphasis on the social purpose of adult education in developing a notion of responsible citizenship" (ibid., 47). Its chairman, the Master of Balliol, A.L. Smith, regarded adult education not as luxury but as "a permanent national necessity, an inseparable aspect of citizenship" (quoted in ibid., 48). Despite opening up a harmful rift between liberal and vocational education, it influenced the Board of Education's subsequent decision to provide special funding for adult education and encourage the universities to become involved through establishing extramural departments and working with voluntary movements that became key features of British adult education.

The issue was again theoretically addressed during WWII by a group of intellectuals who were drawn together by the new Master of Balliol, A.D. Lindsay (formerly Professor of Moral Philosophy at Glasgow). The most articulate statement of the group came from a Jewish exile from Nazi persecution, the German sociologist Karl Mannheim (1943).

Although Mannheim immigrated to Britain from the theoretical hothouse of Frankfurt, he belonged to the "other Frankfurt" from the one that nurtured Critical Theory, which was more inclined to a Christian Socialism rather than revolutionary Marxism (although in many respects, it was not so different from the later Habermas) (Steele 1997). Mannheim's view was that the postwar reconstruction should be on the basis of a *planned* democracy rather than the older notion of *liberal* democracy that had produced such divisive social inequality. Under a planned democracy, he argued, citizenship was based on intellectual understanding of the needs of the whole as well as the liberal ability to argue the case for the needs of the individual or group. Education should therefore aim to develop the whole person, not just a specialist in the division of labor, for whom a rational morality replaced blind obedience, and who valued argument and agreement through rational accord about first principles.

Mannheim was also concerned with a problem that occupied Habermas later (as we shall see), which was: How could social solidarity be achieved under such secular, abstract principles? So to this recognizably Enlightenment view he brought the Christian duty of "love thy neighbor": "The equal political rights of citizens in a democracy are the abstract equivalent of the concrete primary virtues of sympathy and brotherliness" (Mannheim 1943, 18). In a planned society, unity should be achieved through the "spiritual" (though not necessarily Christian) integration of all members within a common philosophical outlook.

Mannheim provided a useful taxonomy of the contradictory philosophies of life current in post-Enlightenment modernity: (1) Christian religion of love and universal brotherhood; (2) Enlightenment liberalism with its emphasis on freedom and personality and its appreciation of wealth, security, happiness, tolerance, and philanthropy; (3) Socialist priorities of equality, social justice, basic security, and planned social order; (4) Fascist demands for fertility, race, power, tribal/military virtues of conquest, discipline, and blind obedience. Such was the theoretical disparity of such views that modern societies had not been successful in formulating an agreed educational policy for normal citizens; there was no agreement either for creating rationalists who discarded custom and tradition or, contrarily, for handing on a social inheritance focused on religion and "national culture." At the higher level there was also little agreement as to whether to concentrate on creating specialists for the industrial division of labor or all-round philosophically grounded personalities.

The only acceptable form of modern society for Mannheim and the social democratic left was one based on collective deliberation, which required an educational approach that developed intellectual powers strong enough to "bear the burden of skepticism." Democracy required decentralization of functions to allow a creative social task for everyone so that education must enable all to understand the "pattern" of life. But such a society needed also to plan for the continuity of "irrational" beliefs among the mass of ordinary people. Democratic progress implied the struggle against all forms of authoritarian order, replacing brutal forms of social integration by more human forms of education—Mannheim cites the way Reformation Protestantism demanded a more rational form of morality than Catholicism, for example.

Mannheim therefore placed the question of citizenship education firmly within the struggle for cultural unity, though not necessarily based on either nationality or religion, but one based on common agreement over human aims loosely derived from a belief in love. Democratically controlled, planned society required agreement for action and spontaneous consent to an *internalized* belief in what was right rather than external coercion. However, Mannheim recognized the coming struggle with popular, mass culture for that internalization. In the coming mass society, school and church would have to compete with commercialized interests for guidance on how to be free, how to love, whom to obey, and so on. But no matter how important the *cultural* struggle, the crux of the problem still lay with the system of *economic* production and for Mannheim it would be impossible to humanize leisure and factory life if the basis of calculation was money and profit rather than social welfare. But as the century progressed, Mannheim's enormously influential sociological argument for cultural unity came increasingly under fire from pluralistic and deconstructive accounts.

2. Citizenship and the Imagined Community

In the light of this criticism, Habermas posed the question of how was it possible for the individual to identify with a set of abstract rights and regulations of which she knew little in detail, but which ensured for her the right to live freely and securely (Habermas 1999). Without these legal relations guaranteeing rights, modern citizenship in the Western tradition was not possible, nor was the power vested in the state legitimate. However, the very state that guaranteed these freedoms most frequently appeared to the individual less as a source of freedoms than as the unwelcome collector of taxes and the instrument of retribution on behalf of the dominant class. The answer to this paradox historically seems to be the imagined community of the *nation,* which created that sense of social solidarity that was lacking in the regulatory state. The nation could offer an identity with people that spoke the same language, who had tilled the same land "since time immemorial," who shared the same customs and festivals, and, most importantly, were of the same "blood." This elaborate fiction seems to have filled the space that dry-as-dust abstractions, beloved of lawyers and bureaucrats, left vacant, and created above all "solidarity between strangers." She still found, however, that male strangers (and brothers and husbands) seemed to possess more of these rights and fewer of the duties.

Hence two not necessarily complementary ideas became fused in the modern system to form the European *nation-state*. This formed the bedrock of the system of rights and duties and social solidarity that became the condition of modern life for both Western communities and many of those that came under the influence of European colonialism during the nineteenth and twentieth centuries. However, under the pressure of late-twentieth century "globalization" of commerce, communications, international finance, and production, the nation-state as guarantor of rights and identity was increasingly vulnerable. Ecological and military risks also increasingly posed problems that could not be solved within the conventional frameworks of the nation-state or by traditional interstate agreements. The territorial sovereignty of nation-states was never secure and was profoundly compromised by the emergence of superpowers claiming their spheres of interest following World War II. With the collapse of the Soviet Union and its satellites under the economic superiority of American capitalism, military pressure, the ideological desirability of liberal rights, and the "shop till you drop" free market, individual nations found that they were joyfully free of external political control, but simultaneously deeply exposed to external corporate exploitation.

The challenge for citizenship now is to understand whether this epochally unique situation of the global dominance of one hyperpower can be made subject to the founding and expansion of political institutions on the *supra*national level, such as had been proceeding since WWII, or whether the nation-state has had its day. Despite criticism from the left, Habermas vests increasing significance in the growth of international political and legal institutions such as the United Nations, the European Court of Human Rights, the international legal agreements that internationalize crimes and restrict the traditional immunity of national elites from prosecution, and commercial regulation. Clearly Habermas is not wedded to the nation-state as such, but more to the project of *civic autonomy*, which first evolved within this institution. Some notion of "global citizenship" (though it is not a term he uses much) would have to embrace such a supranational project and would overcome the parochial restrictions of the nation-state. Without this system of international regulatory frameworks, he is deeply pessimistic. He concludes that if such a regulatory project fails along with the nation-state, then effectively all forms of political integration will cease to exist. This catastrophic failure would leave only the model of the multinational corporation, which encourages uncritical identity with the firm and all its products and hostility to competitors, resulting in what he calls "a disordered mass of self-steering functional systems" (Habermas 1999, 124).

Nationalism vs. Republicanism

Habermas's account of the historical formation of the nation-state, while contested, concentrates on unpacking its twin terms "nation" and "state" and exposing a different and potentially incompatible source for each. The term "state" is associated with the institutional regulation of rights and duties, governance and punishment exercised usually at a distance by monarchy, aristocracy, or elected body. "Nation," however, is associated with land, kinship, and historical destiny and not specifically with any legal enactments. Subsequently, Habermas uses the Greek terms *demos* and *ethnos* to suggest the different set of associations.

This dualistic aspect of nation-states implies that they are Janus-faced. In the first place, it suggests a political legitimation founded on the voluntary nation of citizens or *demos*. The modern state, in principle, owes its legitimacy to classical practices of free democratic elections carried out by individuals acting as citizens of the republic rather than as subjects of the monarch. The elected body has their consent to rule and carry out decisions which affect all, but can also be recalled by the sovereign wish of the people. In practice however, the combination of state bureaucratic and corporate power creates a "system" that perpetually threatens to overwhelm the "lifeworld" of the citizen.

But coupled with this highly abstract form of the state is the "felt community." This has historically ensured social integration based on the inherited or ascribed nation founded on ethnic membership or *ethnos*. This form of identity draws its strengths from known relationships of family and kin that can be traced in the immensely powerful signifier of "blood," which are then projected onto the imagined community of language speakers, physically resemblant and habitually similar, elsewhere within the borders or in exile beyond. Such identity has the politically important function of disguising class, gender, and racial inequalities.

The transition from absolutist monarchy to democratic republic was facilitated by invention of the "nation," since, despite the important shift in the legitimation of rule, the subjects of the monarch now became (subject) citizens of the republic. Nation-states therefore solved two problems. Firstly, the mode of legitimation had to be secular since, because of the schism of confessional religions, the divine right of kings could no longer be evoked. Secondly, social integration was accomplished through national identity, which was further achieved by urbanization and modernization.

The conceptual move from subject of the king to national republican citizenship (even in the face of constitutional monarchies) eased the process of unmooring populations from corporative late medieval social ties. The "rights of subjects" became transformed and augmented into human and civil rights of the voluntary political order as imagined by Kant and Rousseau.

The idea of nation facilitated this shift since it implied continued subjection to state power. But it sets up a problematic double coding in citizenship as, firstly, a legal status in terms of civil rights, and secondly, membership in a culturally defined community. Hence an operative tension is set up between the universalism of legal rights to which the republic of citizens aspires and the particular "historical" community which forms the identity of the nation. Habermas regards this tension as harmless so long as republican cosmopolitanism exercised hegemony over what he calls the naturalistic, pre-political, ethno-nation. He suggests that however useful such an identity was for creating the fusion of nation and state, the vulnerability of civic republicanism to nationalistic fervor ultimately led to Nazism and the genocidal suppression of other nationalities and ethnicities, both internal and external. Thus, under the pressure of multiculturalism, all forms of ethno-nationalism should be renounced.

But how is the unity of a political culture to be sustained in the absence of a strong sense of national identity? Because of the postcolonial and global migrations of labor in recent decades, republicanism now has to stand for the integration of an increasingly differentiated society. While it should no longer take the conventional historical path of fusing the majority culture into the national culture, despite conservative opposition, can we be sure that the constitutional patriotism of the republic is strong enough to attract immigrant and ethnic minority groups? Are the traditional rights of liberal individualism and participation powerful enough to include those groups whose collective identity is cemented by a "fundamental" religion and ethnicity?

During the later twentieth century, the answer modern, liberal, Western states (and for that matter Communist states) found for the problem of social integration was *welfare*. The post-WWII secular state was to various degrees (from the United States to Scandinavia) a Welfare State which extended social and material rights during periods of economic growth to the lower classes into which the ethnic and immigrant groups were integrated. Thus, Habermas notes, public and private autonomy presupposed each other.

Even in prosperous Western states, the cutback in welfare policies and abdication of a common politics that has characterized the neoliberal governments of the last two decades has produced a volatile underclass with no power of political veto through the normal processes. Many of the jobless or low-waged poor in post-Communist societies also look back nostalgically to the era of full employment and cheap housing of their former authoritarian state. For Habermas, this leads ultimately to the undermining of the universalistic core of republican politics. Neo-Nazi groups parade openly and violently in many countries while ultra-right-wing political parties regularly command a significant percentage of votes. Reflecting this turn away from the liberal secularism that characterized earlier social democratic politics, ethnic minorities frequently embrace authoritarian, fundamentalist ideologies that dismiss equal rights for women and internal minorities as "Western" and are often militantly intolerant of other cultures.

The nation-state seems to have come up against its limits. Its boundaries, though always contested, are increasingly permeated by global flows of finance, goods, people, and "alien" ways of thought. The turnover of many international corporations now exceeds the entire revenue of many small countries, while the wealth of a small minority of capitalists exceeds the entirety of sub-Saharan Africa. This phenomenon is often referred to as "globalization," although it is clear that the term covers many contradictory applications. It is not yet clear what effects these are having on public consciousness and the public spheres in which politics has to operate. While some, such as Hardt and Negri, as we shall see, celebrate the democratic potential of the Internet, the actual Internet public is fragmented into serial "village" publics which are largely closed to each other (excepting perhaps the truly international male public for pornography).

Habermas believes that collective cultural rights have to be offered to minority groups in multicultural societies, but under the overall hegemony of liberal individual rights, so that the abused individual member of the community or culture can find redress through the state's or international legislation. But Mannheim's question of "spiritual" unity or a "felt" human commonality needs also to be addressed if the Enlightenment preoccupations with equality and social justice are to be honored, as they must be. Is education, especially the education of mature citizens, a credible starter here?

3. Education and the World Citizen

It is an interesting paradox that America creates both the greatest threat to world citizenship, through its hyperpower exceptionalism, yet produces some of the most creative thinking about it. We shall comment here on two recent offerings. The first is from Martha Nussbaum, a celebrated feminist theorist and Aristotelian philosopher from the Chicago School. Nussbaum over the past decade has strongly defended the liberal humanistic tradition in education in the face of pluralistic attacks upon it. She is not opposed to pluralism; on the contrary she believes that classical liberal humanism is *per se* pluralistic. But against extreme relativist tendencies she insists that all particular forms of humanity are underpinned by a common humanity which can itself be discovered through dialogue and analysis. Her fundamental position is that cultural traditions are not monolithic and unitary, but are subject to internal as well as external rational criticism:

> Since any living tradition is already a plurality and contains within itself aspects of resistance, criticism and contestation, the appeal to reason frequently does not require us to take a stand outside of the culture from which we begin. The Stoics are correct to find in all human beings the world over a capacity for critical searching and a love of truth. . . . In this sense any and every human tradition is a tradition of reason. (Nussbaum 1997, 63)

To this extent we are "fellow citizens in a community of reason." Nussbaum recognizes that we are necessarily historically and culturally located, but that if norms are human and historical and not immutable or eternal, then the search for rational justification of moral norms is not futile. She seems to operate with a kind of qualified universalism that shares neither the absolutist certainty of religious transcendentalism that believes in divinely given truth nor the absolute relativism of some versions of identity politics that insist on the incommensurability of cultures.

Nussbaum takes the Enlightenment view that ethical enquiry requires encouraging a critical attitude to habits and conventions rather than unqualified acceptance of authority. This is enhanced by cross-cultural understanding, which removes the false air of naturalness and inevitability of our practices. She takes as examples both Socrates's argument for equal treatment of women and Aristotle's description of the Athenian constitution, which compares it often unfavorably with other forms. The true basis for human association for Aristotle is not any preexisting cultural or religious "identity," but what can be defended as "good for human beings." Hence the Stoics developed from Diogenes a critique of conventions and cross-cultural study to generate the idea of "World Citizen" or *Kosmoi polités* as the center of their educational program. They held that national identity is accidental and should not be a boundary. The true moral community is humanity itself with its fundamental ingredients of reason and moral capacity (which becomes the source of Kant's "kingdom of ends").

While loyalties based on nonrational cultural or religious identity are more open to manipulation by traditional (usually male) elites, nevertheless some form of local identity may be more desirable. The special love of nearest and dearest, for the Stoic emperor Marcus Aurelius, was preferable to an abstract equality of love. Even though locatedness or roots seems to be important for humanity, closest is not necessarily best. Hence Nussbaum recommends the project of the "examined life," which can distinguish between what is merely parochial and what can be recommended to all.

Nussbaum insists that it is possible to recognize the virtuous life in all cultures and hence a common humanity. But local group loyalties frustrate world citizenship by neglecting commonalities and prioritizing the identity of the group. While it is desirable that oppressed groups should find pride in their identity and deny the representations of them by the hegemonic culture, this cannot take an inflexible supremacist form which merely mirror-images that of the oppressing group, a stance that makes it impossible to evaluate other groups with fairness and justice. The world citizen therefore has to be a "sensitive and empathetic interpreter" cultivated through education.

World Citizenship Education

Nussbaum conducted a wide-scale survey of programs of multicultural education in American liberal arts colleges and universities. Her recommendations fit well into adult educational and lifelong learning parameters. Firstly, education must be multicultural in the sense that it examines the fundamentals of all major religions and cultural groups. Secondly, it should demonstrate awareness of cultural difference accompanied by a critical understanding of one's own traditions, habits, and conventions, with the capacity to question the "inevitable naturalness" of our own ways. Thirdly, local identity should be explored through regional or group history, but in a global context. Finally, education should start early with stories of or from other traditions so that, by the time they encounter higher education, students are well-equipped for the study of diversity, not simply as a way of confirming the superiority of their own identity.

Not surprisingly, Nussbaum is suspicious of programs of multicultural education limited to uncritical recognition or celebration of differences, as if all cultural practices were morally neutral or legitimate. She prefers the term "interculturalism" by contrast, which connotes a comparative searching for common human needs across cultures and of dissonance and critical dialogue within cultures. Such "interculturalist" programs embrace a number of principles: (1) Resist the impression of a "marketplace" of cultures, each asserting its own claim. (2) Emphasize the importance of imagination in crossing cultural boundaries and thinking oneself into the place of the other. (3) Acknowledge certain common human needs. (4) Doubt the unqualified goodness of one's own ways through structured encounters with other cultures. Programs of education that attempt to enter into other cultures and seek their human core are an essential part of the "examined life."

It seems to us that Nussbaum has contributed an important defense of liberal education that reflects many of the rational priorities articulated by Mannheim while counteracting the problems of nondifferential cultural unity. Nussbaum recognizes the strength of religious, national, and local identities but appeals to the classically argued paradigm of cosmopolitanism. Cultural identity may properly strengthen oppressed communities in their struggle with hegemonic forces, but may not protect individuals or minority groups within. As Bauman also notes, in a very rewarding short study of the idea of "community," cultural distinction can often take more malignant forms than language, dress, or ritual expression and may include practices such as female humiliation that cannot be made palatable simply because they are "traditional." Bauman comments:

> We (western intellectuals) may be readier to accept that, as much as we should respect the right of a community to protection against assimilatory or atomizing forces administered by the state or the dominant culture, we must respect the right of individuals to protection against choice-denying or choice-preventing communal pressures. (Bauman 2001, 138).

Mannheim, Habermas and Nussbaum all inhabit a conceptual framework derived from classical, Enlightenment, and Marxist thought, and in Nussbaum's case, feminist theory. Their engagement with current politics reflects a pessimistic distance from revolutionary socialism and a more or less qualified embrace of Western liberal traditions allied to the social-justice project of socialism and a postcolonial sensitivity to cultural difference. As Mannheim notes, however, the cultural project implied in their analysis in the end always runs up against the economic requirements of capitalist social relations.

Empire Against World Citizenship?

Finally then we consider a contrasting view deriving from the revolutionary libertarian Marxist analysis of the Italian *autonomista*. Hardt and Negri's book *Empire* (2000) caused a stir on the jaundiced Left when it was published during the millennium year. Indeed it was millenarian in its implications.

For Hardt and Negri, this is the golden age of the Left, not its defeat. Despite the unraveling of nation-state systems of power, globalization is not just about deregulating markets, but is actually a supranational order of interlocking regulations or "empire." It is an epochally original phenomenon, a Foucauldian, diffuse, and anonymous network that cannot be monitored from metropolitan control centers, for which conventional Marxist analyses are wholly anachronistic. The old dichotomies of ruling class/ proletariat, core/periphery are now broken down into an intricate pattern of inequality, a volatile totality that transgresses inherited divisions of political thought.

This new historical order is based on the classical tripartite order of the "monarchy" of U.S. nuclear supremacy, the "aristocracy" of G7 wealth, and the "democracy" of the Internet. But, *pace* the Roman Empire, it is now in decline at the hands of barbarian migrants. The iconoclasm of their approach rests on the proposition that Empire rose, *not* through the defeat of systemic challenges to capital, but because of the success of heroic mass struggles that shattered the old Eurocentric regime of national states and colonialism.

Now the increasing importance of intellectual labor in high-value-added sectors is shaping a new collective laborer, in the Marxist sense, with acutely potential subversiveness. This new productive force displays a plebeian desire for emancipation through increasing malleability of social relations and permeability of borders. But conservative forces frustrate this desire: The functioning ideology of Empire is a supple, multicultural aesthetic that actually deactivates revolutionary potential. Hardt and Negri argue that academic theorists of multiculturalism, far from subverting hegemonic relations as they imagine, actually serve the interests of hegemonic inclusion. Similarly NGOs, the white hope of radicalism, are not necessarily the resistance agencies of civil society, but mobilize support for "humanitarian" intervention.

But is Empire a coherent legal structure or a permanent state of emergency? Balakrishnan (2000) argues that Hardt and Negri seem to want it both ways. They deny it is a specifically American empire because sovereignty has no purchase, any power or decision-making center. Empire, on the contrary, is brought about by the "multitude," a collective subject (but not yet "for itself" in the Hegelian sense). Negri's position seems to be derived from his 1970s autonomist position when he abandoned the working class as revolutionary agent but turned, via a reading of Marx's *Grundrisse,* to the "dispossessed" and "disaffected." There is, he argues, a new collective worker taking shape that rejects politics as a strategic field for a pervasive, diffuse, popular desire for liberation. Although local rebellions do not connect globally or strategically, they become immediate media events and attack the virtual center vertically. Thus Empire is permanently vulnerable to marginal but highly publicized events. Empire is Debord's "society of the spectacle," seemingly powered by the pursuit of happiness, but actually based on mobilization of desires that are intimately related to fear of failure, exclusion, and loneliness.

The masses no longer need Machiavelli's Prince or any leader but immediate, if episodic, empowerment. They are hostile to borders and restrictions on cosmopolitan freedom; "the general right to control its own movement is the multitude's ultimate demand for global citizenship." But who will guarantee this right if there are no global or international regulatory institutions?

American Exceptionalism

A rather less benign analysis of Empire to emerge from a recent American source is that of a former U.S. General, Andrew Bacevich

(2002). It is clear that the emergence of the United States as *the* global superpower creates enormous challenges for democratic movements and the prospects of a global democratic order throughout the world. Traditional justifications of American power abroad were to liberate Europe and Japan from Fascist and then Communist power. Why, now that these are no longer a threat, Bacevich asks, are American global operations not scaled back?

His answers are not especially comforting. America is revealed as a special kind of imperial state with huge military and civil bureaucracies flanked by massive business organizations. Since at least World War II, "war and conquest had to be accepted as the price of social peace at home," leading to what some have called "Warfare Keynesianism."

The foundations of postwar U.S. imperial strategy were fuelled by a massive military budget against the serious recession of 1949 when, according to Dean Acheson, "Korea saved us." The Cold War to contain the "Evil Empire" of the Soviet Union also delivered key domestic benefits: a popular anti-communist ideology, state-funded R&D support to a range of U.S. industries, and cross-class constituencies with direct stake in imperial expansion.

In this context, "Globalization" can be seen as an extension of an old strategy with a new name, a euphemism for American economic expansionism, a doctrine which goes back to McKinley in 1901 who commented, "How near one to the other is every part of the world. Modern inventions have brought into close relation widely separated peoples and made them better acquainted. . . . Distances have been effaced. . . . Isolation is no longer possible or desirable" (quoted in Gowan 2003, 150).

Bacevich also demonstrates that the U.S. military has also developed the policy of "Full Spectrum Dominance," or decisive strategic superiority over all other powers, which has spawned an intercontinental network of "proconsular powers." These are located in four great regional commands—CINCPAC (East Asia), CINCSOUTH (Latin America), CINCEUR (Europe, Africa, Israel) and CINCENT (Middle East, Central Asia)—the office of each of which now commands greater resources than the President's office and which have greater power than the traditional diplomatic service. Under the new National Security Strategy announced in

September 2002, no comparable power to the U.S. is now tolerated, which is supported by the doctrine of "preemptive war," of which Iraq is the first beneficiary.

The consequences of the new doctrine are far reaching. Key to this, as Chomsky has maintained frequently, is that the U.S. public is kept on permanent alert to potential threats, real or imagined, by an "economy of fear." The huge new internal "security" Department of Homeland Security threatens domestic civil liberties and recasts citizenship in authoritarian ways around patriotic obedience rather than individual or group freedoms, although protection of the latter is given as the reason for suspending them. Suppression of dissent is achieved also by ideological massification, the "War on Terror" serving as a blanket for invasion of privacy and silencing criticism.

The external complement to this policy of internal containment was already signaled by the Bush government's readiness to withdraw from international agreements when they do not suit U.S. strategic interests and strategic retreat from Internationalism. Already the signs of this change are obvious: the downgrading of the U.N. as a forum for solution of international problems and international peacekeeper; the promotion of generic American commercial interests over internationally agreed ecological treaties, such as the Kyoto Protocol; the refusal to submit to key aspects of International Law—one of the great post-WWII signs of progress that limited power of states and immunity from prosecution.

The threats to Global Citizenship of these changes are also clear: a reassertion of national interest over global agreements, weakening of moves toward global rule of law, and the reassertion of brute force as solution for international disagreement. These are hardly the messages of optimism that the young Habermas and his fellow students found in the U.S.-supported advances to international regulation that succeeded the Second World War.

Reasons for Hope

American exceptionalism in global terms is a major concern as is the impact of various kinds of religious fundamentalism, some of which also emanate from the United States. However, the United

States has also been the source of many of the radical movements that have altered the texture of everyday life: The women's movement, the black consciousness movement, the gay pride movement and disability groups have all developed into significant social forces and created global popular literatures in the United States. Despite the enormous ideological leverage that neoconservative regimes are able to mobilize through the popular media, there is clearly a radical otherness in American society which has its roots in the freedoms guaranteed by the Constitution. The same freedoms, particularly of the press and of information, can also question the massive corporate corruption that funds the regime. The speed of global communications, especially through the Internet—again originated in the United States—does imply, as Hardt and Negri have maintained, the potential for truly global democratic movements, even if, as Habermas says, it is pervaded by digital parochialism.

The paradox of this global dominance of American corporate capitalism is that the liberal values of the Constitution and the democratic impulse of the Puritan Founding Fathers are also rhetorically present as justification. The Bush regime can defend its invasion and destruction of other sovereign nations through the language of democracy and an appeal to "the People" even if the actuality is ever so slow in coming.

Arguably, a commercially driven popular culture is also fueling a demand for democracy in traditional or ethno-religious societies (Urry 1998). A global youth culture fueled by cheap cultural consumption goods such as fast food, clothes, and music, subverts local patriarchal traditions and authoritarian norms. Liberal humanism and secular civil rights are carried by nongovernmental organizations (NGOs) and movements to otherwise isolated and oppressed groups. Even the global prevalence of the English language means an unprecedented amount of information and, perhaps more importantly, radical democratic theory is available to resistance movements.

As with the global seduction of American popular culture, U.S. foreign policy is enormously unpopular. This is the natural consequence of economic policies that impoverish "developing" countries through the enormous debts generated by the neoliberal reconstruction of failing economies through the American-dominated International Monetary Fund. The United States is also widely perceived as propping up unpopular regimes, in Asia and Latin America, and siding in ethnic and religious conflicts, as crucially with Israel in Palestine (the Bush "Road Map" merely limiting its excesses).

As a consequence, antiglobalization currents have flourished, of which the most divisive current is the growth of ethnicity and religion. Paradoxically, religious revivalism in the South has replaced socialism as the leading anticapitalist movement. Islam is now the leading edge of the fault line, due to historic resistance to Western imperialism and the warrior sect tradition of puritanical fundamentalism. As Mann (2001) notes, "Combat Fundamentalism" is epitomized in the Palestine/Israel conflict where the poor South (and East) meet the affluent North (and West) and thrives on the consequences of Western economic exploitation. Ironically, regional fights against corrupt and authoritarian regimes are imaged as part of a global struggle of the faithful against the infidel, thereby giving cosmic significance to local conflicts.

Recently, it has been argued that such fundamentalism is already on the wane as liberal reforms in Iran, the first Islamic fundamentalist state, may confirm. Terrorist movements like al-Qaeda, Anderson maintains, are not so much the expression of the vigor of Islamic fundamentalism but a sign of its popular decline and marginalization (Anderson 2003, 13).

If so, nonfundamentalist forms of cultural identity may emerge that are more conducive to democratic citizenship. It appears to be equally the case that, as Iraq testifies, not all aspects of Americana are desirable. Then the case for a separation of ethnos from demos in a form of representative government free from religious, ethnic, or gender discrimination, but respecting local traditions, may be possible. The collective rights that Habermas talks about will have to be enshrined in a way that leaves individual freedom from group oppression unharmed. Even the "multitude" so dramatically interpellated by Hardt and Negri will need formal procedures and structures, if goodwill, neighborliness, and brotherhood are to be projected into global solidarity. If so, then social movements must embed Freirean educational priorities, as with the Zapatistas and other Latin American land movements in their campaigns.

References

Anderson, P. (1974a) *Passages from Antiquity to Feudalism*. London: Verso.
———. (1974b) *Lineages of the Absolutist State*. London: Verso.
———. (2003) "The Casuistries of War," *London Review of Books*, 25(5), 6 March 2003, 12–13.
Bacevich, A. (2002) *American Empire: The Realities and Consequences of US Diplomacy*. Cambridge, MA:, Harvard University Press.
Balakrishnan, G. (2000) review of Hardt and Negri's *Empire*, in *New Left Review*, 5, Sep/Oct, 142–148.
Bauman, Z. (2001) *Community, Seeking Safety in an Insecure World*. Oxford: Polity Press.
Faulks, K. (2000) *Citizenship*. Key Ideas Series. London: Routledge.
Fieldhouse, R., et al. (1996) *A History of Modern British Adult Education*. Leicester: NIACE.
Gowan, P. (2003) "Instruments of Empire," *New Left Review* 21 (May/June), 137–146.
Habermas, J. (1999) *The Inclusion of the Other: Studies in Political Theory*. Oxford: Polity Press.
Hardt, M., and Negri, A. (2000) *Empire*. Cambridge, MA: Harvard University Press.
Held, D. (1996) *Models of Democracy*. Oxford: Polity Press.
Jordan, B. (1989) *The Common Good*. Oxford: Blackwell.
Mann, M. (2001) "Globalization and September 11," *New Left Review* 12 (Nov/Dec), 51–72.
Mannheim, K. (1943) *Diagnosis of Our Time: Wartime Essay of a Sociologist*. London: Kegan Paul, Trench Trubner & Co., Ltd.
Marx, Karl (1973) *Grundrisse* (trans. Martin Nicholas). Harmondsworth: Penguin Books.
Nussbaum, M.C. (1997) *Cultivating Humanity, A Classical Defense of Reform in Liberal Education*. Cambridge, MA: Harvard University Press.
Urry, J. (1998) "Contemporary Transformations of Time and Space," in P. Scott (ed.), *The Globalization of Higher Education*. Milton Keynes: SRHE/OpenUniversity Press.

Chapter Three

Globalization and Critical Feminisms Post-9/11

Rhonda Hammer

Although "terrorism" has taken on new meanings within the context of post-9/11 events, its concept and scope continues to be a contested terrain. The Bush administration has generated ideological discourses that associate the term "terrorism" exclusively with anti-Western philosophies and practices. Yet terrorism is hardly particular to Islamic fundamentalists and is a complex process that characterizes a multiplicity of dimensions of local and global human relations. Terrorism does not exist in a vacuum. Indeed, in order to understand and discuss the realities of terrorism and/or terror war, a theoretical and practical, contextually mediated approach must be employed that engages terrorism within globalization and a range of social relations and forms. My argument is framed by a critical feminist perspective that includes analyses of individualized, local, and global dimensions of what I am calling "family terrorism."

I further argue that this kind of approach owes much to its incorporation and retranslation of dimensions of colonization theories that emphasize the role of alienation in terrorist practices. Moreover, the patriarchal nature of terrorism, which finds significant grounding in the familial relations of the so-called domestic sphere, public domain, and globalized world of neoliberal capitalism, must be recognized and critiqued as a predominant dimension of a plethora of terror relations. Hence, I propose the need for the kinds of radical shifts in thinking and praxis that embrace a globalized, coalition politics which identifies difference and solidarity, in a dialectical, both/and fashion, grounded in an epistemology of social justice. Such a transformative critical perspective is especially cognizant of the hierarchical natures of a multiplicity of patriarchal relations. These include pathological families and overt and blatant segregated communities, governments and businesses, nation-states, nationalized organizations, fundamentalist religious ideologies, and especially, contemporary forms of militarism, which, many argue, are provoking genocidal terrorist policies directed, primarily, at women, children, and the elderly.

Before continuing with my arguments, however, I should indicate the manner in which I am employing some of these terms and ideas, given that most of them (like feminism or globalization, for example) evoke contested and sometimes ambiguous meanings due to the complex and often multidimensional experiences they attempt to describe. Indeed, there is rarely a universally agreed upon collective consensus on the denotative or connotative essence of much of this language. As Zillah Eisenstein puts it: "There is no one feminism. No one nationalism. No one patriarchy. No one colonialism. They take different shapes, are defined in and through different contexts, and have different histories" (1996, 139).

Hence, I begin with some general explications of notions of globalization, family terrorism, colonization, alienation, and militarism as significant interrelations to explain how I understand and employ these concepts in my research, and to give a better sense of my argument. Radical pedagogies need to incorporate these categories into their teaching to help enlighten students concerning the global context of terrorism and its multiple dimensions, including what I call family terrorism.

Globalization

"The concept of globalization," as Carmen Luke reminds us, "is contested, overused and trapped in dangerous dualisms" (2001, 24). Rather than employing globalization in an essentialist or bifurcated manner, I attempt to employ it in a dialectical sense. Hence, I don't reduce it solely to the neoliberal, political, economic, paradigmatic component that, according to Robert McChesney, refers to "the policies and processes whereby a relative handful of private interests are permitted to control as much as possible of social life in order to maximize personal profit" (McChesney 1999, 7). Yet, the economic consequences of these kinds of policies have provoked "a massive increase in social and economic inequality, a marked increase in severe deprivation for the poorest nations and peoples of the world, a disastrous global environment, an unstable global economy and an unprecedented bonanza for the wealthy" (ibid.). For example, over 800 million people are starving in the world (Eisenstein 1998, 1). According to UNICEF, "one out of 6 or 47 million children are living in poverty" in industrial nations; 11.6 of those children live in the United States, "while 600 million children in developing countries live in abject poverty" (www.sustreport.org/news/poverty.html; www.tufts.edu/publications/hunger/pub/paradox of our times/highlights; www.wsws.org/articles/2002/ap2002/chila22.shtml).

It is hardly surprising that starvation in Afghanistan has escalated since the 9/11 bombings and Afghanistan war, with thousands of new widows and orphaned children joining the ranks (*LA Times*, Jan. 7, 2002). Failure of the so-called allied coalition to implement promises of massive financial aid and reconstruction, as well as U.S./British support for what has been identified as a puppet regime, have contributed to rising poverty, disease, human rights violations, and an environment of fear which permeates all human relations in that country.[1] The same has been the case for Iraq, since the so-called Gulf War 2. In fact, Alexander Cockburn describes these kinds of warped dehumanizing practices as the "Terrorism of Everyday Life." At the most elemental level, some terrorism is aimed at "the weakest in our midst: no money for food, for shelter, for the kids. . . . " Thus, he asserts, "do we nourish the next generation of Enemy Combatants" (2002, 9).

One thus needs to recognize the escalation of what Gore Vidal (2002) and Howard Zinn (Dec. 2001) describe as perpetual illegal wars and "crimes against humanity" (ibid, 8). These necessarily encompass burgeoning transnational criminal activities which include the odious increase in what has been identified as one of the fastest growing organized criminal global activities: Trafficking in Human Beings. Needless to say, the majority of these human beings are women and children, according to UNICEF, Amnesty International, and the U.S. Congress, to name a few (Hammer 2002). An international rights group, Anti-Slavery International, reported to the United Nations session on slavery, in March 2002, that there were at least 27 million people forced into slavery in the world today. These figures are growing, due in large part to the escalating poverty, and sexual exploitation and forced labor of children (Reuters in *Metro Today*, May 27, 2002).

Citing 1997 statistics, Zillah Eisenstein points out that corporations are displacing countries in this brave new world, and that "of the world's largest one hundred economies, fifty-one are corporations not countries"(1998, 1). "The five hundred biggest corporations account for 70 percent of world trade" (ibid.). Moreover, "women and girls represent approximately 60 percent of the billion or so people earning one dollar a day or less" (ibid.).

Yet, at another level, globalization has manifested a technological revolution in communications, which has the potential for new kinds of democratic process which can and does provide counterhegemonic information to a growing concerned and activist audience. Within this context, new computer technologies are also assisting and provoking the development of organizations that challenge the system of global neoliberalism, colonization, dictatorial powers, and terrorist practices. Indeed, what Kellner (2002) describes as "globalization-from-below" involves the formation of powerful social movements that are "proactive rather than reactive," such as feminism, environmentalism, human rights (often working within NGOs), and anti-neoliberal, transcapitalism movements (Castells 1997, 109). Yet, we cannot forget that resistance to globalization has also helped construct what Castells describes, as "reactive" movements, that often disseminate cyberhate propaganda and mobilize antimodernist groups. Moves toward commercialization and restrictive practices may also define the future of the new global technologies that could neutralize their applications for progressive reform and struggle. Interrogations of this contradictory and multileveled process do, however, reveal foundational relations associated with patriarchal, familial, terrorist values and practices.

Family Terrorism

The Sept. 11, 2001 terrorist attacks on the U.S. and their aftermath dramatized the centrality of globalization and the dangers and vulnerabilities of the entire world to destructive violence. These events have provoked, not only heinous subsequent terrorist practices, but also widespread discussions that have problematized the definitions of terrorism and have done serious damage to the true nature and contextual meaning of the term. These kinds of erroneous and restricted employment of terrorist discourse conceal and ignore the multidimensionality of terrorism in regards to individual and global human rights, including multiple forms of violence directed at massive numbers of disenfranchised peoples, especially women, children, and the elderly. Moreover, these kinds of delineations generally fail to recognize that terrorism often finds its basis in patriarchal codes that permeate and organize a variety of political, social, economic, and cultural relations of everyday life.

Critical scholars like Manuel Castells emphasize that it is "analytically, and politically essential" to recognize "the roots of patriarchalism in the family structure" (1997, 134). "Patriarchalism," he contends, "is a founding structure of all contemporary societies" and is characterized "by the institutionally enforced authority of males over females and their children in the family unit" (ibid.). This authority is exercised through the permeation of the entire economic, political, and social organization of society by patriarchalism. Hence "interpersonal relationships and thus personality, are marked, as well, by domination and violence originating from the culture and institutions of patriarchalism" (ibid.). Yet it is the patriarchal family, Castells argues, which shields recognition of the "sheer domination" of patriarchalism.

Indeed, to recognize the ideological nature of family terrorism and patriarchal violence combats popular myths regarding feminism's anti-male bias and demonstrates that critical feminists have always recognized that "men were not the problem, that the problem was patriarchy, sexism, and male domination" (hooks [*sic*] 2000, 67). It is, however, essential to recognize that patriarchal tendencies "vary in surprising ways across cultures. Patriarchy does not come in 'one size fits all'" (Enloe 1993, 5)

Hence, deleterious effects of patriarchal values and beliefs on men, in a variety of cultural, localized, and global environments, have been a significant part of critical transformative feminisms. Because violence is systemic and hierarchical, rigid bifurcated descriptions of gender violence must be negated and retranslated into a more complex and contextual analysis of violence at a variety of levels.

It is, in this sense, that I have developed the expression "family terrorism." I employ it to provoke a dialectical shift in addressing issues of violence against women, children, and the elderly that is far more extensive and interrelated to social, political, and economic dimensions (which necessarily includes relations of gender, race, ethnicity, class, and sexuality) than conventional thinking about what violence or abuse of women and children usually signifies. A discussion of the effectiveness of this polysemic term, "family terrorism," which is mediated by patriarchalism, for understanding a multiplicity of social, political, psychic, and economic relations, is especially necessary within this context.

Family terrorism, in its first sense, reveals and critiques the problematic nature of such inept ideological descriptions as "domestic violence," or its latest incarnation, "intimate partner abuse"—which even further neutralizes and reduces the real complexity of relationships it is allegedly delineating. According to bell hooks, "domestic violence" has been used to cover up the severity and the systematic nature of family terrorism. She argues that it is "a 'soft' term which suggests it emerges in an intimate context that is private and somehow less threatening, less brutal, than the violence that takes place outside the home" (2000, 62). Moreover, she is one of a number of feminists who are concerned with the abuse and neglect of children and discuss this within a contextual framework which includes the roles of women in terrorizing and/or neglecting their children and the contexts in which this takes place. It is in this sense that bell hooks's employment of the term "patriarchal violence" is especially appropriate. As she explains it:

The term "patriarchal violence" is useful because unlike the more accepted phrase "domestic violence" it continually reminds the listener that violence in the home is connected to sexism and sexist thinking, to male domination (2000, 61–62).

The patriarchal abuse of children and elderly, as well as the escalating nature of global violence against women and children, must therefore be understood as a systemic, familial mediated process. For example, Linda Gordon points out that even "a mother who might never be violent but who teaches her children, especially her sons, that violence is an acceptable means of exerting social control, is still in collusion with patriarchal violence" (1988, 64). She clarifies the relationship of patriarchal violence to parental violence and women's role as collaborators and/or colonizers in this relationship. And Riane Eisler further argues, in her analysis of the events of September 11 and fundamentalist terrorist extremism, that we must begin with examining gender and parent-child relations since these "are the critical, formative relations . . . where we first learn what's normal and moral, where we learn values and behaviors" (2001, 33). She asserts that you must examine the context of hate and terror, which involves a transformative and dialectical analysis: "Clearly most women do not use violence to dominate men (even though small numbers of women batter the men in their lives), but lots of women believe that a person in authority has the right to use force to maintain authority" (hooks 2000, 64).

Given that violence, abuse and/or terrorism against children and teenagers is escalating, it is mandatory that many feminisms expand upon their definitions of family violence. This is especially relevant given transnational globalization's emphasis on the commoditization of people (primarily women and children), the current "politics of greed," and rising government cutbacks, including the downsizing and dismantling of the so-called welfare state in much of the overdeveloped and developed first-world. For example, the Amnesty International *Children's Report for the 2000 Campaign to Stamp out Torture* provides us with a shocking pronouncement on the global state of family terrorism, specifically violence against children:

[V]iolence against children is endemic: children are tortured by the police or security forces; detained in appalling conditions; beaten or sexually abused by parents, teachers or employers; maimed, killed or turned into killers by war.

Some are victims many times over, first of the chronic poverty and discrimination that renders them vulnerable to torture and ill-treatment, then to the injustice and impunity that allows it to continue unpunished (www.stoptorture.org).

Moreover, in many countries children are kidnapped or purchased from families (often due to extreme poverty provoked by war). Children are kidnapped not only for sexual slavery but also for military use.

Child soldiers are part of the largest problem of child abuse. . . . Human Rights Watch did a report on child soldiers in which they showed that there are about 500,000 child soldiers in 87 countries. . . . In some countries you have children as young as ten years old killing people (Maier, 2002, 78).

As we have witnessed in myriad contemporary terror wars, most of these children do not understand what they are fighting for. They are physically and psychologically brutalized and often fed drugs. In some cases, boys and girls are forced to kill their own parents with semi-automatic weapons (ibid.). Moreover, the systemic nature of family violence is further established by the escalating rate of violence against the elderly. In the United States, for example:

The National Elder Abuse Incidence Study (NEAIS) found that an estimated total of 550 thousand elderly persons experienced abuse, neglect and/or self-neglect in domestic settings in 1996. . . . Abusers are more likely to be male and family members, especially adult children (Soto-Aqino, Congressional Research Service, 1999, 2).

Officials have estimated that "as many as 2 million older Americans become the victims of crimes such as physical and mental abuse, neglect, abandonment, and financial exploitation" every year (*Los Angeles Times*, Aug. 1, 2003). The notion of patriarchalism and its oppressive familial relations that operate in all dimensions of human life, as well as the escalation of family terrorisms, demand a further examination of these sociopolitical, economic, and psychological dimensions within a context of colonization and alienation.

Alienation and Colonization

The employment of colonization theory, which is applied by many transformative, visionary, and/or transnational feminists to dissect terror relations which take place at local/global levels, provides for a deeper understanding and analysis of the complexities and multidimensional nature of family terrorism. Translating from classic works on colonization illuminates the multifarious relationships of violence and terror, especially those directed against women, children, and the elderly. In reality, colonization is not just restricted to physical deprivation, legal inequality, economic exploitation, and classist, racist, and sexist unofficial or official assumptions. Sandra Bartky identifies a pathological dimension which is essential to the process of colonization and terrorisms that Frantz Fanon described as "psychic alienation" (Bartky, 1990, 22).

> To be psychologically oppressed is to be weighed down in your mind; it is to have a harsh dominion exercised over your self-esteem. The psychologically oppressed become their own oppressors; they come to exercise harsh dominion over their own self-esteem. Differently put, psychological oppression can be regarded as the "internalization of intimations" (Bartky 1990, 22).

Yet alienation, as Marx and Hegel point out, is hardly restricted to the psychological domain. In fact Fanon's concept of alienation, which can be generally described as the alienation of humans from their own potentialities—is close to Marx's analysis in his *Early Texts* (Zahar 1974, 13ff.). Indeed, Fanon's method, which interrogates the relations of colonial societies under the aspect of alienation, has been characterized as "a synthesis of the sociological, psychological and Marxian concepts" (cited in Zahar 1974, 14ff). In fact, many translations of colonization and alienation theory and praxis understand that "alienation has a political objective; the intellectual alienation of the colonized," which is evident in their identification with inferiorized stereotypes (Zahar 1974, 15).

It is deplorable that the complexities of intellectual and/or psychological states of the mindset of peoples involved in the pathologies of colonization and terrorisms are often subordinated or ignored in many analytical discussions of these kinds of relations.

Understandings of patriarchal family terrorisms as individualized, nationalized, and globalized relations necessitate recognition of this most sophisticated dimension of colonization. Indeed, these pathological characteristics of colonization and its role in family terrorisms reveal the complexities involved in what is often called a "master/slave dialectic."[2] Moreover, the distinctions between patriarchal codes and values and erroneous essentialized behaviors of a generalized "class of men" become even more apparent when discussed within the context of colonization as an elaborate process which usually involves colonizer, colonized, and collaborator. In relation to women's and children's situations, for example, transformative feminists, like Cynthia Enloe, maintain that

> to describe colonization as a process that has been carried on solely by men overlooks the way male colonizers' success depended on some women's complicity. Without the willingness of 'respectable' women to see that colonization offered them an opportunity for adventure, or a new chance of financial security or moral commitment, colonization would have been even more problematic. (Enloe 1989, 16)

Moreover, colonization cannot be addressed in simplistic manichean, reductionist terms that essentialize men as oppressors and women as oppressed, or infer that all women suffer the same degrees of subordination; for women can be both colonizer and colonized and can be instruments of family terrorism against children and the elderly, as well as instruments of colonization in relation to other women and even men. Hence, colonization is a dialectical set of hierarchical relations which involves class, race, ethnicity, gender (sexuality), age, nationalism, and other determinations, which are often interconnected and multiple.

It is in this sense that a transformative feminist approach expands upon the notions and realities of battery, terrorization, and abuse of women and children to include relations of state, cultural, and global terrorism of women and children in the forms of the feminization of poverty, hunger, exploited labor and slavery, prostitution and the sex trade, arguing that these are expansive forms of the ideology of family terrorism, especially given that family members, cultural communities, and the family of the state are actively involved in these kinds of atrocities. Moreover, as many transformative feminists argue, violence against men—especially during war—is often mediated through the abuse, murder, rape, and torture of familial women and children of the enemy.

Family Terrorism and Militarism

For example, the gender politics and relationship between localized and globalized family terrorism, alienation, and colonization is rarely discussed in terms of violence against women and children in relationship to militarism. Yet violence against women, by men, escalates during conditions of war, and many experts argue that modern or contemporary wars are in themselves acts of terrorism. For example, Howard Zinn argues that: "Terrorism and war have something in common. They both involve the killing of innocent people to achieve what the killers believe is a good end" (2001, 16). "Collateral damage," as it is now euphemistically called, has been extensive in contemporary wars, especially within the latest so-called wars against terror in Afghanistan and Iraq (Herold 2002). Indeed, as Julie Mertes and Jasmina Tesanovic demonstrate, "the startling fact [is] that in contemporary warfare, 95 percent of the casualties are civilians, the majority of them women and children" (cited in Waller and Rycenga 2001, xviii). Further: "Families constitute primary sites of belonging to various groups: to the family as an assumed biological entity; to geographically identifiable, racially segregated neighborhoods conceptualized as imagined families; to so-called racial families codified in science and law; and to the U.S. nation-state conceptualized as a national family" (Hill-Collins 1998, 63)

These kinds of patriarchal family values are especially consequential in comprehending, critiquing, and countering "nationalist, communalist, and religious fundamentalist social movements which have emerged all over the world," which, as Meredith Tax argues, have moved into "the power vacuum created as local elites have been overwhelmed by the new global financial ruling class" (1999, 24).

It is within this translation of the patriarchal family to the "localized, national, or globalized family" that violence, torture, and rape of women and girls are better understood and situated. In fact, many critical feminists have associated patriarchal familial attitudes and violence with militarism. Moreover, a number of feminist studies demonstrate increases and changes in modes of family violence during wars and wartimes (Kesic 2001, 26).

The forms of violence inflicted against women in wars vary in form, scale, and intensity from killing, rape, torture, forced impregnation, body searches at checkpoints, imprisonment, settlement in concentration camps and refuges, and forced prostitution, to verbal insults and degradation, psychological suffering for losses, and the burden of responsibility that women carry as survivors (Kesic 2001, 25).

Eisenstein argues that "war rape is sexualized violence that seeks to terrorize, destroy, and humiliate a people through its women":

> [G]enocidal rape has its own horrors. It takes place in isolated rape camps, with strict orders from above to either force the woman's exile or her death. Rape is repeatedly performed as torture; it is used to forcibly impregnate; it is even used to exterminate. Women in the camps are raped repetitively, some as many as thirty times a day for as long as three consecutive months. They are kept hungry, they are beaten and gang-raped, their breasts are cut off, and stomachs split open. (Eisenstein 1996, 59)

Yet, even under these conditions, women cannot be perceived as universal in that, as Enloe reminds us, rape in war is often structured by class, ethnic and racial "inequalities between women" (1993, 168). The commoditization and colonization of different women become evident in that the rape of these women, in times of war, upheaval, or political disputes, "represents conquered territories" (Eisenstein 1996, 41).

In other words, women and girls are treated as possessions of husbands, fathers, sons, brothers, etc., and their violation, torture, and murder is intended to demoralize and humiliate their enemy. Not to forget that boys and men are wounded, killed, and often tortured in these kinds of contexts, the women's mediating role finds its basis in that the "external enemy is imagined to be other men, men who would defile or denigrate the nation" (Enloe 1993, 239) This was also the strategy of the Japanese during World War II, when they "conscripted" at least 200,000 girls and women from

Korea, China, Taiwan, Indonesia, and the Philippines as sex slaves or "comfort women." Countless impoverished Asian girls and women were snatched from their homes to serve Japanese soldiers, who beat, raped, and murdered them. Some were recruited by force, coercion, and deception into sexual slavery from 1931–1945. (K. Connie Kang, *LA Times*, July 22, 2001). It would be absurd to deny the elements of family violence involved in these kinds of militaristic outrages and sometimes genocide, especially given that the Japanese recorded these sex slaves as "ammunition," and refused until 1993 to even acknowledge that its military ran the program (ibid.).

I believe that the term *family terrorism* is even more appropriate given the nature of the devastating effects of September 11 and its further implications, especially since certain forces are appearing to restrict the meaning of the term to exclude particular Western actions, as well as different dimensions of patriarchal violence and terror. It is imperative that the dialectical relationship between personal, familial, individual/group, organizational, religious/ethnic, national, state, and global terrorisms be analyzed and discussed in academic and public forums. Hence, it is within this contestatory field that feminists and critical pedagogists need to better address and begin to further develop critical definitions and studies of terrorisms which go beyond identifying it as purely individual and collective crimes but as an ideology. It is within this context that describing particular patriarchal relations of abuse, rape, murder, starvation, poverty, exploitation, torture, and genocide is especially relevant.

References

Castells, M. (1997). *The Information Age. Economy, Society and Culture. Volume II: The Power of Identity.* Malden, MA: Blackwell Publishers.

Cockburn, A. (2002). "Terrorism as Normalcy." *The Nation*, July 1, 9.

Chomsky, N. (1999). *Profit over People.* New York: Seven Stories Press.

Eisenstein, Z. (1998). *Global Obscenities: Patriarchy, Capitalism, and the Lure of Cyberfantasy.* New York: New York University Press.

Eisenstein, Z. (1996). *Hatreds: Racialized and Sexualized Conflicts in the 21st Century.* New York: Routledge.

Eisler, R. (2001). "The School for Violence." *LA Weekly,* Sept. 28–Oct. 4, 33–35.

Enloe, C. (1990). *Banana Beaches & Bases: Making Feminist Sense of International Politics.* Berkeley: University of California Press.

Enloe, C. (1993). *The Morning After: Sexual Politics and the End of the Cold War.* Berkeley: University of California Press.

Freire, P. (2001). *Pedagogy of the Oppressed.* New York: Continuum.

Gordon, L. (1988). *Heroes of Their Own Lives: The Politics and History of Family Violence—Boston 1880–1960.* New York: Viking.

Hammer, R. (2002). *Antifeminism and Family Terrorism: A Critical Feminist Perspective.* Lanham, MD: Rowman & Littlefield.

Hill-Collins, P. (1998). "It's All in the Family: Intersections and Gender, Race and Nation." *Hypatia* (Summer), 62–82.

hooks, b. (2000). *Feminism Is for Everybody: Passionate Politics.* Cambridge, Mass.: South End Press.

Kellner, D. (2004). "The Conflicts of Globalization and Restructuring of Education." In M. Peters (ed.), *Education, Globalization, and the State in the Age of Terrorism.* Boulder, CO: Paradigm.

Kojève, Alexandre (1969). *Introduction to the Reading of Hegel.* New York: Basic Books.

Luke, C. (2002). *Globalization and Women in Academia: North/West-South/East.* Mahwah, NJ: Lawrence Erlbaum Associates.

Maier, K. (2002). "Inquiry: Interview with Dr William Aldis, Regional Advisor for Africa for Humanitarian Action at the World Health Organization." *Journal of Children & Poverty,* 8(1), March, 67–83.

Marx, K., and Engels, F. (1978). *The Marx-Engels Reader.* New York: Norton.

McChesney, R.W. (1999). "Introduction." In N. Chomsky, *Profit over People.* New York: Seven Stories Press, 7–16.

Rius, E. Del Rio. (1976) *Marx for Beginners.* New York: Writers and Readers Publishing Co-operative.

Vidal, G. (2002). *Perpetual War for Perpetual Peace: How We Got to Be So Hated.* New York: Thunder Mouth Press.

Waller, M., and Rycenga, J. (eds.) (2001). *Frontline Feminisms.* New York: Routledge.

Zahar, R. (1974). *Frantz Fanon: Colonialism and Alienation* (trans. W.F. Feiser). New York: Monthly Review Press.

Notes

1. See Robyn Dixon, "Afghans on Edge of Chaos: As opium production and banditry soar, the country is at risk of anarchy, some warn, and could allow a Taliban resurgence." *Los Angeles Times,* Aug. 4, 2003.

2. The master/slave dialectic finds its foundations in the work of nineteenth century philosopher G.W. Hegel. It has been employed and translated from in much critical scholarship which attempts to understand the complexities of power relations and relations of domination and subordination. Alexandre Kojève provides for an indication of Hegel's interpretation and explains that a seminal aspect of this relationship is characterized by the needs of the dominant member to be recognized by the slave as the master. To do so, he must overcome him dialectically. That is, he must leave him life and consciousness, and destroy only his autonomy. He must overcome the adversary only insofar as the adversary is opposed to him and acts against him. In other words, he must enslave him. (Kojève 1969, 15).

Chapter Four

Technologies of the Self and *Parrhesia*

Education, Globalization, and the Politicization of Youth in Response to the Iraq War

Tina Besley

Introduction

For Foucault, "technologies of domination" and "technologies of the self" produce effects that constitute the self, both defining the individual and controlling their conduct. His focus is on questions of subjectivity and the shaping and regulation of identities, on a relational self where intersubjectivity becomes central—a self that acknowledges and is constituted by difference and the Other. This chapter comprises two sections: first, an introduction to Foucault's "technologies of the self" and *parrhesia,* and second, an analysis of new kinds of youth who are constituted in response to globalization, the mass media, information technology, and consumer society.[1] From being seen as focused predominantly on style and lifestyle, many youth throughout the world have recently become politically radicalized in response to the 2003 war against Iraq. In the United Kingdom, in particular, despite the influence of some formal curricula, for example citizenship education, much of the information, communication, and organization for youth antiwar protests took place outside the classroom—located through the Internet and text messaging. An example of this kind of project can be seen in the way in which the Hands Up for Peace campaign, which is detailed later in the chapter, was organized by youth. I argue that teachers now need to pay attention to the ways that youth construct themselves in a globalized postmodern world in relation to the Other, and in response to threats to the security of their world—threats that currently include terrorism and war.

Foucault's "Technologies of the Self" and *Parrhesia*

Late in his life, when discussing his work, Foucault (1988b) said that his project had been to historicize and analyze how in Western culture the specific "truth games" in the social sciences, such as economics, biology, psychiatry, medicine, and penology, had developed knowledge and techniques for people to understand themselves. Foucault never focused specifically on education or pedagogy, although he did make some highly original and suggestive comments in earlier works like *Discipline and Punish* (Foucault 1977), which emphasized the application of technologies of domination through the political subjugation of "docile bodies" in the grip of disciplinary powers, and the way the self is produced by processes of objectification, classification, and normalization in the human sciences. Other commentators have addressed the relevance of his writings to education and some have applied his methods to educational issues (see, for example, Ball 1990; Marshall 1996; Olssen 1999; Baker 2001). Foucault defended the "determinist" emphasis in *Discipline and Punish*, admitting that not enough was said about agency, so once he redefined power to include agency as self-regulation, he overcame some of the problematic political implications in his earlier work (see Afterword in Rabinow 1997; Foucault 1985, 1988a, 1990; McNay 1992). He emphasized that individuals are continually in the process of constituting themselves as ethical subjects through both technologies of the self and ethical self-constitution, and a notion of power that is not simply based upon repression, coercion, or domination. By this later point Foucault saw individuals "as self-determining agents capable of challenging and resisting the structures of domination in modern society," doing this for themselves without necessarily needing a priest or a therapist (McNay 1992, 4).

In his later works, Foucault not only provided quite a shift from earlier discourses on the self, but also brought in notions of disciplinarity, governmentality, freedom, and ethics as well as focusing on corporeality, politics, and power and understanding the self in its historico-social context. His own understandings about the self shifted over his lifetime, and he was strongly influenced by both Nietzsche and Heidegger. Nietzsche inspired Foucault to analyze the modes by which human beings *became* subjects without privileging either power (as in Marxism) or desire (as in Freud). In turn, Foucault developed Nietzschean "genealogy" (Nietzsche 1956).

Foucault took up Heidegger's critiques of subjectivity and Cartesian-Kantian rationality in terms of power, knowledge, and discourse—a stance against humanism that is tantamount to a rejection of phenomenology. Foucault harnessed Heideggerian notions of *techne* and technology, rather than an instrumental understanding of technology, innovatively adding these notions to his understanding of the self to formulate technologies of the self in his reconsideration of Greco-Roman antiquity and early Christianity (Foucault 1988b). However, unlike Heidegger (1977), who focused on understanding the "essence" or presence of being (*dasein*), Foucault historicized questions of ontology and was not concerned about notions of *aletheia* or uncovering any inner, hidden truth or essence of self. Foucault substituted genealogical investigations of the subject for the philosophical attempt to define the essence of human nature, aiming to reveal the contingent and historical conditions of existence. For Foucault, the self or subject "is not a substance. It is a form, and this form is not primarily or always identical to itself" (Foucault 1997, 290). Once we realize that there is no universal necessity of human nature, we will feel much freer than we ever experienced ourselves.

In *The Question Concerning Technology,* Heidegger questions our relationship to the essence of modern technology, which, he argues, treats everything, including people, "as a resource that aims at efficiency—toward driving on to the maximum yield at the minimum expense" (Heidegger 1977, 15). Dreyfus (2002) points out that both Foucault and Heidegger believed that the practices of modern technology produce different kinds of subjects—subjects who do not simply objectify and dominate the world through technology, but who are constituted by technology. This forms a fundamental point in the second part of the chapter where I argue that communication technology is an aspect of globalization that enables youth to construct the self in new ways.

In the seminar "Technologies of the Self," presented at the University of Vermont in 1982, Foucault set out a typology of four interrelated "technologies"—namely, technologies of production, technologies of sign systems, technologies of power (or domination), and technologies of the self. Each was a set of practical reason that was permeated by a form of domination that implied some type of training and changing or shaping of individuals. Technologies of power "determine the conduct of individuals and submit them to certain ends or domination, an objectivizing of the subject" (Foucault 1988b, 18). Technologies of the self are ways the various "operations on their own bodies and souls, thoughts, conduct, and way of being," that people make either by themselves or with the help of others, in order to transform themselves to reach a "state of happiness, purity, wisdom, perfection, or immortality" (Foucault 1988b, 18).

Foucault admitted that he had concentrated "too much on the technology of domination and power" (Foucault 1988b, 19). Nevertheless, for him both technologies of domination and technologies of the self produce effects that constitute the self (or subjectivity). They define the individual and control their conduct as they make the individual a significant element for the state through the exercise of a form of power, which Foucault coined as "governmentality," in becoming useful, docile, practical citizens (Foucault 1988c). In turn, Foucault's two notions of technologies of domination and technologies of the self (1988b) can be used as a means for investigation of the constitution of postmodern youth under the impact of globalization.

In "Technologies of the Self" (1988b), Foucault examined the first two centuries AD of Greco-Roman philosophy and the fourth and fifth centuries of the Roman Empire when Christian spirituality and monastic principles were prevalent. Foucault argued that the Delphic moral principle "know thyself" (*gnothi sauton*) became dominant, taking precedence over another ancient principle and set of practices, "to take care of yourself," or to be concerned with oneself (*epimel ésthai sautou*) (Foucault 1988b). According to Foucault, "care of the self" formed one of the main rules for personal and social conduct and for the art of life in ancient Greek cities. The two principles were interconnected, and it was actually *from* the principle of care of the self that the Delphic principle was brought into operation as a form of technical advice or rules to be followed when the oracle was consulted. Foucault accepted that the ancient Greek notion of care of the self was an inclusive one that involved *care for others* and precluded the possibility of tyranny because a tyrant did not, by definition, take care of the self since he[2] did not take care of others. Foucault stated that *care for others* became an explicit ethic later on and should not be put before care of the self (see Foucault 1984, 1997).

In contemporary Western culture the two ancient moral principles (care of the self and know thyself) have been transformed such that care of the self is often viewed as immoral, narcissistic, and selfish, even as an escape from rules. This has occurred because know thyself was the principle that Plato privileged and which subsequently became hugely influential in philosophy and because Descartes privileged the *cogito* or thinking subject and knowledge of the self. Yet Foucault argued for the return of the ancient maxim of care of the self because since the Enlightenment the Delphic maxim had become overriding and linked inextricably with constituting subjects who are able to be governed.

Foucault pointed out that for the ancient Greeks the ethical principle of self consisted of *self-mastery*, but by comparison, it shifted to become *self-renunciation* in the Christian era (Foucault 1988b). Thus the crucial difference revolved around two quite different ethical notions. Self-mastery implied both a control of the passions and a moderation in all things, but also a worldliness that involved being in and part of the world of the free citizen in a democratic society. Self-renunciation as a form of Christian asceticism involved a set of two interlinked truth obligations: one set surrounded "the faith, the book, the dogma" and another "the self, the soul, the heart" (Foucault 1981, cited in Foucault 2001, 139). The tasks involved in the latter include, first, a "clearing up all the illusions, temptations, and seductions which can occur in the mind, and discovering the reality of what is going on within ourselves" and, second, getting free from attachment to the self, "not because the self is an illusion, but because the self is much too real" (ibid.). These tasks implied self-negation and a withdrawal from the world, in what forms a "spiral of truth formulation and reality renouncement which is at the heart of Christian techniques of the self" (ibid.). Confessional practices form a technology of the self—speaking, reading, and writing the self—that shifted from the religious world to medical then to therapeutic and pedagogical models in secular contemporary societies (Foucault 1988b; Peters 2000). Foucault concluded his seminar on technologies of the self with the highly significant point that the verbalization techniques of confession have been important for the development of the human sciences into which they have been transposed and inserted and where they are now used "without renunciation of the self but to constitute, positively, a new self. To use these techniques without renouncing oneself constitutes a decisive break" (Foucault 1988b, 49).

In a later series of lectures at the University of California, Berkeley, October–November 1983, Foucault problematized the practices of *parrhesia*, of "free speech" or truth-telling speech activities in classical Greek culture where "the *parrhesiastes* is one who uses *parrhesia*, i.e., the one who speaks the truth"—a set of deep-seated cultural practices for the West that evolved to take political, philosophical, and personal forms (Foucault 2001, 11). Foucault investigated the use of parrhesia in education to show that education was central to the "care of the self," public life, and the crisis of democratic institutions (see Peters 2003). Foucault's intention was "not to deal with the problem of truth, but with the problem of truth-teller or truth-telling as an activity" (Foucault 2001, 169). He claimed that truth-telling as a speech activity emerged when Socrates pursued his "confrontations with the Sophists in dialogues concerning politics, rhetoric and ethics" (170). Truth-telling was a distinct set of philosophical problems that revolved around four questions: "who is able to tell the truth, about what, with what consequences, and with what relation to power" (ibid.). Foucault pointed out that the problematization of truth since the end of pre-Socratic times created two major branches of Western philosophy—a "critical" tradition and an "analytics of truth" tradition that is primarily concerned with "ensuring that the process of reasoning is correct in determining whether a statement is true (or concerns itself with our ability to access the truth)" (ibid.). He stated that he aligned himself with the "critical" philosophical tradition that is concerned "with the importance of telling the truth, knowing who is able to tell the truth, and knowing why we should tell the truth," rather than the analytic tradition (ibid.). Foucault demonstrated that these practices link truth-telling and education in ways that are still operative in shaping our contemporary subjectivities; thus, they are relevant in understanding the exercise of power and control and of contemporary citizenship, especially in situations where there is some risk for a person in telling the truth to a superior—a situation that clearly can occur in schools, in the student-teacher relationship, and which certainly occurred for some youth in their anti-war activities in 2003.

Over time, the meaning of parrhesia in Greek and Roman culture developed five major characteristics—frankness, truth, danger, criticism, and duty—which Foucault summarized thus:

> *Parrhesia* is a kind of verbal activity where the speaker has a specific relation to truth through frankness, a certain relationship to his own life through danger, a certain relation to himself or other people through criticism (self-criticism or criticism of other people), and a specific relation to moral law through freedom and duty. More precisely, *parrhesia* is a verbal activity in which a speaker expresses his personal relationship to truth, and risks his life because he recognizes truth-telling as a duty to improve or help other people (as well as himself). In *parrhesia,* the speaker uses his freedom and chooses frankness instead of persuasion, truth instead of falsehood or silence, the risk of death instead of life and security, criticism instead of flattery, and moral duty instead of self-interest and moral apathy. (Foucault 2001, 19–20)

Frankness was required in a special parrhesiastic relationship between the speaker and a man[3] of more power and status. There was an exact coincidence between belief and truth where the parrhesiastes "has the moral qualities which are required, first, to know the truth, and, secondly, to convey such truth to others" (14). The compulsion or duty to sincerely and frankly tell the truth to a superior required moral courage because the parrhesiastes risked putting himself in danger and his life at risk, for example in challenging a tyrant or a teacher or father. Rather than demonstrating truth, the function of parrhesia was criticism, which could be directed either toward oneself or another, and could hurt or anger the interlocutor, who is always a superior.

Foucault selected and analyzed three aspects of "the evolution of the parrhesiastic game in ancient [Greek] culture (from the fifth century BC) to the beginnings of Christianity" (20). The first aspect was parrhesia's opposition to rhetoric. The second was its political role. In the Athenian democracy, parrhesia was, not only "an ethical and personal attitude characteristic of the good citizen," but also a guideline for democracy (22). Subsequently, in Hellenistic monarchies it was the sovereign's advisors' duty to help the king make decisions and prevent him from abusing his power. The third aspect was its importance in philosophy "as an art of life (*techne tou biou*)" as exemplified in the life of Socrates and in "the care of oneself (*epimeleia heautou*)" (23 and 24). For the Epicureans, in terms of care of the self, parrhesia "was primarily regarded as a *techne* of spiritual guidance for the 'education of the soul'" (24).

Foucault examined and problematized some parrhesiastic practices as exemplified in the Stoic philosophies of Epictetus and Seneca, and in six tragedies of Euripides: *Phoenician Women, Hippolytus, The Bacchae, Electra, Ion,* and *Orestes.* He noted that in *Orestes* there was a crisis in the function of parrhesia in democracy. Democracy threw up the discrepancy between having the right to speak freely—where even bad, ignorant, or immoral men had such a right—and the ability to speak the truth in a way that benefited the city. Furthermore there were no legal means of protecting the parrhesiastes from potential harm nor of determining who was able to speak the truth, because there also existed negative parrhesia—garrulousness and ignorant outspokenness. The first issue involved "who was entitled to use parrhesia?" (Foucault 2001, 72). The second involved "the relation of *parrhesia* to *mathesis,* [learning or wisdom] to knowledge and education," because pure frankness or sheer courage had become insufficient as the means of establishing the truth (73). What was now required was a good education, intellectual and moral development, and some sort of personal training.

In time parrhesia shifted from the political domain to the philosophical and to the personal. Socrates in the dialogues of *The Last Days of Socrates* exemplifies parrhesia in both the political and philosophical domains, as someone who was courageous and willing to tell the truth, risking his life despite facing a death sentence pronounced by the Athenian city fathers. Socratic parrhesia, which Foucault analyzed in Plato's dialogue *Laches* ("On Courage"), was a new personal form that emerged, one that required education in order to achieve a prominent role in city affairs. Socrates pointed out that education concerned the care of the soul. In the practice of philosophical parrhesia, Foucault argued that the techniques of parrhesiastic games shifted from the classical Greek conception where the game was constituted as someone being "courageous enough to tell the truth to *other people*," to "another truth game which now consists in being courageous enough to disclose the truth about *oneself*" (Foucault 2001, 143). Confronting the truth about oneself required *askésis,* which in the Greek broadly meant *"any* kind of practical training or exercise" directed at the art of living (*techne tou biou*) (ibid.). The Greek conception and practice of askésis differed significantly from the Christian counterpart of ascetic practices. Although the word "asceticism" is derived from askésis, the meaning changed under Christianity. In the Greek, the goal is establishing a specific relationship to oneself—self-possession, self-sovereignty, self-mastery. In the Christian, it is renunciation of the self. Thus, in this series of lectures, Foucault continued the arguments he put up in "Technologies of the Self" (1988b) that Christian asceticism involved detachment from the world, whereas Greco-Roman moral practices were concerned with "endowing the individual with the preparation and the moral equipment that will permit him to fully confront the world in an ethical and rational manner" (Foucault 2001, 144)—a cry that is taken up by various citizenship education curricula in our contemporary world.

Foucault indicated that Socratic parrhesia required, first, close proximity in a personal, face-to-face context, between the parrhesiastes and the interlocutor; second, that the listener is led or persuaded "by the Socratic *logos* [discourse] into 'giving an account' (*didonai logon*) of himself, of the manner in which he spends his days and the kind of life he has lived hitherto" (ibid., 96). Foucault specifically warned against reading "giving an account of your life or *bios*" as a "confessional autobiography" or as a narrative of the historical events of your life because it was

> to demonstrate whether you are able to show that there is a relation between rational discourse, the *logos*, you are able to use, and the way you live. Socrates is inquiring into the way that *logos* gives form to a person's life; for he is interested in discovering whether there is a harmonic relation between the two. (Foucault 2001, 97).

Foucault pointed out that philosophical parrhesia in Greco-Roman culture was "a *practice* which shaped the specific relations that individuals have to themselves" and which partly defined the roots of our moral subjectivity (Foucault 2001, 106). The target of the new parrhesia was "to convince someone that he must take care of himself and of others; and this means that he must change his life"—a conversion theme that became important from the fourth century BC to Christianity (ibid.). These new practices "imply a complex set of connections between self and truth" aiming "to endow the individual with self-knowledge . . . to grant access to truth and further knowledge" (ibid., 107).

The question that this chapter poses is whether either ethical and moral position—the pagan ancient Greek one of self-mastery or the Christian self-renunciation—provides a useful way of understanding youth self-constitution in a postmodern, globalized world. In turn, does globalization encourage an apolitical, apathetic youth that is focused primarily on issues of style and lifestyle in a consumer society? Or does it enable a greater understanding and empathy with the Other and in turn more altruistic and politicized constructions of youth? Or are the youth reactions to the threats of terrorism and war simply youth acting rationally in terms of self- interest, as a means of protecting themselves from the negative consequences of terrorism and war?

Youth 2003—Becoming Politically Radicalized in Response to the Iraq War

Government educational goals for young people often refer to the type of person they are trying to form or construct in terms that are variations on the philosophical theme of a "good" citizen. In pedagogy, educational policy and cultural and sociological theory, the category "youth" tends to be used as a "universal." The totalizing effect of this is to negate any sense of difference or of multiple identities that reflect gender, sexuality, ethnicity, culture, class, etc., when talking about youth. Under postmodernity, many of our assumptions and "truths" about youth that have been theorized within the dominant discourses of psychology and sociology have become outmoded. In fact, discourses "psychologizing adolescence" and "sociologizing youth" have constructed standard, if not universal models of youth that have become widely used in pedagogical and educational discourses (Besley 2002a, 2002b).

New kinds of youth are constituted in response to the impact of globalization, the mass media, information technology, and consumer society (Giroux 1990, 1996, 1998; Luke 2000; Luke & Luke 2000). While not wanting to essentialize or universalize, we need to begin to recognize the differences in the ways youth constitute their identities in response to both terror and war. In some countries, like Afghanistan and some African countries, child-soldiers who know little other than conflict have emerged. In most armed conflicts, the biggest "losers" in almost every sense of the word are children, youth, and women—i.e., those who are relatively powerless.

There have been markedly different constructions for youth identity in response to the Iraq war in different Western nations, depending on the official stance taken and the information presented in the media, for example, in the U.S.A. and United Kingdom compared with European and Australasian youth. For Muslim youth worldwide, the reactions to the Iraq war have been similarly mixed. British Muslims have had particularly difficult issues of identity to resolve about whether allegiance to their country of birth or residence, Britain, took precedence over their religion. Many Muslims in the United Kingdom and elsewhere saw the conflict as a continuation of the crusades and wars between Christians and Muslims, of Westerners invading, not liberating an Arab country, and were consequently encouraged to believe that this was *jihad*, a holy war. Thus some were persuaded to join militant groups and even become suicide bombers, while others welcomed the overthrow of a brutal dictator. During the war, many Muslims were outraged at the cultural inappropriateness of male soldiers frisking female civilians after two female suicide bombers in Iraq killed U.S. troops. Yet, even the opinions of Iraqi exiles in the United Kingdom were contradictory.

Apart from locational and cultural differences, gender differences also came into play; for example, in the United Kingdom, many of the youth protests were led by young women (e.g., the Hands Up For Peace campaign and youth anti-war protests in Scotland, as evidenced on the BBC program *Frontline Scotland*, 6 May 2003). Some boys became very hawkish, gung-ho, and excited by a "real" war happening, rather than simply a video game, and were very impressed by the "shock and awe" of the munitions used. They related very positively to seeing men in combat on TV in ways that contributed to their construction of what it means to be a man. This conveniently ignored the fact that the armed forces actually included some women, but they were seldom shown on TV except for the likes of 19-year-old Private Jessica Lynch's rescue by Special Forces. The media did not focus anywhere near to such an extent on any rescue of male soldiers, thereby unthinkingly reinforcing traditional notions of women being weak and inept enough to get caught and needing to be rescued by men risking their lives—a real-time TV version of children's damsel-in-distress fairy tales. Moreover, for those closely associated with the tragedies and traumas of terror and war on each side, as victims or as soldiers (many soldiers are teenagers, from age 18 upward) and their families, constructions of identity will most likely differ. Clearly, pedagogies that deal with difference and identities are required in schools, rather than some blanket one-sided approach.

Globalization tends to destabilize local ethnic identity at the same time as it accelerates cultural contact, intermarriage, and the development of hybridized multicultural ethnic communities (Besley 2003). With the emergence of new cultural hybridities, many youth identify themselves as cultural or ethnic blends having multiple identities, of being part of and between many different worlds where they navigate myriad "texts" that include written, aural, and visual technologies, all of which produce their/our culture(s) (Luke 2000). But these are much more than simply texts that attempt to position and define youth as they construct their identities; they are extratextual, multiple technologies that youth learn to use and negotiate and even to create, e.g., text messaging. Text messaging has become a new form of communication and one that youth (rather than adults) particularly favor, becoming almost a new language in itself—certainly one with new signs and codes. Global telecommunications technologies are simultaneously technologies of sign, of domination, and of the self—clearly interlinked, overlapping, and reinforcing each other, as Foucault (1988b) pointed out in 1982, prior to the advent of such new mass technologies.

The curriculum of some U.K. schools (and certain teachers), especially through such subjects as media studies, history, modern studies, citizenship, etc., can be given some credit for teaching students to "know" about and empathize with different cultures and identities, to analyze texts, and to be concerned about such values as tolerance, peace, and cooperation. Citizenship education has become a government priority for the whole of the United Kingdom and is expected to be covered within the school curriculum. The Qualifications Curriculum Authority (QCA) is the official curriculum organization for all U.K. schools, except for Scotland, which has a separate education system with the relevant authority being Learning and Teaching Scotland (LTS). The LTS paper "Education for Citizenship in Scotland" forms the basis of Scotland's national framework for citizenship education from age 3–18 (see http://www.ltscotland.com/citizenship/). The aim is

> to teach pupils respect for self and one another and their interdependence with other members of their neighbourhood and society and to teach them the duties and responsibilities of citizenship in a democratic society . . . to work towards a more inclusive society where inequalities are addressed effectively and cultural and community diversity is celebrated. Ways and means are being sought to tackle disaffection and disengagement from society and, more broadly, to address issues of social injustice and of personal identity. (See http://www.ltscotland.com/citizenship/.)

Unlike the QCA document (see below), Scotland's curriculum does not mention racism and neither document specifies peace or war. Both documents, especially the Scottish one, are couched in very general terms (a full critique is beyond the scope of this chapter). It is noteworthy that several other organizations provide further curriculum assistance, e.g., the Development Education Association (DEA) e-noticeboard on the War in Iraq provides some Web-based resources for U.K. schools (http://www.dea.org.uk).

The QCA Web site issues "General guidance for teachers: Respect for all: valuing diversity and challenging racism through the curriculum" (http://www.qca.org.uk/ca/inclusion/respect_for_all/guidelines.asp). This Web site provides both general guidance and specific ways for teachers to use appropriate resources, present a broad and balanced view of cultures, challenge assumptions, understand globalization, and create an open climate. However, it is somewhat alarming that the emphasis should be *in* the classroom, for this seems to ignore ways of dealing with such issues *beyond* the classroom, surely one of the important goals of education for diversity and living in a multiethnic society where cultures in fact influence each other. Despite opting for a broad and balanced view of cultures that challenges assumptions, the position taken remains one that does not sufficiently acknowledge the dominant culture and its often Anglocentric viewpoint, except to note the emphasis on a "somewhat anthropological stance," on the Other *within* the United Kingdom—i.e., on minorities themselves—with limited engagement of situations *beyond* the United Kingdom. The overall emphasis in this document is from the viewpoint of the United Kingdom—a decidedly Anglo bias. When it refers to "*Understand globalisation*," the implied definition, albeit one that looks at positive and negative aspects, narrowly focuses primarily on globalization's politico-economic aspects and the media portrayal of less developed countries with no mention of addressing how it affects developed countries, again an anthropological approach:

[F]or example, the allocation and distribution of natural resources, its effects on food supply, the environment, natural resources, political activity, world and domestic economics and individual standards of living.

Investigate how the media portrays less-economically developed countries, including how it covers such topics as natural disasters and internal conflict in those countries, and those countries' lack of advanced technology.

Examine how political decision-making contributes to, for example, environmental management, relationships between countries and conditions of various countries. (Qualifications Curriculum Authority, http://www.qca.org.uk/ca/inclusion/respect_for_all/guidelines.asp, accessed 6th April 2003).

This rather simplistic depiction of globalization does not adequately take into account its five broader interlinked dimensions (listed below in table 1), nor the part played by a host of transnational organizations that drive globalization, e.g., transnational corporations (such as Microsoft, Nike, Coca Cola, McDonald's, Time-Warner, and News Corp), intergovernmental organizations (United Nations, NATO, World Bank, IMF, World Trade Organization, NAFTA, etc.), and nongovernmental organizations (NGOs, such as Greenpeace, Oxfam and Amnesty International).

New information and communication technologies emphasize individualism, since using a computer or mobile phone is overall a solitary activity that does not generally require the presence of another (e.g., playing a computer game or writing an email or text message does not require the presence of another at the other

Table 1: Five Broad Interlinked Dimensions of Globalization

1. *economic* (involving transnational capital, foreign investments, economic and corporate concentration, deregulation of labor markets, management, trade liberalization, "McJobs," credit cards)
2. *political* (democratization, closing borders, asylum seekers, migration, "illegal" migrant workers, increased neoliberal, right-wing and fundamentalist movements)
3. *cultural* (English as "lingua franca," "Westernization," "Americanization," popular culture)
4. *ecological* (extinction of species, global warming, global pollution)
5. *communications* (news, images and data flows, Internet, simultaneous translation, air travel) (see http://www2.hawaii.edu/~fredr/glocon.htm).

end as does a phone call or a conversation). They also encourage engagement with consumer culture and the uptake of new and the latest "cool" brands as youth construct the self in the marketplace—maybe buying online, e.g., through Amazon or e-Bay. Yet, as well as having solitary aspects, these same global technologies enable communication (e.g., through chat rooms, discussion boards, text messaging) with others throughout the world and the development of virtual communities. They also create both a sense of alienation and of boredom with schools and teachers who can no longer compete with such "exciting" technologies (Giroux 1990). Many youth get online without learning what are seen as "the basics" (reading, writing, and arithmetic). Contrary to developmental stage/readiness hierarchies that many educators seem to recommend, the critical literacies they now need involve new forms of analysis of the world that enable them to navigate and critique online texts and their relations with extratextual practices.

Youth Identities in the Postmodern, Globalized Era

In the postmodern, globalized era, as the market logic penetrates the social fabric ever more deeply, youth have become consummate consumers in a culture of consumption (Baudrillard 1998; Corrigan 1997; Jameson 1983; Ritzer 1998). Style and identity have become inextricably mixed and hybridized, such that youth self-constitution is played out in terms of international global styles that are clearly influenced by the logics of fashion, advertising, music, the cult of celebrity, video games, and the plethora of multimedia sites. Such hybridization involves negotiating both the local and the global that intrude, impose, and are interconnected spatially, temporally, and culturally—assembling identities in the global marketplace on the basis of one's local cultural predispositions. Hence, postmodern theorizing has emphasized dual cultural processes of constructing youth identities first through the global marketplace as an aspect of the culture of advanced consumerism, and second through the agency of youth themselves. "Youth" is highlighted as a socio-cultural construction based on concepts of style, and lifestyle, reflecting Foucault's notion of the "aesthetics of existence" and of making one's life a work of art.

This has potential to become a new sociology of youth that emphasizes an aesthetics of self and questions of self-stylization that follows both Nietzsche and Marx (Besley 2003; Best & Kellner 2003; Foucault 1990). A sociology based on an aesthetics of existence has conceptual strengths that help to unpick and unpack processes of what might be called a "consumption of the self"—that is, patterns of self-constitution in consumer culture centered on "investments" in the self at important points in one's lifetime. This is what Peters (2003) calls the new prudentialism that elucidates an actuarial rationality determining points, patterns, and levels of self-investment. At the same time, it is not clear how much such a new sociology can interpret recent anti-war protests and struggles by youth in both Western and non-Western contexts. I say this because clearly a principle of political agency and self-constitution—maybe even political self-education—is required to analyze recent protests by youth.

Youth have recently proven themselves to be concerned about much more than just style and lifestyle choices. The most recent change that seems to have occurred has been a marked political radicalization of many youth throughout the world in response to threats of terrorism and the 2003 Iraq war. Here is one young woman's comment:

> Of all the carnage to come from a war in Iraq, one positive element has emerged. Young people of my generation are becoming more and more politicised. You can see it around you. It is now normal for me to overhear 14-year-olds discussing the pros and cons of military intervention, on the bus on the way home from school. Badges carrying anti-war slogans, such as "Not In My Name" are appearing on the lapels of school blazers and ties. It is common to turn on the television and see students under the age of 18 defying their teachers, waving banners and megaphones, and protesting in Parliament Square. . . . (Zoe Pilger, "Generation Apathy Has Woken Up," *The Independent,* 23 March 2003 [http://argument.independent.co.uk/low_res/story.jsp?story=389745&host=6&dir=140]).

The atrocities of 9/11 shook up a somewhat complacent Western world such that subsequently many young people became fearful of the possibilities of future terrorism—something new for most Western youth. There were some general warnings about terrorist threats with particular concern about the vulnerability of London and the Tube. Prior to war, and in response to terrorism warnings, some people stocked up with water and essential foods, but there seemed to be nothing on the scale of fear that the media had promulgated in the U.S.A. during February 2003 when various supplies (e.g., duct tape) became scarce. As 2002 proceeded, once war with Iraq shifted from a possibility to a probability to an actuality in early 2003, many commentators and youth alike worried that such a war would potentially create hundreds of new terrorists from among the ranks of angry, disaffected, politicized, radicalized, fundamentalist Islamist Arab youth. Once war began, a virulent anti-Americanism emerged in much of Europe and in the Middle East, even in moderate Muslim states friendly to the U.S.A., such as Morocco and Egypt. This anti-Americanism was shown in TV news clips and on the BBC1 Panorama program *The Race to Baghdad,* shown on 6 April 2003 (for script, see http://news.bbc.co.uk/nol/shared/spl/hi/programmes/panorama/transcripts/racetobaghdad.txt).

People worried at the shift in geopolitics and the changing balances of power and about the U.N. possibly becoming irrelevant. The pedagogic response to the war varied throughout the United Kingdom Geraldine Bedell, in *The Observer,* 23 March 2003, posed a pertinent question: "While thousands of teenagers march against the war, others fear Saddam is about to bombard them with nerve gas. Amid all the division and confusion, what do parents and teachers tell a generation brought up on computer battle games?" (http://education.guardian.co.uk/Print/0,3858,4631332,00.html).

For various reasons, many people, including youth, oppose war as a solution to the world's problems. On 15 February 2003, as war with Iraq became imminent, there were large antiwar demonstrations throughout the world. On that day, in the United Kingdom, huge demonstrations were held in many cities, and thousands of British school students joined approximately 800,000 in Glasgow and 1 million in London in antiwar protests prior to the war. In Glasgow, the Scottish Coalition for Justice Not War, which included trade unions, the Muslim Association of Britain, and Scottish Campaign Against Nuclear Disarmament, organized a protest that marched through the center of town to the Scottish Exhibition and Conference Centre, where the Labour Party annual conference was being held. As part of a comparative international research project, a team led by Catherine Eschle and Wolfgang Rüdig from University of Strathclyde, Glasgow, conducted a survey at the 15 February protest that involved the distribution of postal questionnaires during the march plus over 400 face-to-face interviews both before and after the march. Their preliminary analysis of these interviews revealed that the majority of protesters came from similar political and social groupings to those on other peace marches; from a mainly secular, highly educated, and professional background. The Scottish Muslim community was strongly represented. Conservative voters, manual workers and those with little formal education were largely absent. What was particularly noticeable was the number of young people (22% were 17–24), including school students, who were demonstrating—a much higher proportion compared with the Scottish Census. Clearly the Iraq war had mobilized young adults (http://www.strath.ac.uk/government/awp/demo.html).

The Hands Up For Peace campaign, which was "designed, funded, and implemented entirely by young people to demonstrate their opposition to an unjust war in Iraq" provides one example of a protest initiative taken by school children in the United Kingdom (http://www.messengers.org.uk). From their inner city London comprehensive school common room, a group of students with coursework requirements, GCSE and A-Level exams looming asked, "If two middle aged men can start a world war how many young people would it take to stop it?" They argued, "It's not just exams that will determine our future, it's the decisions made by Bush and Blair. As young people we know that we are to inherit a future shaped by our leaders. We know that unless we stop this coming war, the blood that is spilled will be left on our hands" (http://www.messengers.org.uk). Significantly, they painted their banner on the school stage without the knowledge of teachers, and harnessed the technology of the Internet (emails, a website, a Hotmail account), amongst other means (an assembly, leaflets, badges, and posters) to gain widespread local, United Kingdom, and global support from other youth. It seems appropriately respectful to give these young people their own voice about what they did and the instructions they provided so that others could contribute. Therefore, an extract from their website is provided:

Excerpts from Hands Up for Peace Campaign

The plan: To gather thousands of handprints from children everywhere, with their name and age on one side and their message for peace on the other. To attach these hands to sticks and plant them all in Parliament Square under a 25 metre banner 'Hands Up For Peace'. Like flowers, this display will spring up in a single night before the end of March and will leave a vibrant creative message screaming silently in the early morning rush hour.

The 'field of hands' will be beautiful, creative and probably very chilling. The idea is straightforward, but the connotations powerful and disturbing, as is the nature of war. It will be a visual statement from the people who have a right to decide what kind of future they wish to inherit. . . .

Although thirty of us painted the banner in the hall with paintbrushes brought from home no teachers knew what we were doing behind the closed curtains of our school stage. . . .

So while the banner was under construction, leaflets, badges and posters were being designed and made by other students; packs were being sent out to friends, friends of friends; emails were starting to spread to kids from primary to uni, from Clapham to Camden, Bradford to Belfast. We held a meeting for students at the Tricycle Theatre where students from all over London flocked to hear about the campaign and literally lend a hand.

One of Our Workshops

The finished banner

We held an assembly. We made a website. We created the declaration on the front of this web-site together by writing it, passing it round, redrafting, improving and approving it. We asked questions about the war, sought information and strengthened our arguments. We started a Hotmail account which we can all access, reply to questions from all over the world. We got interest from TV companies, newspapers, photographers, teachers. We received messages of solidarity from students everywhere and members of youth organisations such as Woodcraft and Children's Express.

Word spread like inspectors in Iraq. Decorated hands started pouring in from all over the UK.

We all wear our Hands Up for Peace badges because we're all part of something. But we don't have a leader, we don't have a boss. We are just a group of young people of every age, race, and religion coming together without help or instruction from any adult to do something we believe in. Time might be running out for Saddam Hussein but patience is running out for Bush and Blair. We're not going to stop until we're listened to, until our hands are raised in Parliament Square one night in March.

Until our hands are counted (http://www.messengers.org.uk).

This website provided steps for other school pupils in the United Kingdom and overseas to take, including how to make a "digital hand" to join the protest by putting their hands up for peace. From the photos, it appears that most of the participants were girls. This extract displays that they not only had considerable empathy for others and obviously concern for themselves and the world to come but also a high degree of technological literacy. They had become sufficiently politicized to take action without recourse to teachers—an example of political self-education or possibly, considering there was a group of students, group self-education that in effect constituted new identities for the participants.

Some young people left school during the day to attend anti-war marches, which, in some instances, were instigated by them (e.g., in Edinburgh on 19 March 2003, school children staged street-theater of a mass "die-in," an act which was also carried out in London). Press releases from the StopWar organization website provided the following evidence of school student anti-war protests:

> In Queensbridge School in Birmingham 300 students walked out of school and marched to the city centre where they held a rally outside the council house. Sidcup Girls School led a march to Forest Hill Boys and then onto Sedgehill School. In Sheffield 500 marched to the council offices and held an anti-war rally. In North London over 80 pupils from Fortismere School and 100 from Acland Burghley left their lessons to join a demonstration in Parliament Square at 1pm against the war. (Press release, March 5, 2003, http://www.stopwar.org.uk/release)

Another press release reported on schools and the numbers leaving to protest throughout United Kingdom:

> Sydenham 100; Forest Hill Boys; Sedgehill; Fortismere 60; Alexandra Park School; William Ellis; Acland; Burghley 100; Camden School for Girls; Hampstead Secondary School 1500; Belfast 500; Milton Keynes; Bedford; Cambridge: Hills Road and Long Road Schools; Liverpool: Calderstones 250; Toxteth 50; King William 80; Wallesley 120; Birkenhead 90; Birmingham: Queensbridge 300; Norfolk: North Walsham; Fakenham; Sheffield 500; Newcastle: Heaton Manor; Hexham and one other, 300 marched to Newcastle Civic Centre. In London students assembled in Parliament Square before marching to Downing Street where they staged a sit down. Although peaceful the students were penned in by the police who used horses and behaved aggressively towards them. (http://www.stopwar.org.uk/release)

Once war broke out there were further protests:

School students disrupted many city centres, stopping traffic. Four thousand school students massed in Parliament Square in London. In Liverpool, police were called to remove protesters including many school children who blocked the Mersey tunnel. Many hundreds of schools were affected across the UK. (Press release 20 March, 2003, http://www.stopwar.org.uk/release)

In an article entitled "Voices of tomorrow don't wait to protest," Geraldine Bedell wrote in *The Observer*, 23 March 2003:

On the balmy early spring afternoon the day after the war started, more than 500 children massed on the lawns of their school in south London. They had permission to go home half an hour early, but had chosen to stay and wave placards, listen to speeches and read the poems they had written for peace.

The protest was indicative of the impact the war has had already on a generation commonly deemed benignly apathetic about politics. Representatives of every year at Graveney School, a large comprehensive in Tooting with no previous history of political activism, addressed the crowd in speeches of an impressively high quality. They ranged over the Palestinian question, the role of the International Court of Justice, analyses of contemporary imperialism, and, from a Muslim girl, an explanation of the misconceptions of the Islamic idea of jihad. (*The Observer*, 23 March 2003 [http://education.guardian.co.uk/Print/0,3858,4631332,00.html]).

Despite the influence of some formal curriculum lessons, much of the information, communication, and organization would have taken place outside the classroom and through the Internet and text messaging, as for example with the Hands Up For Peace campaign.

Many teachers were alarmed to find that youthful students took their citizenship lessons and civic responsibilities seriously enough to take action in protest against the Iraq war. Many teachers and adults were worried at the rapid, wildfire-like spread of school pupil-led protest action. Some adults did not see youth as being media-savvy or "mature" enough to have informed opinions, but rather as being unduly swayed by propaganda from antiwar groups. Dea Birkett's article entitled "It's their war too," in *The*

Guardian, Tuesday 25 March 2003, pointed out that "some schools [were] arguing that the curriculum provides appropriate channels for children to express their beliefs without leaving school." Not surprisingly considering the widespread condemnation by police amid concerns about safety and the conservatism of some teachers who think that education that takes place within a classroom is of overriding importance, the pupils who took time out of school to protest without school permission were considered as truant by many local authorities and the teacher unions and punished accordingly. "Treat it as normal truancy and take appropriate action," said the Secondary Heads Association (http:// education.guardian.co.uk/Print/0,3858,4632153,00.html), which is exactly what happened to 16-year-old sixth-former, Sachin Sharma, who was suspended from Prince Henry's Grammar School, Otley, for urging pupils to walk out in protest over war in Iraq. Rather ironically, Sachin noted that "the majority of our school does not have democratic rights. They have no means to express themselves, and they don't have a voice in real terms. The only way we can, as minors, express ourselves is through demonstration" (*The Guardian,* 25 March 2003 [http://education.guardian.co. uk/Print/0,3858,4632153,00.html]). A representative of the Educational Institute of Scotland (the main teachers' union in Scotland, see http://www.eis.org.uk/latest.htm) appeared on TV suggesting that parents should be jailed for letting their children be truant (something that had happened in 2002 to a single mother in Oxford whose child was a persistent truant).

Such comment was in marked contrast to reaction from East Dunbartonshire Council, Scotland, that permitted its workers time off to protest (incidentally, schools come under the control of such local authority councils in both Scotland and the United Kindgom). The significance of being suspended for what some schools constructed as encouraging other students to "truant" was in stark contrast to how the pupils conceived of their actions to promote peace not war. In terms of their statements and actions, such youth protests are arguably a current-day example of parrhesia in action—they embody frankness, truth, risk, criticism, and a sense of duty in their challenge to teachers, school authorities, parents, and political leaders. In terms of the attitude of schools and teachers to the current pressing issues of our world, some are in danger of being accused of a lack of genuine moral leadership and courage, especially if we value being a society that encourages and teaches our young people about peace, citizenship, and critically engaging with media and the messages that politicians are trying to make the public believe. Ironically, it was because youth had been perceived as disaffected and politically apathetic that government and schools had introduced citizenship curricula (usually within modern studies in Scotland). Citizenship curricula are partly designed to engage pupils in the political process, yet when they actually take a political stand, youth are generally condemned—a Catch-22 situation. It seems that many schools are only interested in their young people *talking about,* but not *acting upon* such issues and curricula.

Whether or not schools should encourage pupils to form and express their own political views and if the current curriculum allowed for this became key questions that schools answered very differently. Some schools focused on a standard curriculum, largely ignoring the war. In contrast, other schools made space available for discussion, trying at the same time to avoid scaring students who were understandably afraid of the consequences of war and of potential terrorism. In London, for example, Alfred Salter School often started the day with "Metro time"—a half-hour when children picked out news stories from a free paper and discussed the issues raised, e.g., the U.N. and its future role or comparing America and Saddam Hussein as bullies (http://education.guardian.co.uk/Print/0,3858,4632153,00.html).

Prior to hostilities beginning, the National Union of Teachers urged schools to be ready to deal with any increase in bullying and racism, especially anti-Semitism and Islamophobia, as a result of the Iraq war, pointing out that such issues can be addressed through the new citizenship curriculum which requires students to be taught about national and religious identities and social justice, which provides an opportunity to discuss the war (see http://www.nut.org.uk/). However, once war began, one of the consequences was the development of virulent anti-Americanism in the Middle East, even in moderate Muslim states friendly to the U.S.A. (e.g., Morocco and Egypt), and in Europe, amidst fears that hundreds of fundamentalist Islamic youth have been radicalized and are likely to become terrorists in the future (see

BBC1, Panorama, *The Race to Baghdad* 6 April 2003; http://news.bbc.co.uk/nol/shared/spl/hi/programmes/panorama/transcripts/racetobaghdad.txt). Furthermore, some, considering the multicultural nature of many U.K. schools (e.g., in London about 30% of the population is considered "ethnic," i.e., people of color and/or non-British—see *The Observer Review*, 6 April 2003, 5), will have students with family and friends engaged in the hostilities on both the British side and the Iraqi side, or who are Islamic. So ways of dealing with such differing ideas, values, and emotions need to be found.

Schools must be relevant to the outside world and engage students in issues that affect them and which they care about. They cannot reasonably say that they are only in the business of delivering a set of subjects and getting pupils to pass exams. Education is far more than this simplistic, albeit important part. When the major issues of the time become war and terrorism, understandably there are innumerable questions for pupils, such as: Why war? Why now? How else could we do things? How is this liberation when it is an invasion? The USA calls this war "Operation Iraqi Freedom," but why did no one ask the Iraqi people if bombing was the price they were prepared to pay for liberation from Saddam? What is the difference between guerrilla warfare, terrorism, and suicide bombing? What is a just and moral war and what is an illegal one? Is this about oil and unfinished Bush family politics? Does Iraq still have weapons of mass destruction? How can we understand competing patriotisms and nationalism? Who should manage the peace? Which component of our identity and values (if any) takes priority—being British, Christian, Islamic, Jewish, atheist, Iraqi, Pakistani, Scots, European, male, female, black, white, Asian? And so on.

Pedagogies that study difference, cultural identity, and citizenship have contributed to the radicalization of youth and to how youth construct their identities to a certain extent, but they cannot take full credit. With many youth having computers at home and with the huge uptake of mobile phones and text messaging as the latest communication trend among youth, students learn (with or without the help of schools) to negotiate and use new ICT technologies and the Internet, developing multiple, new literacies (Lankshear & Knobel 2003). They use these mediums for much more than chatting and arranging social events; they also use them to access information about the issues and questions about war within or outside the classroom. While many youth are media savvy, well-aware of the ways and ruses the media uses to target-market them and able to construct understandings of the world that acknowledge power relations and possible exploitation, others, especially poorer students, who are less likely to have home computers, remain on the wrong side of the digital divide. Those students who have developed the relevant literacies, critical thinking skills, and reasoning are able to analyze and decode, not only the consumer world, but also the whole gamut of advertising, P.R., spin, and propaganda of politicians, military spokepersons, and commentators on the 2003 Iraq war. Students have learned how to decipher the multiple meanings of current politico-war language: e.g., collateral damage, benign invasion, regime change, friendly bombs, cluster bombs, daisy cutters, shock and awe, precision guided munitions, surgical strikes, mouse-holing, friendly fire, and illegal combatants, etc. Once schools teach students to resolve conflict and bullying through negotiation or mediation rather than fighting and violence, many see this as a preferable way of addressing international crises. Unsurprisingly, when U.S. foreign policy under the Bush regime shifted to the notion of "pre-emptive strike" and military action, many youth saw this as an aggressive action akin to bullying. This became increasingly apparent since Iraq clearly had far more limited military technology than either the U.S.A. or Britain. The incongruency between what is taught in schools and the behavior that the adults who hold powerful political leadership positions display in relation to other countries was not lost on many students.

Many years ago, Marshall McLuhan argued that the information level was higher outside the classroom than inside it. Considering the current age of technological sophistication of many youth, McLuhan's thesis could be added to in a variety of ways. Not only is the level or amount of information higher, it is also more diverse, more open to indoctrination without the authority of the teacher, and comprised of multiple sources of differing quality. Certainly, traditional news broadcast media provide a technological transmission that cannot be easily equaled in the classroom. Access to information is also higher outside the classroom for some groups, especially if there is access to home computers. Also access to information is self-governed by youth rather than controlled (unless parents chose to censor it through various means), hence the new media and ICT tend to decenter the authority of the teacher.

The newly politicized youth generation in the United Kindgom has become acutely aware of geopolitics and the new world order. Unlike the days of the Cold War, with its nuclear threat and notion of maintaining a balance of power between the U.S.A. and U.S.S.R., the world is, arguably, now uni-polar, with the U.S.A.'s immense military, technological, and economic power leaving it as the only superpower that furthermore is now dominant in popular culture. Not only has English become the *lingua franca,* but *American* English is increasingly gaining supremacy. Altogether this constitutes an American hegemony that is hard to resist, despite being much resented, especially when President Bush simplistically asserts that people/countries are either with us or against us. There is increasing worry that after this current war we face a series of wars, maybe for decades, against states that threaten our security—Syria, Iran, and North Korea have already been mentioned by Bush and Rumsfeld as part of an "axis of evil." Some worry that rather than the Iraq war making the world safer, as Bush and Blair have maintained throughout the conflict, quite the reverse will happen, especially considering the anger that has been generated within the Arab world and the continued problems between Israel and the Palestinians.

Schools and teachers now need to pay more attention to the ways that youth construct themselves rather than to the traditional academic discourses which retain "truths" that are becoming increasingly challenged and outdated (Besley 2002a). In the globalized postmodern world, through tapping into ICT and new associated literacies, many youth are now producing the self through constructing identities that address the Other. These include understandings of difference in culture, power, politics, gender, class, values, and ideals—identities that are relational at the same time as they are individual at a particular historical moment. As the historico-cultural context changes, so too are their constructions of identity likely to change. Youth actions, especially in response to the Iraq war, indicate an example of choice-making in producing the self through the moral choices—a relational self where intersubjectivity has become central, a self that acknowledges and is constituted by difference and the Other. Therefore, Foucault's notion of technologies of the self becomes central in ethically constituting the self in relation to the Other as the production of selves/identities is constructed through the social apparatus where clearly the curriculum and ICT technologies play a part.

References

Baudrillard, J. (1998) [orig. 1970]. *The consumer society: Myths and structures.* London: Sage.

Besley, A. C. (Tina). (2002a). "Psychologised adolescents and sociologised youth: rethinking young people in education in the 21st century." In B. Cope & M. Kalantzis (eds.), *Learning for the future: Proceedings of the Learning Conference 2001.* (www.theLearner.com)

Besley, A. C. (Tina). (2002b). *Counseling youth: Foucault, power and the ethics of subjectivity.* Westport, CT & London: Praeger.

Besley, A. C. (Tina). (2003). "Hybridized and globalized: Youth cultures in the postmodern era," *The Review of Education, Pedagogy & Cultural Studies,* 25(2), 153–177.

Best, S., and Kellner, D. (2003). "Contemporary youth and the postmodern adventure," *The Review of Education, Pedagogy & Cultural Studies,* 25(2), 75–94.

Corrigan, P. (1997). *The Sociology of Consumption.* London: Sage.

Dreyfus, H. (2002). *Heidegger and Foucault on the Subject, Agency and Practices,* Regents of University of California, Berkeley. Accessed October 2002 (http://socrates.berkeley.edu/~hdreyfus/html/paper_heidand foucault.html)

Foucault, M. (1977). *Discipline and Punish: The Birth of the Prison.* London: Penguin.

Foucault, M. (1984). "Space, knowledge and power." In P. Rabinow (ed.), *The Foucault Reader.* New York: Pantheon Books, pp. 239–256.

Foucault, M. (1985). *The Use of Pleasure: The History of Sexuality,* Vol. II. New York: Vintage.

Foucault, M. (1988a). "Truth, power, self: An interview with Michel Foucault," in L.H. Martin, H. Gutman, and P.H. Hutton (eds.), *Technologies of the Self: A seminar with Michel Foucault.* Amherst: University of Massachusetts Press, pp. 9–15.

Foucault, M. (1988b). "Technologies of the self," in L.H. Martin, H. Gutman, and P.H. Hutton (eds.), *Technologies of the Self: A seminar with Michel Foucault*. Amherst: University of Massachusetts Press, pp. 16–49.

Foucault, M. (1990). *The Care of the Self: The History of Sexuality*, Vol. III. London: Penguin.

Foucault, M. (1997). "The ethics of the concern for self as a practice of freedom, trans. Robert Hurley and others," in P. Rabinow (ed.), *Michel Foucault: Ethics, Subjectivity and Truth, The Essential Works of Michel Foucault 1954–1984*, Vol 1. London: The Penguin Press, pp. 281–301.

Foucault, M. (2001). *Fearless Speech*, edited by J. Pearson. Los Angeles, CA: Semiotext(e). (www.repb.net)

Jameson, F. (1983). "Postmodernism and consumer society," in H. Foster (ed.), *Postmodern Culture*. London & Sydney: Pluto Press.

Giroux, H. (1990). *Curriculum Discourse as Postmodern Critical Practice*. Geelong, Australia: Deakin University Press.

Giroux, H. (1996). *Fugitive Cultures: Race, Violence and Youth*. New York: Routledge

Giroux, H. (1998). "Teenage sexuality, body politics, and the pedagogy of display," in J. Epstein (ed.), *Youth Culture: Identity in a Postmodern World*, Oxford: Blackwell, pp. 24–55.

Heidegger, M. (1977). *The Question Concerning Technology and Other Essays*, translated and edited by W. Lovitt). New York: Harper & Row.

Lankshear, C. & Knobel, M. (2003). *New Literacies: Changing Knowledge and Classroom Learning*. Buckingham: Open University Press.

Luke, A. (2000). "The jig is up: an alternative history of psychology or why current concepts of identity and development are part of the problem rather than part of the solution," *NZAC Newsletter*, 20:3: 12–26.

Luke, A. & Luke, C. (2000). "A situated perspective on cultural globalisation," in N. Burbules & C.Torres (eds.), *Globalisation and Educational Policy*. New York: Routledge.

McNay, L. (1992). *Foucault and Feminism: Power, Gender and Self*. Boston: Northeastern University Press.

Nietzsche, F. (1956 [orig. 1887]). *The Genealogy of Morals*, translated by F. Golffing. New York: Doubleday.

The Observer Review, 6 April 2003, 5.

Peters, M. A. (2000). "Writing the Self: Wittgenstein, Confession and Pedagogy," *Journal of Philosophy of Education*, 34(2), 353–368.

Peters, M. A. (2003). "Truth-Telling as an Educational Practice of the Self: Foucault, parhessia and the ethics of subjectivity," *Oxford Review of Education*, 29(2), 207–223 forthcoming.

Rabinow, P. (1997). "Afterword," in P. Rabinow (ed.), *Michel Foucault: Ethics, Subjectivity and Truth, The Essential Works of Michel Foucault 1954–1984*, Vol. 1, translated by Robert Hurley and others. London: The Penguin Press.

Ritzer, G. (1998). "Introduction," in J. Baudrillard, *The Consumer Society: Myths and Structures*. London: Sage.

Websites

http://www.strath.ac.uk/government/awp/demo.html, accessed July 2003

http://www.messengers.org.uk, accessed April 2003

http://www.stopwar.org.uk/release, press release 20 March 2003, accessed April 2003

http://education.guardian.co.uk/Print/0,3858,4632153,00.html, accessed April 2003

http://www.eis.org.uk/latest.htm, accessed April 2003

http://www.nut.org.uk/, accessed April 2003

http://news.bbc.co.uk/nol/shared/spl/hi/programmes/panorama/transcripts/racetobaghdad.txt, accessed April 2003

http://www.ltscotland.com/citizenship/, accessed April 2003

http://www.qca.org.uk/ca/inclusion/respect_for_all/guidelines.asp, accessed April 2003

http://www.dea.org.uk, accessed April 2003

http://socrates.berkeley.edu/~hdreyfus/html/paper_heidandfoucault.html, accessed October 2002

http://education.guardian.co.uk/Print/0,3858,4631332,00.html, Geraldine Bedell, "Voices of tomorrow don't wait to protest", *The Observer*, 23 March 2003, accessed April 2003

http://education.guardian.co.uk/Print/0,3858,4632153,00.html, Dea Birkett, "It's their war too," *The Guardian*, 25 March 2003, accessed April, 2003

http://argument.independent.co.uk/low_res/story.jsp?story=389745&host=6&dir=140, Zoe Pilger, "Generation Apathy has Woken Up," *The Independent*, 23 March 2003, accessed April 2003.

Appendix

Some Web Resources for UK schools: Development Education Association (DEA) e-noticeboard on the War in Iraq (www.dea.org.uk)

a. Citizenship Foundation: Iraq Q & A. Michael Brunson, former Political Editor of ITN, writes this briefing paper for teachers and older students and provides background and arguments surrounding the current situation in Iraq—available online as a series of sequential questions or a PDF file at:

http://www.citfou.org.uk/teaching_support/iraq_intro.php4

b. Children's Express: War—what is it good for? The media is full of views about the war with Iraq—from politicians to religious leaders to military experts. But war affects everyone, including young people. Children's Express interviews children from four different cities around the world—New York, Tokyo, London, and Belfast—to see how the prospect of war and the threat of terrorism are affecting them.

http://www.childrens-express.org/

c. Expresso News—Interactive multimedia activities for weekly news lessons.

http://www.espresso.co.uk/visitors/efs/staffroom/

d. Global Express: the rapid response information series for schools on world events in the news. The November 2002 issue, *Iraq: in search of resolution,* focuses on the underlying issue that many think is central to the current situation—the role of the United Nations and that of the United States as the sole remaining superpower. It contains photocopiable classroom activities aimed at 8 to 14 year olds, linked to national curriculum subjects including Citizenship, Literacy and History.

http://www.dep.org.uk/globalexpress/index.htm

e. Learn.co.uk (based on contemporary articles from the *Guardian* and the *Observer*). Opposition to War: a Key Stage 4 topical lesson pack— Protests: This lesson explores some of the issues surrounding how and why people participate in protests, particularly focusing on the opposition to a war with Iraq.

http://www.learn.co.uk/glearning/secondary/topical/default.htm

f. Newsround: Conflict with Iraq. BBC TV's Newsround team explains the issues around the conflict with Iraq in a language which younger people will understand.

http://news.bbc.co.uk/cbbcnews

g. Oxfam: free web and print resources for teaching about war in Iraq. Information that supports teachers answering questions from pupils, gives ideas for activities in the classroom, and gives some leads about further action and information gathering that pupils could undertake. The resources include:

1. background info about Iraq, its people, geography, economy, history.

2. thought-provoking info about current debated issues and terms, e.g. weapons of mass destruction, media coverage of the war, the role of the UN, the future of Iraq postconflict.
3. activities for the classroom.

For printed booklet, phone Oxfam on +44 (0)1865 312610 or email (put "Iraq resource" in subject line): education@oxfam.org.uk. Oxfam's Cool Planet Web site will carry additional information and a downloadable PDF version of the booklet available at:
http://www.oxfam.org.uk/coolplanet
h. Parents online: Following Iraqi war development on the web.
Links to the Web sites of the main U.K. television stations and newspapers, U.K. and U.S. governments, United Nations, and the antiwar movement.
http://www.parentsonline.gov.uk/articles/2003/3/21–1048257578.html
i. Talking and Teaching—for teachers, parents, and youth workers. Guidance and resources for teachers, youth workers, carers, and parents, compiled by the Runnymede Trust and the Commission on British Muslims and Islamophobia. Includes Web site links, "Hard Questions for Adults," "Understanding, Solace, Coping and Hope," and "Handling Controversial Issues."
http://www.runnymedetrust.org/meb/islamophobia/talking_teaching.html
j. Teaching for Change: Building social justice starting in the classroom. A Washington DC-based not-for-profit organization promoting social and economic justice through public education. Site contains a range of resources on the War on Terrorism and Iraq, including books, videos, documentaries, and posters.
http://www.teachingforchange.org/body_index.html

Acknowledgment

Thanks to Professor Michael A. Peters, University of Glasgow, for his helpful comments on an early draft of this paper.

Notes

1. Earlier variations of this chapter were presented at the Foucault Pre-session, AERA, Chicago, April 2003; The Big Day Conference, Centre

for Global Citizenship, University of Glasgow, June 2003 and the GENIE conference, Cyprus, July 2003.

2. The pronoun "he" was used because these discussions about ancient Greek society only referred to free males, not slaves nor women, as citizens.

3. Along with "aliens, slaves and children," women were oppressed in Ancient Greek society and so were generally deprived from using *parrhesia*; therefore; the male pronoun was used by Foucault in this text (see Foucault 2001, 12).

Chapter Five

Globalization, the Third Way, and Education Post-9/11

Building Democratic Citizenship

Mark Olssen

The possibility of acts of terror, whether committed by rogue states or transnational groups, forces a new consideration of the themes of democracy, community, and individual rights. And there must also, I believe, be a new understanding of what citizenship entails, and what the role of education is in relation to creating citizens. The new realization that the world is full of dangers is leading to a reappraisal of the relations between the state and the individual and between collective interests and individual rights. What confronts us now, more than at any time since the seventeenth century, is the prospect of a new political settlement that involves a radical revision and restriction of traditional rights and liberties given to individuals. At the same time as states are encouraged to adhere to the "steer" but not "row" philosophy of neoliberalism in economic affairs, in the political sphere the state's need to know, involving increased surveillance and data gathering for the purposes of fighting crime and fraud, and preventing acts of terror, has now become an *explicit agenda of states*. What is being ushered in, indeed, is a new postliberal political settlement. Within this scenario there are possibilities, openings, and dangers. In this chapter, I will seek to reassess the significance of globalization, neoliberalism, human rights, community, democracy, and the role of education taking the events of 9/11 into account.[1]

Neoliberalism, Globalization, and the Move to the "Third Way"

Neoliberalism is that form of economic reason encapsulated in the notion of *homo economicus*, which represents individuals as rational self-interested choosers, which was based on a revitalization of neoclassical economic liberalism and which, as Peters (2001, 9) says, "has been remarkably successful in advancing a foundationalist and universalist reason as a basis for a radical global reconstruction of all aspects of society and economy." During the last several years neoliberalism has been adapted, rescued one might say, under the mantle of the "third way," which aims to retain the neoliberal concern in the economic sphere with efficiency, while avoiding traditional policies of redistribution, still defining freedom in terms of autonomy of action, but now mixed in with a concern for the values of social justice and democracy and increased involvement and participation in the local community.

Critics suggest that the third way is an amorphous linking of disparate elements, lacking any distinctive economic policy, based upon an attempt to find a middle way. Giddens (2000, 163) suggests that the third way is not an attempt to occupy the middle ground but rather is "concerned with restructuring social democratic doctrines to respond to the twin revolutions of globalization and the knowledge economy." What the third way tries to do—in my view, unsuccessfully—is theorize the need for a more active state intranationally, in order to deal with the crucial national issues concerning social democracy, while retaining economic commitment to neoliberalism as its central orientation to both domestic and global relations. In this sense, the third-way politics of New Labour in Britain maintains that it constitutes a melding of traditional concerns of social democracy while retaining the central neoliberal insights over economic policy, the role of the state, and the need for accountability. This is the political discourse that presently dominates New Labour's policies toward education, health, crime, and the role of social services. Dubbed the "new localism," it is based on the state philosophy of "steer" but not "row," and signals the end of the centrally planned Welfare State as established in Britain in 1945. It entails the move from what British Prime Minister Tony Blair calls a "one size fits all" model of public service provision, whereby spending and direction was effected from the center, to a model whereby spending and direction is effected at the local level via the people directly affected and involved. As such, the third way effects fundamentally a shift in the role of the state. As Tony Blair stated at the 2001 Labour Party Conference at Bournemouth: "Just as mass production has departed from industry, so the monolithic provision of services has to depart from the public sector. Out goes the big state. In comes the enabling state" (Wintour 2002).

This idea of an enabling state is central to the third way politics of New Labour, and to new policy initiatives on education and health. In education, it has involved the expansion and development of specialist schools as part of the "post-comprehensive era." This has resulted in new legislation to encourage successful specialist schools to operate autonomously and to expand, as well as to encourage school takeovers. Choice policies which enable parents to secure the school of their preference are being encouraged, and privatization initiatives are also being encouraged in order to extend private sector involvement in public services through a proliferation of public-private partnerships (PPPs), private finance initiatives (PFIs), and public interest companies (PICs). As such, the enabling state constitutes a model of semiautonomous public services supposedly free of Whitehall control. Both schools and hospitals are being granted autonomy where they can establish new directions of travel. Controls are being released on local councils, and voluntary organizations are being allowed to run public services. New Labour theorists, such as the New Economics

Foundation, the New Local Government Network, and the Institute of Public Policy Research, represent this agenda as moving beyond old distinctions between the state and the market. The idea is that services funded by the state need not be run by the state. Such a model thus entails an increased role for the private sector and increased choice.

Whether this third way model really does manage to reconcile neoliberal and social democratic agendas is a much-contested issue. Whether state control is any less, or any different, than it was in the pre-Thatcher years is indeed a meaningful question. Supposedly, according to Rhodes (2000), the new governance narrative which is espoused by New Labour is based on networking, partnerships, autonomy of providers, interdependence between organizations, and trust. The state's role is to facilitate and coordinate without treading on the autonomy of foundation hospitals, schools, or higher education institutions. In reality the state underemphasizes its control, for although it may not actively be delivering services, it can still be seen to be effecting control, and at least some studies claim that this control is, rather than being less, is simply taking a different form (Rhodes 1997a, 1997b, 2000; Cloke et al., 2000, 130). In addition, in that the power of the state is being reorganized rather than reduced, in its relationship to local groups, the organization of governance in networks and partnerships is producing new obstacles as far as traditional democratic forms of accountability are concerned. A governance model which delegates power to local agencies is producing problems relating to representation, accountability, openness to criticism, as well as to the rights of consumers or users. The ability of local agencies to work together, or coordinate service provision, is offset by the differences in power and influence between them; by the adherence to traditional norms of exclusivity and noncooperation; by the inequalities between the different partners or actors providing services in the state, voluntary, and private spheres; and by the fragmentation of services across different sectors.

Thus, whether new models of governance based on networks and partnerships can constitute a solution to traditional forms of state bureaucracy or markets, or overcome the limitations inherent in forms of state bureaucracy or markets is unlikely. Research by Rhodes (2000), Mayo and Taylor (2001), Cochrane (2000), Cloke et al. (2000), Glendinning et al. (2002), and others cast doubt on whether patterns of state control have significantly altered, and whether ad hoc adjustments and interference are not constantly required to overcome inequities, unfairness, and inequalities that arise when localistic solutions and policy operate. As Karl Polanyi (1944) observed with reference to the rise of the welfare state, the growth of central state involvement in economic and social policy arose, not because of any predetermined political plan or conspiracy, but because of the sheer complexity of government. This complexity is likely to increase at pace given the inherently individualist and self-serving nature of neoliberal reason. In the end, the resources and manpower invested in "steering" becomes as great, if not greater, than in "rowing," until it is not clear what the differences between them are.

Indeed, we might be tempted to say that the bride is too beautiful for any marriage of private investment with state "steering" will likely result in a greater and greater role for the state as it attempts to level-out the bumps and imperfections, provide reasonable mechanisms of representation and accountability, and ensure some measure of rights and fair treatment for the unsuspecting and often unenlightened public whose education and welfare is at stake. This seems to be what is indeed happening in third way policy delivery. Britain's *Railtrack*, privatized under Thatcher, has recently returned to public ownership due to the sheer operational chaos that private ownership produced. More recently, *British Energy* has had to be bailed out by the State. The government had to underwrite its risks due to the sensitive place it occupies in the economy, which of course was one of the reasons for nationalizing it in the first place. Under private ownership it has become obvious that neither managerial efficiency nor public safety are guaranteed. The history of the past year in Britain is littered with examples of the failings of privately run prisons, schools, and hospitals. It is a situation, as Roy Hattersley (2002, 18) has quipped, of "taxpayers servicing the debt, and shareholders receiving the dividends."

If the third way attempt to marry social democracy and neoliberalism in terms of governance is problematic, the rise of the third way does suggest a more positive message in that it speaks to a more active state than was entailed under traditional laissez-faire models. Indeed, even if the state under the third way seeks to change the form of its operation from traditional bureaucracy to governance through networks, the model still speaks to the idea of a strong state. The idea of an enabling state is indeed quite compatible with a conception of the state that sets up the rules of the game, that passes legislation to enforce minimum conditions of acceptable treatment for all of the various groups in society (children, the aged, women, ethnic minorities, etc.), and that seeks to ensure adequate protection and rights for all through the framing and introduction legislation. The notion of "enabling," like that of "steering," does not of itself speak to the size of the state, and conceivably, a state that "steers" might be just as big as a state that "rows." At the same time, so long as the state can assure the important platforms of universal entitlement, equality of opportunity, and equality before the law, then the attempt to actively co-opt the citizenry in running their own lives can only be seen as positive and a major back-down from the discourse of a reduced state which became the catch-cry of neoliberal reason during the Thatcher years.

What Is Globalization?

What is thus most positive about the third way's conception of the enabling state is the very recognition of a *role for the state* in an age of globalization. The central thesis of the doctrine seems to suggest that the state can act as a powerful force to regulate and supervise, and to initiate and direct policy within national contexts. This recognition of the power of the state would seem to contradict the thesis of a "powerless state," as writers like Manual Castells (1997) (who used this phrase as the title to a chapter), or Naomi Klein (2000), or Kenichi Ohmae (1990, 1995) have depicted, and which has been generally the dissertation of so many globalization theorists of recent years.

In my view, globalization does not spell the end, or even, necessarily, the demise, of the nation-state as an autonomous force. Writers who suggest that it does are failing to differentiate the different theses entailed in the notion of globalization. In order to make this thesis clear it is important to distinguish the senses of globalization. For a start we can note how this concept has functioned to displace other related concepts and theories to do with cultural, economic, and political "colonialism," "neo-colonialism," or "imperialism." It is as if suddenly these more specific theories, which were more politically charged and made explicit the relations of power and knowledge entailed in state actions in international affairs, were replaced by a more general concept where the relations of power are not so obvious, or were seen to be manifested in a different way. Yet, the concept is clearly important, and it has become more so post-9/11 in that it gives recognition to the undeniable fact that our lives are becoming more intertwined. This, it may be argued, has always been the case, and there is a certain sense in which that is true, as David Held (1995) has argued, but a number of twentieth-century developments in technology, science, communication and travel, and economy have arguably increased, or at least changed, the sense in which it is so. Developments in communications technology, the mass media, the Internet, the increasing availability and possibility of travel, the growth in multinational trade and international marketability of goods and services, and the general growth in the circulation of money and goods, through to developments in science, and the spread and democratization of knowledge, which make weapons of mass destruction and acts of terror within the sphere of capability of private citizens, transnational groups and rogue nations, all serve to reinforce the "intertwined" nature of our existence. September 11 and Bali '02 have brought home dramatically the sense in which what happens in one part of the world affects what happens everywhere. Cultures mix through migration, education, GATS, news and information, ideas and fashions, brands and marketing. Like crises in health (AIDS, SARS) or climate change, terrorism increases at the political level the degree of interdependence in terms of political governance and regulatory arrangements between nation-states and amongst transnational political and economic agencies and organizations such as the EU, WB, IMF, OECD, NAFTA, APEC, and WTO.

The fact that globalization is promoting greater integration between countries and regions is not of itself of concern. One must take each issue and each effect separately in order to assess its positive or negative consequences, and one must do this one issue at a time. That one can discern many issues of exploitation and oppression is clearly evident. At the cultural level, for instance, it can be observed that the spread of information technology and the communications revolution tend to operate as forms of imperialism, in that the ideas, images, and even language of communication is provided by the more powerful Western states, led by the U.S.A. and Britain. If globalization increases the speed and intensity of the circulation of ideas across the globe, then the effect on small, relatively powerless states will be the same as has always been the case: The cultural and intellectual sovereignty of their customs, beliefs, and ways of life will be undermined.

At the same time, one must be open to the fact that there are some possible positive effects of globalization. Recent moves to internationalize in higher education have resulted in the large-scale international movement of students and staff across national borders. Ph.D. students at Surrey, to give one very local example, are now selected from many countries. Similarly, as with most universities, and many other institutions, higher education staffs are recruited internationally. Growing internationalization leads to increasingly innovative attempts to standardize procedures such as criteria of admission and recruitment, resulting in new forms of global communication and regulation. These trends, which are merely small examples of how global cooperation and exchange can have positive effects, are not without elements of injustice and oppression, of course, and this is especially so in that they are structured within neoliberal economic frameworks.

They are also not really new, but as with international travel and migration, the scale and scope have both increased. We can, in this sense, I believe, agree, at least in part, with Held (1995) in the relevance of a new concept of *cosmopolitanism*. This is so in a number of senses. Firstly, with changes to the material bases of culture in the West since the scientific revolution, but especially during the twentieth century, it has become increasingly true that there are a great number of events and developments (Chernobyl, acid rain, oil slicks, climate change, AIDS, SARS) which have impacts across national borders. Secondly, relatedly, in relation to international trade and twentieth-century economic developments, there have been huge increases in the global circulation of goods, ideas, and information, as well as money, all of which are more global in terms of both the speed and scale of distribution than at any previous time in history. If these speak to a new sense of cosmopolitanism, which I see as an extension of the idea of republicanism, it is only partly in the sense elaborated by Held, however. For while both these developments clearly entail a growth in the importance of international agencies and regulatory bodies, as Hirst and Thompson (1996) argue, any mandate for the democratic functioning of these agencies still resides within individual nation-states. It is at the national level, ultimately, where accountability resides.[2]

A New Political Settlement?

At the political level, globalization can also be represented as a dynamic process. In that the scale and scope of communication and travel have increased, so we can say that since 9/11 the potential risks and dangers have also increased. It is at this level that 9/11 serves to denote a major epistemological-political break with previous discursive systems. Since 9/11 we can say indeed that there has been a keener interest by Western states in the uniform global imposition of standard systems of security and surveillance which is altering the traditional nature of the relations between individuals and the state. What private individuals do in Baghdad, Afghanistan, Cairo, Naples, London, or Auckland, or what they carry through airports, is now of vital concern to policy makers and ruling elites, as well as to ordinary citizens, in all parts of the globe. In a way, the reality of terror, like that of climate change, makes us painfully aware of our *interrelatedness*. The effects of this show the signs of crystallizing a new political settlement that has been perhaps embryonic as an emergent discourse for some time, but after 9/11 has been given a new impetus. Whether it represents a "permanent settlement," or just a "temporary tendency," is as yet uncertain, and while I will refer to the former, I leave open the possibility, and the hope, that it is only the latter. At least some early signs are appearing as emergent forms within the existing political milieu.

The emergent new tendency/settlement has two elements: At an economic level, it is based on neoliberal freedom, which is now more obviously confined to the "freedom of commerce,"

153

or to "free trade." In this sense, neoliberalism must clearly be seen as a particular element of globalization in that it constitutes the form through which domestic and global economic relations are structured. Yet, neoliberalism is only one form of globalization, and only pertains to economic globalization. It is not something that has evolved naturally as a consequence of changes in technology or science. And it must not be confused with globalization as such. Rather it must be seen as a specific economic discourse or philosophy which has become dominant and effective in world economic relations as a consequence of superpower sponsorship. Neoliberalism is a politically imposed discourse, which is to say that it constitutes the hegemonic discourse of Western nation-states. As such, it is quite independent of the forms of globalization that we have spoken of above, based as they are on changes in technology and science, nor can it be seen as part of their effects, although this is not to say that there is no relationship at all. Its major characteristics emerged in the U.S.A. in the 1970s as a forced response to stagflation and the collapse of the Bretton Woods system of international trade and exchange, leading to the abolition of capital controls in 1974 in America and 1979 in Britain (Mishra 1999; Stiglitz 2002). This made it extremely difficult to sustain Keynesian demand management. Financial globalization made giant strides. Exchange rates were floated and capital controls abolished, giving money and capital the freedom to move across national boundaries. The changes in technology did certainly facilitate these changes, for developments in microelectronics and computers made it possible to shift financial reserves within seconds. To the extent that neoliberalism was effective it certainly compromised the autonomy of national governments in the sphere of managing their economies. This depended upon political alliances to support such policies however. By this I mean that there was nothing necessary about this decentering of the nation state. The very emergence of the third way, and of new leftist traditional Labour adaptations within the third way, some of which are now claiming "limits to privatization,"[3] make the latent power of the state in an age of globalization eminently visible. The equation is not globalization *or* the nation state, but globalization *and* the nation state.

At a political level, the signs of what could be seen as a new postliberal settlement are premised on greater control, increased surveillance, and an eclipse of liberal rights that have prevailed since the seventeenth and eighteenth century. Terrorism, as Charles Townsend (2002, 137) has noted, constitutes "a calculated assault on the culture of reasonableness," which is central to democratic civic culture. Such a culture is epitomized by norms such as "toleration," "moderation," "the principle of proportionality," and "nonviolence," which form the conditions for the exercise of civil liberties. Townsend (2002, 134) reports the conclusions of the Dutch political scientist Alex Schmid (1993), who has concluded that democracies experience weaknesses when faced with terrorism related to: (a) freedom of movement, (b) freedom of association, (c) an abundance of targets, and (d) the constraints of the legal system.

While the liberal rights of free association and free speech make democracies slow to respond, some significant changes have come in a number of respects. Firstly, as concerns rights within the law, in respect to being imprisoned without being charged and to being detained for an indefinite period. A relaxation of traditional judicial cautiousness has been introduced as the condition upon which the safety of each person can be assured. In Britain, the legislative basis was introduced in December 2001 in the *Anti-Terrorism Crime and Security Act,* which introduced internment without trial or the necessity of leveling charges. October 2002 saw this act being used in London to effect the imprisonment of the radical Muslim cleric Abu Qatada, who was suspected to be an al Qaeda agent. This and other legislation also enable state surveillance and control over banking and information resources.

A second sense in which traditional political settlement has altered relates to the doctrine of "pre-emptive strike" (and the associated notion of "regime-change"), which supercedes the doctrine of deterrence or containment that has been the bedrock of stability, and the traditional Westphalia model of international relations, which established the principle of state sovereignty by a treaty signed in 1648. Under deterrence, a country could retaliate if its national borders were violated. Under the doctrine of pre-emptive strike, a country may anticipate aggression and "retaliate in advance." This enables states to attack who they like, based solely on the perception of a threat. This represents a move beyond what Henry Kissinger called "realpolitik" and casts aside traditional tenets of international law, as well as U.N. and NATO charters. The new doctrine makes no qualification as to its use, so pre-emption becomes a new universal principle available to every nation. In addition, the new doctrine is not required to conform to international law, but can be justified as self-defense for individual countries to take action unilaterally. Except, in these new circumstances self-defense is redefined from meaning "actual attack by another country" to "perceived imminent attack."[4]

In addition to these changes post-9/11, there has been a sharp increase in surveillance and data sharing, which has effected changes in the conception of citizenship. As part of this there has been an increase in the demands for information in the name of the public interest which is affecting the boundaries between the private and the public spheres. A recent newspaper feature on privacy (*The Guardian* 2002) documented a whole range of forms of surveillance across both the private and public spheres, including data trawling, data sharing, visual surveillance (CCTV), DNA testing, fingerprinting, communication interception, and identity cards. In Britain, where liberal protections of the individual privacy and autonomy have a strong tradition, a recent report has been published on *Privacy and Data Sharing* (Performance and Innovation Unit 2002) which aims to balance the dual concerns of protecting the rights of the individual and the state's interest in collecting and sharing data more efficiently across various public and private agencies for the purposes of creating "joined-up" government. Although critics are representing the report as a "snooper's charter," enabling the state to know everything about you, and are doubtful, to use Charles Raab's (2002, 16) words, that "the circle of privacy and data sharing can be squared," certain measures have been taken to protect the individual as well as minority groups within this legislation. These measures range from the establishment of a public services "trust charter" and other devices which oblige all public services to state how data can be shared, how individual privacy can be protected, and how individuals can assert their rights, to the appointment in state bodies of chief knowledge officers with responsibility for managing data and overseeing an organization's privacy commitments. In addition, in Britain, there have been several pieces of legislation which help to protect the rights and interests of individuals. These range from the *Human Rights Act* (1998), which aims to balance the needs of the state and the rights of the citizen, and is arguably one of the Blair government's most significant achievements to date; the *Data Protection Act* (1998), which gives to all citizens the right to know who holds information about them (subject access), as well as rights to object and remedy errors; and the *Freedom of Information Act* (1999) and the *Regulation of Investigatory Powers Act* (2000), both of which seek to ensure that the use of communication data is properly controlled with independent oversight and proper complaints procedures, and which introduce new and supposedly improved regulatory machinery which didn't previously exist. In addition, the *Anti-Terrorism, Crime and Security Act* (2001), although it requires communications companies to retain basic details of Internet activity longer than was the case previously and to report suspicious and irregular activity, also forbids data "fishing" and "trawling" expeditions, confining access to information strictly in relation to specific inquiries about crime or terrorism.

A key question here relates to the issue that in tackling a minority or criminals or terrorists in our midst, are we not trampling on the rights of the vast majority of citizens? The answer to this is of course complex, but we must not see the issue in terms of privacy as a natural right of individuals pitted against the common good. The classical liberal conception of privacy is linked integrally to the conception of the self as the private, self-interested chooser who exists prior to society and is endowed with natural rights. Although utilitarian writers, such as John Stuart Mill, did not subscribe to natural rights theory, they still represented the individual as separate from the sphere of society. What such a conception ignores is that it is a fiction, as Foucault and others have identified. Such rights are indeed internal to, not antecedent to, community, and as such are not absolute. Moreover, as the framers of the recent *Human Rights Act*, as well as the *European Convention of Human Rights*, which was its inspiration, knew only too well, different rights and interests need to be kept in balance. Privacy, like autonomy and freedom, is rooted in human dignity and speaks to the demands for safety and respect. It is not, however, an absolute right, but must be balanced by the right to safety and security of all, including children, women, and employees.[5] In this balance of forces, the state must be seen as both a negative as well as a positive force. It is a negative force in that it protects the safety of all, and it is a positive force in that it empowers and enables people to shape their lives, constituting, as it were, a collective vehicle to achieve progressive change. This notion of positive freedom, which starts with the Greek polis and is evident in writers like John Dewey, sees the full development of human beings as only possible through active participation in the affairs of the community.

Totalitarianism

This form of positive government was seen by liberals like Isaiah Berlin (1969), Friedrich Hayek (1935, 1944) and Karl Popper (1945, 1961) as likely to lead toward totalitarianism. The classic liberal theory of totalitarianism sees it as a form of government that develops out of the structures of the positive state. For liberals, a positive conception of liberty leads the state to promote a single substantive ideal of the good—a description of humans as spiritual beings whose ultimate rationality and reality are grounded in a unified spirit. This leads to a nation-state, which imposes a substantive conception of the good life, eradicating individuality by a concern with "normcentricity."[6]

Positive freedom worries liberals. The positive view of freedom as active self-determination implies, says Berlin (1969), a distinction between two selves—a higher self that determines, and a lower self that is subject to determination. Berlin argues that in the history of political thought, it is all too easy for the higher self to become identified with the state or society, or with a particular political group's conception of what is "rational." Freedom then tends to become defined as obedience to what is rational, or obedience to the will of the state, or conformity to a predetermined pattern of thought or life. As a consequence, claims Berlin, positive freedom is transposed into the opposite of freedom: totalitarianism or tyranny.

In its extreme form, argues Nel Noddings (1996), it is claimed that the positive conception of liberty often leads to the promulgation of a single ideal—a description of "man" as a spiritual being whose ultimate rationality and reality are grounded in a unified spirit. In this model, the state is seen as the expression of collective will (positive freedom), rather than the (mere) protector of individual liberties (negative freedom).

The total community = fascism = the nation-state. If the state is right, then there is no room for dissent, and liberty is equated with full immersion in the community. Liberals claim that individuality is wiped out by normcentricity. In this way, Eric Hoffer maintained that communities foster "unity" and "self-sacrifice" along with conformity to established norms. In Hoffer's words:

> Unity and self-sacrifice, of themselves, even when fostered by the most noble means, produce a facility for hating. Even when men league themselves mightily together to promote tolerance and peace on earth, they are likely to be violently intolerant towards those not of like mind (Hoffer 1951, 92).

While writers like Berlin, Popper, and Hayek believe that any state, over and above a concern with negative liberties, constitutes a threat to the freedom of the individual, as if inherently unable to respect a diversity of lifestyles, their argument falters on a number of grounds which I have summarized more fully elsewhere[7] and can only outline briefly in this context:

Firstly, their arguments technically rule out even a welfare state, for welfare rights are "positive" rights, and for Hayek, the welfare state is the start of the "slippery slope," leading down "the road to serfdom."

Secondly, it is neither logically nor empirically entailed that a state that acts positively in terms of a specific substantive conception of the good must ignore a respect for diversity and difference, or fail to respect the plurality of groups and subgroups in the wider society. As postmodernists and others have suggested, the good can accommodate difference. To suggest, therefore, that any state that does not confine itself to the minimum protection of individual liberties, but acts in terms of a general substantive vision, even if conceived in sophisticated terms, will unleash a pressure toward "unity" or normcentricity is a flawed argument, for it assumes that a theory of the good cannot exist at an abstract enough level to accommodate diversity or pluralism. Further, it attributes a failure of democracy to the particular way the state acts, *as a general orientation,* rather than to a specific analysis of *particular* societies in *particular* historical circumstances.

Thirdly, the liberal theory of totalitarianism depends on presumptions that liberalism constitutes a neutral agenda where freedom is defined as the natural property of individuals outside of society. Based on this argument, writers like Berlin (1969) maintain that liberalism advocates no substantive conception of the good. The identification of a good is impossible, in Berlin's view, as individuals manifest such diversity of opinion over the nature of the good. Because of this irreducible pluralism over values and preferences, and consequent incompatibility over versions of the good, individual freedom is all that remains. It is only as a consequence of this axiom that that the state can be represented as *the enemy,* rather than the *precondition,* of freedom.

Notwithstanding Berlin's view, it can be claimed that liberalism itself implies a substantive conception of the good. The argument by liberals that within its policy prescriptions liberalism does not invoke a particular preferred shape to society, or that it does not advocate the establishment of a social good over and above what individuals desire cannot rule out substantive commitments about what society should be like. As Luke Martell (1992, 156) states:

> It all sounds very nice until you realize that what it does, in effect, is to let in just another particular substantive vision of society as consisting of the sum total of individuals' preferences over which individuals have no overall control. In this sense, liberalism is in fact a highly substantive doctrine—one which posits a competitive individualist society immune to overall democratic direction.[8]

Fourthly, as Steven Heyman (1992) claims with respect to Berlin's (1969) analysis of liberty, what is striking about it is the way it is distorted by the political circumstances in which the essay was written:

> Berlin was writing in the late 1950s, at the height of the Cold War. He casts the debate between negative and positive liberty as a crucial battle in "the open war that is being fought between two systems of ideas" . . . and between the political systems allegedly based

on them—western liberal democracy and totalitarian regimes of
the left and right. . . . With the passing of the Cold War, it may be
easier to understand the relationship between positive and negative liberty in our political tradition (Heyman, 1992: 81–82).

Although we must applaud classical and neoliberals for being
against totalitarianism, their specific theoretical analysis as to *what
causes* totalitarianism became mixed in with both "left-right" politics and analysis of the role of the state in general, and Cold-War
politics in particular. Although Heyman discusses this contention
with specific regard to Berlin, I would claim the thesis is generally applicable to many others, *to varying extents,* including Hayek,
Popper, and Plamenatz, to name but a few.[9]

With the passing of the Cold War, it can be more easily seen
that liberal explanations as to the origins of totalitarianism are
woefully inadequate. To the extent that there are dangers inherent in human societies, such dangers inhere in all sorts of society,
and it is difficult to identify such dangers as belonging specifically to a particular form and organization of the state in promoting the conditions for positive or negative freedom. Although it is
not possible to do justice to such a complex topic in the short space
available here, any adequate explanation for the origins of totalitarianism must take adequate account of the *historical, political,
cultural, and economic specificity of particular states at particular locations in history.* What produces totalitarianism is not a particular
gearing of state power (such as "positive" or "negative," or even
"holist," or "piecemeal" engineering, to use Popper's term), but
quite simply the *absence of democracy,* or of the *conditions* which
enable democracy to flourish. Based on this criteria, the Marxist-
Leninist regimes of Eastern Europe failed in that they lacked a
strong or deep conception of democracy, as well as the range of
specific *mechanisms* by which democracy operates. As democracy
is a structural arrangement, with specific techniques and mechanisms and processes that can be analyzed, the best way to safeguard against totalitarianism is by ensuring that the state is a *democratic* state, and by seeking to *deepen* the specific senses in terms of
which democracy operates.

To the extent that the state is solely concerned with the negative goals supporting the protection of individual liberties, and

does not focus on the expression of a public will, it will be poorly equipped to deal with terrorist attacks. To the extent that terrorism forces the liberal state to reveal its "dormant will," liberals, who always thought that no such thing existed, will, of course, be perturbed.

Many, including myself, who support a "positive" role for the state while acknowledging that there are dangers in relation to this, as there are in relation to any form of social and political organization, believe that the answer is best sought in the strengthening or deepening of democracy.[10]

Rights Talk

The changes to traditional liberal safeguards and forms of governmentality indicative of a new political tendency or settlement, outlined above, signal the sense in which certain liberal discursive patternings of power have constituted the taken-for-granted basis of Western political and educational arguments over the last century. There was a time, not too far back, when the left saw "rights-talk" as having little relevance to their discourses of emancipation or to educational programs, seeing issues to do with "rights" as either part of the regulatory politics of the bourgeois state, focusing too specifically on individual as opposed to collective concerns, or as part and parcel of Cold War politics. The events of 9/11 may hopefully reintroduce a concern for rights, and maybe other themes within liberal constitutionalism, in both educational and political research, as fundamental to emancipatory and progressive concerns. Individual human rights and duties are not just important for the security and survival of all, but constitute the visible precondition for the legitimacy of collective power's right to govern. Indeed, it can be said that within what I am calling (following Held 1995) *the new cosmopolitanism,* human rights and democratic justice must be called upon to fill the void of traditional concerns with socialist politics. In this sense, for educators, 9/11 has introduced much more pressing concerns, for one of the more important functions of education is in citizenship for democratic participation. This unfortunately is something that universal education in the Western world has almost single-mindedly avoided during the twentieth century. While it has been recognized that the concerns with literacy and numeracy and social studies have positive externalities for democratic citizenship, the emphasis has been on "teaching" citizenship in the curriculum, rather than through involvement of students in the active decision-making processes of the school, where it could be argued that democracy is learnt. As Walter Parker (2001, 9) has observed, citizenship education has largely been concerned with *learning about democracy* rather than *involvement in democracy*. What must be implemented is a form of citizenship education which is *extracurricular*, focusing not only on what is taught in the classroom, but on *indirect* learning through participation in the governance of the school (the processes through which both school and classroom policies are made), in school-community forums, and in interschool forums for broader educational-community relations.

A New Multicultural Cosmopolitanism

In this sense, the new cosmopolitanism must embody an educational conception of democracy which is truly *multicultural*. As well as aiming to promote the skills of sharing and deliberation through active participation in democratic processes of the school, what is brought home with the events of 9/11 is the need to involve students in democracy in a genuine multicultural sense. For what is crucial in the world post-9/11 is that it is a global world which urges us to recognize those people and cultures who inhabit the world in addition to us as those others who are inhabiting the cities, libraries, and schools that we think of as ours, a world which is increasingly cosmopolitan, if not in the sense that we all travel more, or at all, but certainly in the sense that what happens in one part of the globe now affects us all. Multicultural citizenship is now a matter of vital concern.

In that democracy must respect multiculturalism, so multiculturalism must respect democracy. Democratic norms must necessarily crosscut multicultural groups to protect three conditions: (1) the basic rights of all citizens individually and as groups (freedom of speech, thought, assembly, expression, lifestyle choice, etc.);[11] (2) that no person or group is manipulated into accepting values represented by public institutions, and (3) that public officials and institutions are democratically accountable in principle and practice.

Democracy in this sense must constitute a new universal. In this sense, it is a more basic set of procedural norms and rules than are the rights of any minority to do what they like. We must move away from any conception of multiculturalism whereby cultural minorities can be completely unresponsive to outside cultures, or where prohibitions against group members leaving the culture can be enforced. No minority and no culture can guarantee their own survival forever, as openness to the world outside is a necessary principle of democracy. This openness is indeed a core principle of cosmopolitan global democracy, which must infuse citizenship education post-9/11. The point here is that a democratic culture, which contains as its basis both an attribution of rights and a specification of duties, must underpin any conception of multiculturalism so defined.

By making a "rights/duties culture" fundamental, in this sense, limits are placed upon the "discourse of diversity" that multiculturalism entails. This does not mean that the recognition of distinct identities and differences, as argued for by multiculturalists, are not important. Liberalism has clearly failed to sufficiently acknowledge such insights from "the politics of recognition," tending to represent justice as the *imposition of a single standard or rule* to all of the diverse groups within the social structure. Yet, while we can accept that multiculturalists have contributed something important in arguing for the recognition of distinct cultural identities, based on ethnicity, race, religion, gender, or class, as Kymlicka (1999) has argued, such arguments cannot be used to legitimate "internal restrictions" (e.g., prohibiting group exit) which violate or contradict democratic principles or interfere with the rights of other individuals or groups. By the same token, multicultural advocacy may result in "external protections" to counter group disadvantage or marginalization. Such claims may themselves vary from one historical period to another and should thus be deliberated and enacted through the democratic process itself.

Although multiculturalism advances a "discourse of diversity," it is different from, and largely unrelated to, the "discourse of diversity and devolution" advanced by neoliberalism. In that the multicultural stress on diversity has been influenced by postmodernist theorizing, neoliberal diversity is sponsored by the market mechanism, which results in compounding and cumulative inequalities. With multiculturalism, diversity may also be dysfunctional to the extent that it undermines the degree of societal cohesion necessary for different groups to work and live together. The extent to which multicultural diversity reinforces norms of intolerance and conflict also takes on a new and altered significance post-9/11. Clearly the balance of contending forces among the common interests of society, and the subgroupings within it, and the overall extent to which diversity is *recognized* and permitted, is itself a question of democratic deliberation and adjudication, which may alter in different places and times.[12]

Democracy

The principle of democracy that I am talking about is *nonfoundational* but *universal*. By this I mean that it is not based upon any fixed conception of human nature, or on a premise, as with Habermas, of universal rationality, whereby conflicts can be redeemed dialogically through communicative action in the ideal speech community. Rather, the principle of democracy which I favor insists on the protection of human rights, recognizes the distinctiveness of subcultures, ensures the principles of inclusion and openness, and ensures the universal application of the rule of law and of open dialogue, not based upon any faith in rationality, but based purely on a principle of a *mutual interest in universal survival*. Thus, while such a conception of democracy is "deliberative," it is pragmatically rather than epistemologically based.[13] This is to say that the safety of all is guaranteed *in the final analysis* on the basis of a common interest in survival. This iterates the same ground which justifies the culture of reasonableness, as well as liberal values such as freedom of association, expression, and the like. *In an age of terrorism, democracy is the condition upon which survival can best be assured.* Such a conception is universal to the extent that it is *willed*. The inspiration is Nietzschean rather than Kantian. It is also very Foucauldian in the sense that it constitutes *a universalism of democracy as a contingent discourse of open protection and facilitation in a world of dangers.*[14]

Although survival may justify democracy, as an end or goal it is too thin to be fully adequate, of course, for mere survival cannot possibly satisfy a complete account of life's ends and aims. And it may not be universally agreed to, if we mean by universal "agreed to by all," for there are no doubt some, including suicide bombers, for whom it holds no sway at all. Ultimately, that is the choice of course, and certainly it focuses the concentration. For if democracy is the *precondition* of survival, then it requires a contractual democratic mandate to be effective, even so.

Beyond this, it is possible to build a much richer conception of democracy on this basis. If survival is a final justification and focuses our attention as to why democracy is important, survival with dignity resonates of a more traditional concern with *ends*. This of course is the classic conception of democracy as a doctrine based on the ultimate worth and dignity of the human being, as espoused in the republican tradition. Thus, it is not the narrow "realist" theory of democracy that has been articulated and advocated by postwar American political science, commonly associated with the writings of Joseph Schumpeter's (1976) *Capitalism, Socialism and Democracy*, which refers to a narrow system of representative government and a means of changing governments through a system of elections (Hindess 2000). Rather, if safety, dignity, and survival are to be possible, the theory of democracy must be deepened, once again, to refer to a substantive end which is something more than mere utility, but encompasses the well-being and safety "of each and all" (Shapiro 1999). That is, it expresses the common interests of all, and allows for responsible liberty within this context. Such a conception must once again entail a certain idea of participation and equality as well.[15] While some philosophers and political theorists will sense a resonance here with Rousseau's *general will*, this would be mistaken, for the model suggested here is not a totalizing one, which presupposes unity between individual and collective, but a *detotalizing* one that is based on the notion of general well-being while recognizing the diversity and differences between cultures and people in relation to the way that ends are articulated and realized. This is what I have referred to elsewhere as "thin communitarianism." The formulation owes its general inspiration to Foucault, whose conception of the "equalization of power relations" and "non-domination" can be used to support, I argue, a general conception of democratic justice (see Olssen 2002; Olssen, Codd, O'Neill 2004, ch. 11). In terms of social ontology, such a conception can be thought of as similar to Martha Nussbaum's (1995, 456) "thick vague conception of the good." Nussbaum advances "a soft version of Aristotelian essentialism" which incorporates a "determinate account of the human being, human functioning, and human flourishing" (ibid. 450). While in formal terms it recognizes that all individuals and cultures have certain developmental and lifestyle needs, this "internal essentialism" is "an historically grounded empirical essentialism" (ibid. 451). As such, it is purely formal, for within this broad end, and subject to the limits necessary for its realization and continuance, it permits and recognizes a multitude of identities and projects and ways of life.[16]

Attempts to reconcile diversity with social unity are not new. John Rawls seeks to account for a "reasonable pluralism" within the context of the "overlapping consensus" as the basis of "justice as fairness" (Rawls 1996, lecture iv).[17] Arguments from postmodernists have also sought to throw new light on how difference and unity can be reconciled. For Foucault (1981, 69), the social whole is never a "sealed" unity, or resistant to change, but is characterized rather by incompleteness, complexity, and chance (*alea*). Such theorizing by Foucault, and others, utilizing models of nonlinear complex causality,[18] has led to fresh interest in how creativity and difference can exist and be safeguarded in a community. Similar initiatives, relating to Foucault and other postmodernist thinkers, are summarized by William Corlett (1989) in his book *Community Without Unity: A Politics of Derridean Extravagance.*

Deepening Democracy Through Education

If post-9/11 makes democracy of more pressing concern, our conception has moved a long way from a narrow theory of universal enfranchisement. To the extent that counterterrorist action now constitutes an important item, it must itself be subject to the democratic norms of public visibility and critical scrutiny, together with open processes of deliberation and debate, as well as traditional rights of contestation in terms of the rule of law. If our substantive conception posits certain general ends which allow for a degree of diversity and pluralism, our procedural view of democracy is as a multifaceted array of mechanisms and processes instituted to ensure the *inclusion, security,* or *safety* (including ethnic, racial, and sexual safety), as well as *development* and *opportunities* of all individuals and groups. In this respect, research needs to focus on the means of *deepening* democracy to satisfy these goals. As a way of concluding this article, we might say that research needs to be concerned with all or any of the following themes:

• *The concern with equality*: The development of any conception of democratic justice must seek to deal with, rather than avoid, issues to do with distribution of resources and life chances. Given a rejection of the classical liberal fiction regarding entitlement to property based on a model of presocial, possessive individuals who, as C.B. Macpherson (1962, 263) puts it, "owe . . . nothing to society," it is important to theorize the implications of a social ontological framework of community for considerations of democratic justice as it pertains to distributional ethics. Community in this sense is definable as an all-encompassing arena without fixed borders or unity, which comprises an assortment of values, norms, and institutions that enable life to be lived. Such a conception of community recognizes social ties and shared values, as well as practices of voluntary action and public institutions like education which constitute the conditions for stability and reproduction of society. Although neoliberal philosophers like Nozick (1975) have shifted political philosophy away from a concern with issues of distributive justice in recent years, my own view is similar to the nineteenth-century social democrat L.T. Hobhouse (1911), who held that one's entitlement to rewards and gain must be balanced by one's obligation to society. What liberal conceptions of democracy obscured, in Hobhouse's view, was the *interdependence* between individuals and the social structure, or the social and moral obligation of the society (acting through the vehicle of the state) to assist in arranging the social futures of each rising generation. As he argued in his book *Liberalism* (1911, 189–190), in his justification for redistributive policies of progressive taxation, the state has an obligation to enforce reasonable conditions of equality on the basis that while a society should provide the conditions for enterprise, all individuals are correspondingly indebted to society for the conditions and structures provided, and on this basis, individuals should contribute in direct proportion to the luck or good fortune they experience.

• *The role of the state*: The role of the state should be concerned with guaranteeing both negative freedom and positive freedom. Negative freedom involves the state's responsibility for ensuring the universal entitlements to safety and reasonable autonomy for all. The trade-off in respect to privacy will be necessitated to the extent that these obligations are threatened. To the extent that greater surveillance is deemed necessary, the proposals must be themselves subject to democratic processes that ensure visibility, openness, deliberation, and debate.

The state's obligations as regards positive freedom involve developing opportunities based on people's rights to inclusion and the development of their capacities. This obligation gives the state a role in the provision of social services, health care, and education. In brief, the role for the positively geared state lies in relation to socially directed investment decisions, to provide for the general conditions for all species needs and development, including education and training, and to create and maintain quality infrastructure such as schools, hospitals, parks, and public spaces.

• *The development of civil society*: A vibrant civil society can constitute a check on the powers of government. Civil society refers to that sector of private associations, relatively autonomous from the state and economy, which spring from the everyday lives and activities of communities of interest. Clearly, one principle of democracy is the idea of multiple centers of power, and of their separation, as suggested by writers like Montesquieu (1989) and de Tocqueville (2003). Another principle of democracy is the right to contest, challenge, or oppose. Institutions of civil society, as writers like Paul Hirst (1995) have maintained, can be seen to constitute an important powerful network of quasi-independent associations, which can strengthen democratic rule through checking the power of the state. If democracy is rule by the people, the ability and opportunity to "speak the truth to power," as Michel

Foucault (2001) has put it, is itself one of democracy's crucial rights, indeed its very condition. According to Cohen and Arato (1992), civil society strengthens democracy in both a defensive and offensive sense. The defensive aspect refers to the way that associations and social movements develop forms of communicative interaction that support the development of people's identities, expand participatory possibilities, and create networks of solidarity. The offensive aspect refers to how associational networks and institutions come to exert influence on, and constitute checks to, the state, and to each other.

• *The role of education*: the role of education is crucial for democracy, as educational institutions, whether compulsory or postcompulsory, intersect with, and therefore mediate between institutions like the family and those of the state and the economy. Although formal institutions of education have been in the main public institutions, there is an important sense in which they are semi-autonomous from the state. This is not the neoliberal sense where management and administration are devolved to the local school, but the sense in which the schools are located in, and represent local community groups. In this sense, schools are important as democratic organizations, through the particular way that they are connected to communities, through their ability to empower families and involve minority groups in participatory projects. Education also is crucial as the central agency responsible for the production of democratic norms such as trust and political decision-making. This is to say, as Mill (1910) recognized in *Representative Government*, educational institutions are important as sites where democracy and self-government are learnt. Deliberative democracy is especially complex, for it involves not just norms and procedures of debate but norms and procedures of contestation, inclusiveness, tolerance, compromise, solidarity with others, generosity, care, the operations of forums, and of checks and balances, the use of sanctions and screens, and the separation of powers. In the republican tradition, schools are instrumental in the development of civic virtue and habits of good citizenship. This is what signals the real importance of the "knowledge economy." For education is essentially important in its role of constructing democratic civic norms, and this must become one of the central aims of government policy in this regard. It is not a case of "brainwashing" or "socialization," but of teaching skills and establishing models of civic conduct based on tolerance, deliberation, conflict resolution, give-and-take, and trust. While educational processes depend upon fairness of political processes, and of the distribution of economic resources, education is necessary to construct the network of norms that permit both the market and democracy to function. As Philip Pettit (1999, 255) puts it, education represents a "stark choice between the invisible hand and the iron hand: between a strategy of marketing and a strategy of management." It is this reason of course why education should ideally be *public, universal, compulsory, and free*. For if education is vital in constructing norms that nurture the market, it cannot be itself subject to the market's disorganizing effects.

References

Arendt, H. (1958) *The Origins of Totalitarianism*. London: Allen & Unwin.

Berlin, I. (1969) *Four Essays on Liberty*. London: Oxford University Press.

Blunkett, D. (2002) "Civic Rights," in "Big Brother: The Secret State and the Assault on Privacy, Part Two." *The Guardian*, September 14, 22–23.

Castells, M. (1997) "A Powerless State," in *The Information Age: Economy, Society and Culture. Volume II: The Power of Identity*. Oxford: Blackwell Publishers.

Cilliers, P. (1998) *Complexity and Postmodernism: Understanding Complex Systems*. London: Routledge.

Cloke, P., Milbourne, P., and Widdowfield, R. (2000) Partnership and policy networks in rural local governance: homelessness in Taunton. *Public Administration* 78(1), 111–113.

Cochrane, A. (2000) "New Labour, New Urban Policy." *Social Policy Review* 12, 184–204.

Cohen, J.L., and Arato, A. (1992) *Civil Society and Political Theory*. Cambridge, MA & London: The MIT Press.

Corlett, W. (1989). *Community Without Unity: A Politics of Derridean Extravagance*. Durham and London: Duke University Press.

Dahl, R. (1999) "Can International Organisations be Democratic? A Skeptic's View," in I. Shapiro and C. Hacker-Cordón (eds.), *Democracy's Edges*. Cambridge: Cambridge University Press, 19–36.

Dennett, D. C. (2003) *Freedom Evolves*. London: Penguin Books.

European Convention on Human Rights. Available at: http://www.hri.org/docs/ECHR50.html

Falk, R. (1995) *On Humane Governance.* Cambridge: Polity Press.

Foucault, M. (1981) "The order of discourse" (trans., I. McLeod), in R. Young (ed.), *Untying the Text.* London: Routledge.

————. (2001) *Fearless Speech* (ed., Joseph Pearson). Los Angeles: Semiotext(e).

Giddens, A. (2000) *The Third Way and Its Critics.* Cambridge: Polity Press.

Gewirtz, S. (2002) "Faith-based schooling and the invisible effects of September 11th: the view from England." Unpublished paper.

Glendinning, C., Powell, M., and Rummery, K. (2002) *Partnerships, New Labour and the Governance of Welfare.* Bristol: Policy Press.

Habermas, J. (1984) *The Theory of Communicative Action,* Vol. 1. (trans., T. McCarthy). Boston: Beacon Press.

Hattersley, R. (2002) "The Silly Season," *Guardian,* August 30, p.18.

Hayek, F. (1935) *Collectivist Economic Planning.* London: Routledge & Kegan Paul.

Hayek, F. (1944) *The Road to Serfdom.* London: Routledge & Kegan Paul.

Held, D. (1995) *Democracy and the Global Order.* Cambridge: Polity Press.

Heyman, S. (1992) "Positive and Negative Liberty." *Chicago-Kent Law Review* 68(1), 81–98.

Hindess, B. (2000) "Representative Government and Participatory Democracy," in Andrew Vandenberg (ed.), *Citizenship and Democracy in the Global Era.* London: Macmillan Press.

Hirst, P. (1995) "Can Secondary Associations Enhance Democratic Governance?" in J. Cohen and J. Rogers (eds.), *Associations and Democracy: The Real Utopias Project,* Vol. 1. (Series Ed., Erik Olin Wright). London: Verso, p. 101–113.

Hirst, P., and Thompson, K (1996) *Globalization in Question.* Cambridge: Polity Press.

Hobhouse, L.T. (1911) *Liberalism.* London: Williams and Norgate.

Honohan, I. (2002) *Civic Republicanism.* London: Routledge.

Hoffer, E. (1951) *The True Believer.* New York: Harper and Row.

Klein, N. (2000) *No Logo.* London: Flamingo.

Kymlicka, W. (1999) "Liberal Complacancies," in S. M. Okin (ed.), *Is Multiculturalism Bad for Women?* Princeton, NJ: Princeton University Press.

MacIntyre, A. (1984) *After Virtue* (second ed.). Notre Dame, IN: University of Notre Dame Press.

Macpherson, C.B. (1962) *The Political Theory of Possessive Individualism: Hobbes to Locke.* Oxford: Oxford University Press.

Martell, L. (1992) "New Ideas of Socialism." *Economy and Society,* 21(2), 151–172.

Mill, J. S. (1910) *Representative Government.* New York: Everyman.

Mishra, R. (1999) *Globalization and the Welfare State.* Cheltenham: Edward Elgar.

Montesquieu, C. de S. (1989) *The Spirit of the Laws,* translated and edited by A.M. Cohler, B.C. Miller, and H.S. Stone). Cambridge: Cambridge University Press.

Noddings, N. (1996) "On Community," *Educational Theory,* 46(3), 245–267.

Nozick, R. (1975). *Anarchy, State, Utopia.* Oxford: Blackwell.

Nussbaum, M. (1995) "Human Functioning and Social Justice: in Defence of Aristotelian Essentialism," in D. Tallack (ed.), *Critical Theory: A Reader.* New York: Harvestor/Wheatsheaf.

Ohmae, K. (1990) *The Borderless World.* New York: Harper Business.

Ohmae, K. (1995) *The End of the Nation State: The Rise of Regional Economics.* New York: The Free Press.

Olssen, M. (1996) "In Defence of the Welfare State and Publicly Provided Education: A New Zealand Perspective," *Journal of Education Policy,* 11(3), 337–362.

Olssen, M. (1998) "Education Policy, the Cold War and the 'Liberal-Communitarian' Debate." *Journal of Education Policy,* 13(1), 63–89.

Olssen, M. (2002) "Michel Foucault as 'Thin' Communitarian: Difference, Community, Democracy," *Cultural Studies—Critical Methodologies,* 2(4), 483–513.

Olssen, M. (2003) "Totalitarianism and the 'Repressed' Utopia of the Present: Moving beyond Hayek, Popper and Foucault." *Policy Futures in Education,* 1(3), 526–552.

Olssen, M., Codd, J., and O'Neill, A-M. (2004) *Education Policy: Globalisation, Citizenship, Democracy.* Sage: London.

Parker, W. (2001) "Educating Democratic Citizens: A Broad View." *Theory into Practice,* 40(1), 6–13.

Parliamentary Acts, UK (1998) *Human Rights Act* (Great Britain). Available at: http://www.hmso.gov.uk/acts1998/19980042.htm

Parliamentary Acts, UK (1998) *Data Protection Act.* Available at: http://www.hmso.gov.uk/acts/acts1998/19980029.htm

Parliamentary Acts, UK (1999) *Freedom of Information Act.* Available at: http://wwwusdoj.gov/04foia/

Parliamentary Acts, UK (2000) *Regulation of Investigatory Powers Act.* Available at: http://www.hmso.gov.uk/acts/acts2000/20000023.htm

Parliamentary Acts, UK (2001) *Anti Terrorism, Crime and Security Act.* Available at: http://www.hmso.gov.uk/acts/acts2001/20010024.htm

Performance and Innovation Unit (2002) *Privacy and Data Sharing: The Third Way Forward for Public Services.* Available at: http://www.strategy.gov.uk/2002/privacy/report/

Peters, M. (2001) Education and Culture in Postmodernity: The Challenges for Aoteroa/New Zealand. *The Macmillan Brown Lectures* (Unpublished paper)

Pettit, P. (1999) *Republicanism: A Theory of Freedom and Government.* Oxford: Oxford University Press.

Plamenatz, J. (1954) *Marxism and Russian Communism.* London: Longmans.

Plamenatz, J. (1963) *Man and Society: A Critical Examination of Some Important Social and Political Theories from Machiavelli to Marx.* (Volume 2). London and Harlow: Longman Green.

Polanyi, K. (1944) *The Great Transformation,* Boston: Beacon Press.

Popper, K (1945) *The Open Society and Its Enemies.* London: Routledge.

Popper, K. (1961) *The Poverty of Historicism.* London: Routledge

Raab, C. (2002) "Data Sharing: Privacy in the Public Interest," in "Big Brother, Part III," *The Guardian,* September 21.

Rawls, J. (1996) *Political Liberalism.* New York: Columbia University Press.

Rhodes, R. W. (1997a) *Understanding Governance: policy networks, governance, reflexivity and accountability.* Buckingham: Open University Press.

Rhodes, R.W. (1997b) "From marketization to diplomacy: It's the mix that matters," *Public Policy and Administration,* 12(2), 31–50.

Rhodes, R.W. (2000) "Governance and Public Administration," in Jon Pierre (ed.), *Debating Governance.* Oxford: Oxford University Press, pp. 54–90.

Sandel, M. (1982) *Liberalism and the Limits of Justice.* Cambridge: Cambridge University Press.

Schmid, A. (1993) "Terrorism and Democracy," in A. Schmid and R. Crelinsten (eds.), *Western Responses to Terrorism.* London: Frank Cass.

Shapiro, I. (1999) *Democratic Justice.* New Haven and London: Yale University Press.

Schumpeter, J. (1976) *Capitalism, Socialism, Democracy.* London: Routledge.

Stiglitz, J. (2002) *Globalization and Its Discontents.* Allen Lane: Penguin.

Talmon, J. (1955) *The Origins of Totalitarian Democracy.* London: Secker & Warburg.

The Guardian (2002) "Special Report: Big Brother," Parts 1, 2, and 3, September 7, 14, and 21. http://www.guardian.co.uk/bigbrother/privacy/0.12377,783005,00html.

Tocqueville, A. de (2003) *Democracy in America (and Two Essays on America)* (Trans. Gerald E. Bevan, with Introduction and Notes by Isaac Kramnick). London: Penguin Books.

Townshend, C. (2002) *Terrorism: A Very Short Introduction.* Oxford: Oxford University Press.

Walzer, M. (1985) *Spheres of Justice.* Oxford: Basil Blackwell.

Wintour, P. (2002) "Parties Consign Welfare State to History," *Guardian,* October 12, p. 13.

Notes

1. An earlier version of this paper appeared in *Access: Critical Perspectives on Communication, Cultural and Policy Studies*, 21(1), 75–90. The editors are thanked for permission to publish.

2. For a more nuanced discussion of cosmopolitanism, see Olssen, Codd, O'Neill (2004), ch. 12.

3. *The Guardian*, Monday November 4, 2002. A headline on page one read "Brown camp seeks sell-off limit," revealing a faction in the government with a more cautious view towards privatization. This reinforces a widely held view amongst journalists that within New Labour there are different factions on privatization.

4. Yet a third sign of a change in the political settlement is the ignoring of the Geneva Convention by the United States in its imprisonment of suspected al-Qaeda terrorists at Guantanamo Bay, Cuba. Other possible signs include proposals in Britain in 2002 to do away with the "double jeopardy" rule, which has traditionally prevented people from being tried twice, as well as proposals to restrict trial by jury, and to reveal a person's previous convictions.

5. In legal terms, this idea of balance is covered by the "principle of proportionality."'

6. See also Arendt (1958), Talmon (1955).

7. See Olssen (1996, 1998, 2003).

8. This objection, which has been formulated many times by many writers, concerns the difficulty of distinguishing "procedural" from "substantive" goals (See Dahl 1999, 25–26; Honohan 2002, 9; Sandel 1982; Walzer 1985; MacIntyre 1984). Given that even "autonomy," or "democratic citizenship" can be construed as "substantive goals," on this basis, all states can be seen as having *some* substantive concerns.

9. See Hayek (1944), Popper (1945, 1961), Plamenatz (1954, 1963). For a brief argument to this effect, see Olssen (1996, 1998). For a more substantial critique of the liberal theory of totalitarianism see Olssen (2003). A great deal more work on this topic needs to be done.

10. Social democrats traditionally have supported a positive view of freedom. For a recent expression, see David Blunkett (2002), the current British Home Secretary, who writes "I prefer a positive view of freedom, drawing on another tradition of political thinking that goes back to the ancient Greek polis. According to this tradition, we only become fully free when we share, as active citizens, in the government of the affairs of the community. Our identity as members of a collective political community is a positive thing. Democracy is not just an association of individuals determined to protect the private sphere, but a realm of active

freedom in which citizens come together to shape the world around them. We contribute and we become entitled."

11. Human rights must underpin group rights to control the possibilities of groups acting in oppressive ways.

12. Sharon Gewirtz (2002) suggests that official government support towards state funding of "faith-based" schools in England has altered post-9/11, suggesting that forms of religious separatism over education are being seen as socially dysfunctional for the production of democratic values, such as tolerance.

13. It thus has the character of a "settlement," rather than a "consensus," or a "reflexive equilibrium," although the latter concept (which is Rawls') may, in this view, form part of a broader conception of citizenship which the state seeks to democratically promote.

14. My view is that a contract in relation to "survival" is a better basis to justify and ground democracy than traditional "social contract" theories, which concern a mythical transition from nature to culture. However, it is not possible to explore the differences in this paper.

15. I will argue in subsequent work that liberty presupposes equality, and that premised on a social view of selfhood, all action, even in language, represents a form of participation.

16. Of course, in that Nussbaum claims to be influenced by Aristotle, there is a clear difference with Foucault, who was more influenced by Nietzsche. Thus Foucault would reject the essentialist teleological conception of the subject as "realizing" their *ends* or *destiny,* in preference for a more Nietzschean emphasis on "self creation." But beyond this, it can be claimed that self-creation presupposes certain "capabilities" in the way Nussbaum claims. Also, the models of social relations, and specifically of the ontological priority of the social to the individual are similar in both traditions.

17. While we can accept much of Rawls' argument in practice, it is Rawls' commitments to liberal contract theory that we find problematic and which prevents him from, amongst other things, developing a viable notion of community. (See Rawls 1996).

18. For Foucault's model of holism/particularism, or system/originality, see my brief summaries (Olssen 1998, 79–80; 2002, 490–491). For a general account of theories of complex determination that are being used to explain how infinite possibilities and unpredictable occurrences are derivable from a set of determined rules or structure, see Cilliers (1998). As Daniel C. Dennett (2003) points out, such approaches still operate within the confines of *deterministic* physics, and hence, while theories like chaos theory can account partially for unpredictability and can "contribute to the plasticity and flexibility human brains display" (106), it

would require a theory of *indeterminism* to account for freedom, at least as conceived in the Kantian sense of *unconditioned* action. To render an account of freedom *compatible* with social and historical determinations is what Dennett seeks to provide, and hence, there is an interesting emergent parallel to the sort of account Foucault would seek to provide. How analytic philosophy adapts!

Chapter Six

Terrorism and the Culture of Permanent War

Democracy Under Siege

Henry A. Giroux

As the state is restructured as a result of right wing assaults by the Bush administration, it has dramatically shifted its allegiance away from providing for people's welfare, protecting the environment, and expanding the realm of public good. As a result of such a shift, the state has nullified the social contract that lies at the heart of a substantive democracy, a contract that provides for social provisions against life's hazards, that ensures a decent education, health care, food, and housing for all, but especially for those who are marginalized by virtue of sickness, age, race, gender, class, and youth. As the social contract is shredded by Bush's army of neoliberal evangelicals, neoconservative hardliners, and religious fundamentalists, government relies more heavily on its militarizing functions, giving free reign to the principle of security at the expense of public service and endorsing property rights over human rights. Under such circumstances, as Arundhati Roy argues, "the fundamental governing principles of democracy are not just being subverted but deliberately sabotaged. This kind of democracy is the problem, not the solution."[1] Fascism's shadow becomes increasingly more menacing as society is organized relentlessly around a culture of fear, cynicism, and unbridled self-interest—a society in which the government promotes legislation urging neighbors to spy on each other and the president of the United States endorses a notion of patriotism based on moral absolutes and a mandate to govern, which as Bush has claimed comes directly from God (of course, with a little help from Jeb Bush and the U.S. Supreme Court). Increasingly, we are told by President Bush, John Ashcroft, Dick Cheney, and others that patriotism is now legitimated through the physics of unaccountable power and unquestioned authority, defined rather crudely in the dictum "Either you are with us or with the terrorists."[2] Such absolutes, of course, have little respect for difference, dissent, or for that matter democracy itself. Politics in this instance has much less in common with public engagement, dialogue, and democratic governance than with a heavy reliance on institutions that rule through fear and, if necessary, brute force.[3]

As a wartime president, Bush's ratings are relatively high, even in the midst of an upcoming presidential election. But beneath the inflated ratings and the President's call for unity, there is a disturbing appeal to modes of community and patriotism buttressed by moral absolutes in which the discourse of evil, terrorism, and security work to stifle dissent, empty democracy of any substance, and exile politics "to the space occupied by those discontented with the West, and dispossessed by it."[4] Shamelessly pandering to the fever of emergency time and the economy of fear, President Bush and his administrative cohorts are rewriting the rhetoric of community so as to remove it from the realm of politics and democracy. In doing so, Bush and his followers are not only concentrating their political power, they are also pushing through harsh policies and regressive measures that cut basic services and public assistance for the poor, offering school children more standardized testing but not guaranteeing them decent health care and adequate food, sacrificing American democracy and individual autonomy for the promise of domestic security, and allocating resources and tax breaks to the rich through the airline bailout and retroactive tax cuts. Bush rhetoric of "permanent war" and antiterrorism has done more than create a culture of fear and a flood of jingoistic patriotism, it has also covered up those neoliberal tax polices for the rich that are part of the war waged against public goods, the very notion of the social and those marginalized by class and race. As Jeff Madrick observes:

> Narrow politics, of course, can partly account for the Bush administration's tax proposals. The tax cuts disproportionately benefit the wealthy, which, after all, is Bush's natural political constituency. But Bush's policies may, in fact, be explained by another, more radical agenda. Extensive tax cuts will require Congress to limit the growth of social programs and public investment and undermine other programs altogether. If that is your vision of the best direction America can take, the strategy makes some sense. So, we were wrong about how dividend tax cuts stimulate growth, you can almost hear the Bush advisers thinking. No problem. Rising deficits will inevitably force Congress to starve those 'wasteful' social programs. The prospective high deficits may even make it imperative to privatize Social Security and Medicare eventually. Social spending is the problem, goes the argument, not tax cuts.[5]

Starving social programs and destroying public institutions and services are now matched by the creation of a politics of fear and a notion of community that increasingly lives under the shadow of the legacy of fascism. For example, under the auspices of a belligerent nationalism and militarism, community is being constructed "through shared fears rather than shared responsibilities" and the strongest appeals to civic discourse are focused primarily on military defense, civil order, and domestic security.[6] Within the rhetoric and culture of shared fears, patriotism becomes synonymous with an uncritical acceptance of governmental authority and a discourse "that encourages ignorance as it overrides real politics, real history, and moral issues."[7] Lost here is any notion of patriotism as a multiple construction, particularly as a self-critical conception organized around a set of critical beliefs and progressive actions. Patriotism as a more critical variant becomes strategic, attentive to the particularities of contexts and place but not limited to a specific geography or history, and it suggests embracing dissent as a fundamental right while extending to all the right to govern and control those forces that bear down on their everyday lives.[8] If patriotism is to be rescued from its morally dangerous uses in the hands of reactionaries, religious fundamentalists, and other conservative ideologues, it must be engaged critically within the broader context of democratic values and rights. In part, this suggests engaging patriotism as both a theoretical referent and a performative social practice through which a country, region, or international organization does everything possible to *question* itself and provide the conditions necessary for its people to actively engage and transform the policies that shape their lives. One possibility is to take up the issue of patriotism as a principle of democratic community transfigured through notions of critical engagement, social justice, and political action. Community in this context becomes fluid, cosmopolitan, closely attuned to its connections to diverse spaces and places that occupy the rest of the globe.

The longing for community seems so desperate in the United States, steeped as it is in the ethic of neoliberalism with its utter disregard for public life, its ethic of downsizing, and its contempt for any mode of sociality based on noncommodified values, that in such ruthless times any invocation of community seems nourishing, even when the term is invoked to demand an "unconditional loyalty and treats everything short of such loyalty as an act of unforgivable treason."[9] How can any notion of democratic community or critical citizenship be embraced through the rhetoric of a debased patriotism that is outraged by dissent in the streets?

The English historian Eric Hobsbawm has observed that "never was the word 'community' used more indiscriminately and emptily than in the decades when communities in the sociological sense became hard to find in real life."[10] Maybe it is the absence of viable communities organized around democratic values and basic freedoms that accounts for the way in which the language of community has currently "degraded into the currency of propaganda."[11] How else can one explain the outrage exhibited by the dominant media against anyone who seems to question, among other things, the United States' support of friendly dictatorships, including Turkey and Saudi Arabia, or the Patriot Act with its suppression of civil liberties, or who even suggests the need for a serious discussion about how United States foreign policy contributes to the poverty, despair, and hopelessness throughout the world that offers terrorist nihilism the opportunity "to thrive in the rich soil of exclusion and victimhood"?[12] Actual democratic communities are completely at odds with a smug self-righteousness that refuses to make a distinction between explaining events and justifying them. As Judith Butler points out: "[t]o ask how certain political and social actions come into being, such as the [September 11th] terrorist attack on the U.S., and even to identify a set of causes, is not the same as locating the source of the responsibility for those actions, or indeed, paralyzing our capacity to make ethical judgments on what is right or wrong . . . but it does ask the U.S. to assume a different kind of responsibility for producing more egalitarian global conditions for equality, sovereignty, and the egalitarian redistribution of resources."[13] Such questions do not suggest that the United States is responsible for the acts of terrorism that took place on September 11th. On the contrary, they perform the obligatory work of politics by attempting to situate individual acts of responsibility within those broader sets of conditions that give rise to individual acts of terrorism while simultaneously asking how the United States can intervene more productively in global politics to produce conditions that undercut rather than reinforce the breeding grounds for such terrorism. At the same time, such questions suggest that the exercise of massive power cannot be removed from the exercise of politics and ethics, and such a recognition demands a measure of accountability to be responsible for the consequences of our actions as one of the most powerful countries in the world. As Jerome Binde observes, "Being able to act also means being able to answer for our actions, to be responsible."[14]

The rhetoric of antiterrorism is important, not only because it operates on many registers to both inflict human misery and call into question the delicate balance of freedom and security crucial to any democratic society, but also because it carries with it an enormous sense of urgency that often redefines community against its most democratic possibilities and realized forms. Rising from the ashes of impoverishment and religious fundamentalism,

terrorism, at its worst, evokes a culture of fear, unquestioning loyalty, and a narrow definition of security from those who treat it as
a pathology rather than as a politics. In part, this is evident in
Bush's "war against terrorism," which, fueled by calls for public
sacrifice, appears to exhaust itself in a discourse of moral absolutes and public acts of denunciation. One consequence is that
antiterrorism as practiced by the Bush administration now mim-
ics the very terrorism it wishes to eliminate. This all-embracing
policy of antiterrorism depoliticizes politics by always locating it
outside of the realm of power and strips community of democratic values by defining it almost exclusively through attempts
to stamp out what Michael Leeden, a former counterterror expert
in the Reagan administration, calls "corrupt habits of mind that
are still lingering around, somewhere."[15] The militarizing of community and the perpetuation of a harsh culture of fear and insecurity not only results in the narrowing of community and the
ongoing appeal to jingoistic forms of patriotism in order to divert
the public from addressing a number of pressing domestic and
foreign issues. It also results in the increasing suppression of dissent and what Anthony Lewis has rightly called the growing escalation of concentrated, unaccountable political power that threatens the very foundation of democracy in the United States.[16] Signs
of the growing forces of domestic militarization are everywhere
in the United States and can be found in the rise of the prison-
industrial complex, the passing of retrograde legislation that
targets immigrants, the undermining of civil freedoms through
antiterrorist legislation, the increasing presence of gated communities, the widespread use of racial profiling, police brutality
against people of color, and the ongoing attacks on the welfare
state. Of course, state repression is not new, but what is unique
about contemporary political culture is that the shift away from
policies favoring social welfare, protecting the environment, and
regulating corporate power is directly correlated with a growth
in prisons and other forces of domestic militarization in the United
States. As Paul Street points out, "The growth in spending on prisons is directly related to a decline in the growth of positive social
spending in such poverty- and crime-reducing areas as education, child care, and job training."[17] We live at a time when the
forces and advocates of neoliberalism are not only attempting to

undermine all efforts to revive politics as an ethical response to the demise of democratic public life but are also aggressively waging a war against the very possibility of creating forums that provide the conditions for critical education, especially those that link learning to social change, political agency to the defense of public goods, and intellectual courage to the refusal to surrender knowledge to the highest bidder.

Against an endless onslaught of images of U.S. jets bombing Afghanistan and Iraq, amply supplied by the Defense Department, the dominant media connects the war abroad with the domestic struggle at home by presenting numerous stories about the endless ways in which potential terrorists might use nuclear weapons, poison the food supply, or unleash biochemical agents on the American population. The increased fear and insecurity created by such stories simultaneously served to legitimatize a host of antidemocratic practices at home, including "the beginnings of a concerted attack on civil liberties, freedom of expression, and freedom of the press,"[18] and a growing sentiment on the part of the American public that people who suggest that terrorism is, in part, caused by American foreign policy should not be allowed "to teach in the public schools, work in the government, and even make a speech at a college."[19] Against this militarization of public discourse, Hollywood and television producers have provided both Spielberg-type patriotic spectacles, such as the made-for-television HBO dramatic series *Band of Brothers,* and Hollywood's uncritical homage to the military in films such as *Behind Enemy Lines, Black Hawk Down,* and *Spy Games.* All of these narratives, especially in the aftermath of the terroristic attacks of September 11th, offered romanticized images of military valor and a hypermasculine, if not over-the-top, patriotic portrayal of war and violence—while hoping to capitalize on the current infatuation with the military experience by raking in big box office receipts. During and following the more recent war on Iraq, almost any vestige of critical commentary on the part of the dominant media collapsed into mindless patriotic support for the war and the Bush administration's policies. In fact, as Mark Weisbrot has pointed out, "American journalists became the Bush administration's major means of promoting it, even through disinformation."[20] So unquestioning was the American media in regard to the invasion of Iraq by the United States and its Coalition of the Willing that Greg Dyke, General Director of the BBC, claimed that he was "shocked while in the United States by how unquestioning the broadcast news media was during this war."[21]

But unreflective patriotism as home-team boosterism promoted by the dominant media runs the risk of, not only bolstering the conditions for what Matthew Rothschild, the editor of *The Progressive,* calls "The New McCarthyism,"[22] but of also feeding a commercial frenzy that turns collective grief into profits and reminds us how easy the market converts noble concepts like public service and civic courage into forms of civic vacuity. Frank Rich, an op-ed writer for *The New York Times,* calls this trend "Patriotism on the Cheap" and captures its paean to commercialism following September 11th in the following commentary:

> "9/11" is now free to be a brand, ready to do its American duty and move products. Ground zero, at last an official tourist attraction with its own viewing stand, has vendors and lines to rival those at Disneyland. (When Ashleigh Banfield stops by, visitors wave and smile at the TV camera just as they do uptown at the *Today* show.) Barnes & Noble offers competing coffee-table books handsomely packaging the carnage of yesteryear. On Gary Condit's Web site, a snapshot of the congressman's own visit to ground zero sells his re-election campaign. NBC, whose Christmas gift to the nation was its unilateral lifting of a half-century taboo against hard-liquor commercials, deflects criticism by continuing to outfit its corporate peacock logo in stars and stripes.[23]

Red, white and blue flags adorn a plethora of fashion items, including hats, dresses, coats, T-shirts, robes, and scarves. Many corporations now organize their advertisements around displays of patriotism—signaling their support for the troops abroad, the victims of the brutal terrorists acts, and, of course, American resolve—each ad amply displaying its respective corporate or brand-name logo, working hard to gain some cash value by defining commercialism and consumerism as the ultimate demonstration of patriotism.[24] Other companies have seized upon the remarkable flood of giving displayed by many Americans after the tragic bombings to sell their products by suggesting they are working with charities associated with September 11th. In many cases, the connections with charities exist, but most of the profits go to the companies rather than to the victims they are supposed to benefit. For instance, Sony Music produced a disc called *God Bless America*, which displays boldly on its cover the message, "For the Benefit of the Twin Towers Fund," which refers to "a charity established by former Mayor Rudolph Giuliani for the families of uniformed rescuers killed in the World Trade Center collapse."[25] On the back of the disc in small print is the message that "a substantial portion" of profits from the disc will be donated to the fund. *The New York Times* reported that the company had no formal agreement with the fund and that no money had gone to the Twin Towers Fund, even though the disc had sold over 1.2 million copies.[26] It gets worse. Steve Madden, the shoe designer (now imprisoned on fraud charges), produced a sneaker emblazoned with an American flag of imitation gemstones that was part of the Bravest shoe line. "The sneakers were promoted across the country as a joint endeavor with a charity run by Denis Leary, star of 'The Job' on ABC, to 'raise money for New York City's fallen firefighters.'"[27] According to *The New York Times*, Madden made $515,783 in profits from the sneakers by February 2002 and at that time none of the profits had been distributed to "the families of the firefighters killed September 11." Under pressure to distribute some of the profits, Madden's company agreed to give at least 10 percent to the charity, while retaining "more than $400,000 in profits from the Bravest." When queried about the refusal of the company to hand over the profits made through an appeal to help the families of the firefighters, Jamie Karson, the Madden chief executive, responded, without irony, by arguing "The most patriotic thing we can do is make money."[28] Of course, making profits is one thing, but making excessive profits through the discourse of compassion and patriotism at the expense of the bereaved families it uses promotionally to sell its products is simply shameful and makes clear how low corporations can reach in their attempts to rake in profits. In this register, consumerism and the squelching of dissent represent mutually compatible notions of a view of patriotism in which citizenship is more about the freedom to buy than the ability of individuals to engage in "critical public dialogue and broadened civic participation leading (so it is hoped) to far-reaching change."[29]

Moral panic following the September attacks has not only re-defined public space as the "sinister abode of danger, death and infection"[30] and fueled the collective rush to "patriotism on the cheap," it also has buttressed the "fear economy" given expression through daily warnings of terrorist attacks and the call to invade Iraq in order to prevent Saddam Hussein from dropping "weapons of mass destruction" on the United States, weapons which after the war's end were never found. Defined as "the complex of military and security firms rushing to exploit the national nervous breakdown,"[31] the fear economy promises astronomical financial gains for those industries supported by the Defense Department, already asking for an additional $48 billion increase from the Bush administration for the 2003 budget, with administration estimates of more than $2 trillion being spent on the military over the next five years and annual budgets rising to $451 billion by 2007.[32] In addition to bloated defense budgets, the fear economy also spells big profits for the antiterrorists—security sectors which are primed to terror-proof everything from trash cans and water systems to shopping malls and public restrooms. But patriotism is more than a consumer good, and the politics of anti-terrorism demands more than a military response.

The greatest struggle Americans face is not terrorism but a struggle on behalf of justice, freedom, and democracy for all of the citizens of the globe. Defended as a war against terrorism, the invasion and occupation of Iraq by the United States has not only squandered resources that could be used to fight al-Qaeda but has energized radical terrorists all over the world while alienating most of the nation's foreign allies and most of the Arabic world. Bush may believe that he is fighting for democracy, a mission sanctioned allegedly by the divine, but democracy cannot be won abroad with bombs or through a high-intensity guerilla war. Nor can it be won at home by shutting down democracy, eliminating its most cherished rights and freedoms, deriding communities of dissent, and reinvigorating the crude logic of American imperialism. On the contrary, the struggle for democracy has to be understood through politics, not moralism, and if politics is to be reclaimed as the center of individual and social agency, it will have be motivated, not by the culture of fear, but by a passion for civic engagement, ethical responsibility, and the promise of a realizable democracy.

The campaign against terrorism signals not only a war being waged against terrorists abroad or against dissent at home, but also a war that feeds off the general decay of democratic politics and reinforces what neoliberals cheerfully call the death of the social. This war is made visible in two quotes. The first quote comes from Debbie Riddle, a current Texas state representative. The second quote comes from Grover Norquist, the president of Americans for Tax Reform and arguably Washington's leading right-wing strategist.

> Where did this idea come from that everybody deserves free education? Free medical care? Free whatever? It comes from Moscow. From Russia. It comes straight out of the pit of hell.[33]

> My goal is to cut government in half in twenty-five years, to get it down to the size where we can drown it in the bathtub.[34]

War, fear, and a particularly virulent contempt for social needs, as these quotes suggest, have now become the dominant motifs shaping the domestic and foreign policies of the United States. This is evident, not only in the all-embracing militarization of public life that is emerging under the combined power and control of neoliberal zealots, religious fanatics, and far right-wing conservatives, but also in the destruction of a liberal democratic political order and a growing culture of surveillance, inequality, and cynicism.[35] As I suggested in the beginning of this essay, these are dangerous times in which a new type of society is emerging in the United States unlike anything we have seen in the past—a society in which symbolic capital and political power reinforce each other through a public pedagogy produced by a concentrated media, which has become a cheerleading section for dominant elites and corporate ruling interests. As the global media becomes even more concentrated, democracy and civic life are undermined through the relentless predominance of a culture of commercialism, advertising, and commodification. Hypercommercialism and privatization expand the power of neoliberalism while simultaneously gutting the welfare state and bankrupting public services, including education and health care. As the dominant media advance the interests of corporate power over democratic considerations and values, public space is replaced by commercial space, and those institutions capable of engaged critiques of institutional power give way to celebrity culture and overtly propagandistic journalism.[36] The United States is a society increasingly marked by a poverty of critical public discourse, thus making it more difficult for young people and adults to appropriate a critical language outside of the market that would allow them to translate private problems into public concerns, or to relate public issues to private considerations. This is also a social order that seems incapable of questioning itself, just as it wages war through its retrograde social policies against the poor, youth, women, people of color, and the elderly.

The war with Iraq has changed the way the United States relates to the rest of the world, as well as how it addresses the most pressing problems Americans face in their everyday lives. But the danger we face as a nation is not only related to the war in Iraq, it is also related to the silent war at home, especially since the Iraqi war and the war against terrorism are being financed from cuts in domestic funding on health care, children's education, and other public services. It would be a tragic mistake for those of us on the left either to separate the war in Iraq from the many problems Americans face at home or fail to recognize how war is being waged by this government on multiple fronts. The war against terrorism is part and parcel of the war against democracy at home.

Slavoj Zizek claims that the "true target of the 'war on terror' is American society itself—the disciplining of its emancipatory excesses."[37] George Steinmetz argues that the current state of emergency represents a new shift in the mode of political power and regulation. He claims that:

> The refocusing of political power on the level of the American national state has been most evident in the area of U. S. Geopolitical strategy (unilateralism and pre-emptive military strikes), but much of the new regulatory activity has focused on the state apparatus itself and the "domestic" level of politics, with the creation of a huge new government agency (the department of Homeland Security), transformations of the legal system (e.g., secret trials and arrests, indefinite detentions), and intensified domestic surveillance: first with the 2001 USA Patriot Act, which dramatically relaxed restrictions on search and seizure; then with the Total Information

Awareness program, which collects and analyzes vast amounts of data on private communications and commercial transactions; and most recently with the proposed domestic Security Enhancement Act of 2003.[38]

Both are partly right. The Bush "permanent war doctrine" is not just aimed at alleged terrorists or the excesses of democracy, but also against disposable populations in the homeland, whether they be young black men who inhabit our nation's jails or those unemployed workers who have been abandoned by the flight of capital as well as all levels of government. The financing of the war in Iraq is buttressed by what Vice President Dick Cheney calls the concept of "never-ending war." This is a concept that declares permanent war as a continuous state of emergency and brings into play a fundamentally new mode of politics. In a commencement speech given in 2003 at the United States Military Academy, Cheney provided a succinct outline of the permanent war concept:

> The battle of Iraq was a major victory in the war on terror, but the war itself is far from over. We cannot allow ourselves to grow complacent. We cannot forget that the terrorists remain determined to kill as many Americans as possible, both abroad and here at home, and they are still seeking weapons of mass destruction to use against us. With such an enemy, no peace treaty is possible; no policy of containment or deterrence will prove effective. The only way to deal with this threat is to destroy it, completely and utterly.[39]

The apocalyptic tone of his comments does more than cover up the fictive relationship between Iraq and 9/11, it also serves to legitimate a bloated and obscene military budget, as well as economic and tax policies that are financially bankrupting the states, destroying public education, and plundering public services. The U. S. Government plans to spend up to $400 billion to finance the Iraqi war and the ongoing occupation, while it allocates only $16 billion to welfare programs that cannot possibly address the needs of the over 33 million people who live below the poverty line, many of them children, or the 75 million without health insurance, or the millions now unemployed because of diminished public services and state resources. While $350 billion are allocated for tax cuts for the rich, state governments are cutting a total of $75 billion in health care, welfare benefits, and education. The sheer inhumanity this government displays toward the working poor and children living below and slightly above poverty level can be seen in the decision by Republicans in Congress to eliminate from the recent tax bill the $400 child credit for families with incomes between $10,000 and $26,000. The money saved by this cut will be used to pay for the cut on dividend taxes. As a result, as Bill Moyers observes, "Eleven million children [are] punished for being poor, even as the rich are rewarded for being rich."[40] These multiple attacks on the poor and on much-needed public services need to be connected to an expanded political and social vision that refuses the cynicism and sense of powerlessness that accompanies the destruction of social goods, the corporatization of the media, the dismantling of workers' rights, and the incorporation of intellectuals. Against this totalitarian onslaught, progressives need a language of critique and possibility, one that connects diverse struggles, uses theory as a resource, and defines politics as not merely critical but also as an intervention into public life. We need a language that relates the discourse of war to an attack on democracy at home *and* abroad, and we need to use that language in a way that captures the needs, desires, histories, and experiences that shape people's daily lives. Similarly, as democratic institutions are downsized and public goods are offered up for corporate plunder, those of us who take seriously the related issues of equality, human rights, justice, and freedom face the crucial challenge of formulating a notion of the political suitable for addressing the urgent problems now facing the twenty-first century—a politics that, as Zygmunt Bauman argues, "never stops criticizing the level of justice already achieved and seeking more justice and better justice."[41]

As Ulrich Beck has argued, the language of war has taken a distinctly different turn in the new millennium.[42] War no longer needs to be ratified by Congress, since it is now waged by various government agencies that escape the need for official approval. War has become a permanent condition adopted by a nation-state that is largely defined by its repressive functions in response to its powerlessness to regulate corporate power, provide social investments for the populace, and guarantee a measure of social freedom. The concept of war occupies a strange place in the current lexicon of foreign and domestic policy. It no longer simply refers to a war waged against a sovereign state such as Iraq, nor is it merely a moral referent for engaging in acts of national self-defense. The concept of war has been both expanded and inverted. It has been expanded in that it has become one of the most powerful concepts for understanding and structuring political culture, public space, and everyday life. Wars are now waged against crime, labor unions, drugs, terrorism, and a host of alleged public disorders. Wars are not declared against foreign enemies but against alleged domestic threats. The concept of war has also been inverted in that is has been removed from any concept of social justice—a relationship that emerged under President Lyndon Johnson and was exemplified in the war on poverty. War is now defined almost exclusively as a punitive and militaristic process. This can be seen in the ways in which social policies are now criminalized so that the war on poverty is now a war against the poor; the war on drugs is now a war waged largely against youth of color; and the war against terrorism is now largely a war against immigrants, domestic freedoms, and dissent itself. In the Bush, Perle, Rumsfeld, and Ashcroft view of terrorism, war is individualized as every citizen becomes a potential terrorist who has to prove that he or she is not dangerous. Under the rubric of emergency time, which feeds off government-induced media panics, war provides the moral imperative to collapse the "boundaries between innocent and guilty, between suspects and nonsuspects." [43] War provides the primary rhetorical tool for articulating a notion of the social as a community organized around shared fears rather than shared responsibilities and civic courage. War is now transformed into a slick Hollywood spectacle designed to both glamorize a notion of hypermasculinity fashioned in the conservative oil fields of Texas and fill public space with celebrations of ritualized militaristic posturing touting the virtues of either becoming part of "an Army of one" or indulging in commodified patriotism by purchasing a new Hummer. War-as-spectacle easily combines with the culture of fear to divert public attention away from domestic problems, define patriotism as consensus, and further the growth of a police state. The latter takes on dangerous overtones, not only with the passage of the Patriot Act and the suspension of civil liberties, but is also evident in the elimination of those laws that traditionally separated the military from domestic law enforcement and offered individuals a vestige of civil liberties and freedoms. The political implications of the expanded and inverted use of war as a metaphor can also be seen in the war against "big government," which is really a war against the welfare state and the social contract itself—this is a war against the notion that everyone should have access to decent education, health care, employment, and other public services. One of the most serious issues to be addressed in the debate about Bush's concept of permanent war is the effect it is having on one of our most vulnerable populations, children, and the political opportunity this issue holds for articulating a language of both opposition and possibility.

Wars are almost always legitimated in order to make the world safe for "our children's future," but the rhetoric belies how their future is often denied by the acts of aggression put into place by a range of ideological state apparatuses that operate on a war footing. This would include the horrible effects of the militarization of schools, the use of the criminal justice system to redefine social issues such as poverty and homelessness as violations of the social order, and the subsequent rise of a prison-industrial complex as a way to contain disposable populations, such as youth of color, who are poor and marginalized. Under the rubric of war, security, and antiterrorism, children are "disappeared" from the most basic social spheres that provide the conditions for a sense of agency and possibility, as they are rhetorically excised from any discourse about the future. The "disappearing" of children is made more concrete and reprehensible with the revelation that three children between the ages of 13 and 15 were held without legal representation as enemy combatants in possibly inhumane conditions at the military's infamous Camp Delta at Guantanamo Bay, Cuba. One wonders how the Bush administration reconciles its construction of a U.S. Gulag for children with their fervent support of family values and the ideology of compassionate conservativism.

The Bush administration's aggressive attempts to reduce the essence of democracy to profit-making, shred the social contract, elevate property rights over human rights, make public schools dysfunctional, and promote tax cuts that will limit the growth of social programs and public investments fail completely when applied to the vast majority of citizens, but especially fail when applied to children. And yet, children provide one of the most important referents for exposing and combating such policies. Making visible the suffering and oppression of children cannot help but challenge the key assumptions of "permanent war" and antiterrorist policies designed to destroy public institutions and prevent the government from providing important services that ameliorate ignorance, poverty, racism, inequality, and disease. Children offer a crucial rationale for engaging in a critical discussion about the long-term consequences of current policies. Any debate about war, regime change, antiterrorism, and military intervention is both unethical and politically irresponsible if it doesn't recognize how such policies affect children. The focus on children may be one place to begin to develop a unifying rallying point of struggle and resistance in order to make clear to a broader public that Bush's permanent-war strategy, discourse of antiterrorism, and rhetoric of moral absolutes promote democracy neither abroad nor at home, and their alleged value can best be understood in the hard currency of human suffering that children all over the globe are increasingly forced to pay.

Fear and repression reproduce rather than address the most fundamental antidemocratic elements of terrorism. Engaging terrorism demands more than rage and anger, revenge and retaliation. If the United States and the international community are to adequately address the politics of terrorism, it has to be confronted as a political act and a crime against humanity. Of course, this would mean that the United States would have to confront its own sordid participation in acts of state terrorism. Instead of succumbing to media-induced moral panics and government-inspired jingoism, people need to recognize that the threat of terrorism cannot be understood apart from the crisis of democracy itself. This suggests that any discourse on terrorism must be accompanied by questions about the shared obligations of human rights, social justice, and a meaningful sense of global democracy.

But there is more at work here than simply recognizing that the rhetoric of war has now become a standard excuse for punishing children, invoking a jingoistic notion of patriotism to silence dissent and gut the welfare state; there is also the use of the politics of fear on the part of the Bush administration both to create one of the most extensive national security states in history and to deracinate the very foundations of a substantive democracy. The most important question that has to be faced is how do progressives theorize a war that is being waged on multiple fronts, how do we theorize a notion of the political for the twenty-first century? The greatest struggle Americans face is not terrorism, but a struggle on behalf of justice, freedom, and democracy for all of the citizens of the globe. This is not going to take place, as President Bush's policies will tragically affirm, by shutting down democracy, eliminating its most cherished rights and freedoms, and deriding communities of dissent. On the contrary, the struggle for democracy has to be understood through politics, not moralism, and if politics is to be reclaimed as the center of individual and social agency, it will have be motivated not by the culture of fear but by a passion for civic engagement, ethical responsibility, collective struggles, and the promise of a realizable democracy.

Notes

1. Arundhati Roy, *War Talk* (Boston: South End Press, 2003), p. 34.
2. President George W. Bush, Address to Joint Session of Congress, "September 11, 2001, Terrorist Attacks on the United States."
3. Within such a set of circumstances, the criminal justice system now serves as one of the primary models for how to manage and contain populations within a wide range of public spheres. In this context, the prison-industrial complex can best be understood as a model for enforcing the criminalization of social problems, policing communities, suppressing dissent, punishing and containing students of color, and reconstructing the state as a force for domestic militarization. The importance of the prison-industrial complex can be seen in the fact that the United States imprisons more people than any other country in the world—more than 2 million, and though it comprises only 5 percent of the world's population it houses more than 25 percent of the world's prisoners.
4. Barnor Hesse and S. Sayyid, "A War Against Politics," *Open Democracy*, (November 28, 2001), p. 3, available at openDemocracy@open democracy.net
5. Jeff Madrick, "The Iraqi Time Bomb," *The New York Times Magazine* (April 6, 2003), p. 50.

6. Anatole Anton, "Public Goods as Commonstock: Notes on the Receding Commons," In Anatole Anton, Milton Fisk, and Nancy Holmstrom (eds.), *Not for Sale: In Defense of Public Goods* (Boulder: Westview Press, 2000), p. 29.

7. Edward Said, "Thoughts About America," *Counterpunch,* March 5, 2002, p. 5, available at www.counterpunch.org/saidamerica.html

8. There is a long tradition of American radicalism which takes up this position. See, for example, Michael Kazin, "A Defense of Patriotism," *Dissent* (Fall 2002), pp. 41–44; Peter Dreier and Dick Flacks, "Patriotism's Secret History," *The Nation* (June 3, 2002), pp. 39–42. For a spirited engagement over the relevance of patriotism as a radical discourse, see Joshua Cohen (ed.), *For the Love of Country: Debating the Limits of Patriotism* (Boston: Beacon Press, 1996).

9. Zygmunt Bauman, *Community: Seeking Safety in an Insecure World* (Cambridge, UK: Polity, 2001), p. 4.

10. Eric Hobsbawm, *The Age of Extremes* (London: Michael Joseph, 1994), p. 428.

11. Lewis H. Lapham, "American Jihad," *Harper's Magazine* (January 2002), p. 8.

12. Susan George, "Another World is Possible," *The Nation* (February 18, 2002), p. 12.

13. Judith Butler, "Explanation and Exoneration, or What We Can Hear," *Theory & Event* 5:4 (2002), pp. 8, 16.

14. Jerome Binde, "Toward an Ethic of the Future," *Public Culture* 12:1 (200), p. 57.

15. Cited in Douglas Valentine, "Homeland Insecurity," *Counterpunch* (November 8, 2001); available online at www.counter punch.org/homeland1.html.

16. Anthony Lewis, *The New York Times* (August 9, 2002), p. A27.

17. Paul Street, "Race, Prison, and Poverty: The Race to Incarcerate in the Age of Correctional Keynesianism," *Z Magazine* (May 2001), p. 27.

18. Eric Alterman, "Patriot Games," *The Nation* (October 29, 2001), p. 10.

19. Cited in the National Public Radio/Kaiser Family Foundation/Kennedy School of Government Civil Liberties Poll. Available online at wsiwyg:5http://www.npr.org/news ... civillibertiespll/011130.poll.html (November 30, 2001), p. 3.

20. Mark Weisbrot, "When the Media Fails," *CommonDreams* (May 17, 2003). Available online at: www.commondreams.org/views03/0507–08

21. Cited in ibid.

22. Matthew Rothschild, "The New McCarthyism," *The Progressive* (January 2002), pp. 18–23.

23. Frank Rich, "Patriotism on the Cheap," *The New York Times* (January 5, 2002), p. A31.

24. This issue was also explored brilliantly by Doug Kellner with respect to the war against Iraq under the senior Bush presidency. See Douglas Kellner, *Media Culture: Cultural Studies, Identity, and Politics Between the Modern and the Postmodern* (New York: Routledge, 1995), especially pp. 213–214.

25. David Barstow and Diana B. Henriques, "Lines of Profit and Charity Blur for Companies with 9/11 Tie-Ins," *The New York Times* (Saturday, February 2, 2002), p. A15

26. Ibid., p. A15.

27. Ibid., p. A15.

28. Ibid., p. A15.

29. Carl Boggs, *The End of Politics* (New York: Guilford Press, 2000), p. vii.

30. Mike Davis, "The Flames of New York," *New Left Review* 12 (November/December 2001), p. 44

31. Ibid., p. 45.

32. Figures cited in "The Pentagon Spending Spree," *The New York Times* (Wednesday, February 6, 2002), p. A26.

33. Cited by Bill Moyers on *NOW*, aired in May 2003.

34. Cited in Robert Dreyfuss, "Grover Norquist: 'Field Marshal' of the Bush Plan," The Nation (May 14, 2001). Available online: http://www.thenation.com/doc.mhtml?i=20010514&s=dreyfuss p. 1

35. Arianna Huffington recently argued that we are being governed by "a gang of out and out fanatics." See Arianna Huffington, "A White House Fluent in Language of Fanatics," CommonDreams News Center (May 21, 2003). Available online at www.commondreams.org/views03/0521-on.htm

36. See Robert W. McChesney and John Nichols, *Our Media Not Theirs* (New York: Seven Stories Press, 2002).

37. Slavoj Zizek, "Today Iraq. Tomorrow. . . Democracy?" *In These Times* (May 5, 2003), p. 28.

38. George Steinmetz, "The State of Emergency and the Revival of American Imperialism; Toward an Authoritarian Post-Fordism," *Public Culture* 13:2 (Spring 2003), p. 329.

39. Dick Cheney cited in Sam Dillon, "Re-elections on War, Peace, and How to Live Vitally and Act Globally," *The New York Times* (June 1, 2003), p. 28.

40. Bill Moyers, "Deep in a Black Hole of Red Ink," CommonDreams News Center. (May 30, 2003). Available online at: www.commondreams.org/views03/0530-11.htm

41. Zygmunt Bauman, *Society Under Siege* (Malden, MA: Blackwell, 2002), p. 54.

42. Ulrich Beck, "The Silence of Words and Political Dynamics in the World Risk Society," *Logos* 1:4 (Fall 2002), p. 1.

43. Ulrich Beck, Ibid. "The Silence of Words and Political Dynamics in the World Risk Society," p. 3.

Chapter Seven

Education and War

Primary Constituents of the Contemporary World-System

Cliff Falk

Education: De- and Re-Territorialization

Education often is conceptualized as a state of being (educated) and as a social practice or process related to material conditions or subjective formation only indirectly.[1] Education, in standard liberal accounts, is viewed as a progressive practice that has a built-in tendency to work toward limiting and controlling socially organized violence and discord.

Most accounts assume the values education carries with it are positive, that the practice of education cannot but be a force for human betterment. Education often is perceived as indiscriminately beneficial, as a good in its own right. It is seen as a *mission civilisatrice*, a means of mitigating or removing the Hobbesian condition of "war of everyman against everyman" and of "natural" life as necessarily fraught with "continual fear, and danger of violent death."

In the Anglophone academy, this force for unilateral good usually is conceptualized as a field of study rather than a discipline. This field in turn is comprised of two elements, knowledge dissemination (e.g., teaching) and the production of knowledge devoted to it (e.g., pedagogy), knowledge defined as information combined with judgment. However, it is important to distinguish between education as a subjectivity-producing process (e.g., teaching) and subjectivity, the product of the process (human attributes, knowledge, dispositions, skills, etc.). It is the educational product (abstracted as academic labor in this instance) that is the source of knowledge production—for example, an academic researcher whose job it is to produce novel knowledge based in new or reconfigured data, information, or already existing knowledge.

Viewed this way, knowledge production is dependent upon subjectivity, which in turn is dependent upon the social practice called education. If persons are not taught (do not learn) that which a society considers "knowledge," they will be incapable of producing more of it. This is no doubt commonplace and obvious, but it is important to recognize that mathematicians for example must be educated in mathematics to produce more mathematics. At the same time it is important to recognize that there is a recursive, mutually reinforcing, mutually constitutive, and mutually determinative (overdetermined) relationship between education, knowledge, subjectivity, and social conditions.[2]

This holds for theoretical and applied fields, for the hard sciences and mathematics, and for "applied" fields like education, law, and medicine. All knowledges stand with feet in two camps: the material economy of quotidian practice—of "know how & who"—and the less-obviously material economy of academic "know what & why," the theoretical economy of "invisible materiality." Of these knowledges, education however merits special attention. Ruth Jonathan (1997, 4) says: "Education is the one social practice that both reflects and produces social circumstances and values." While that comment may not do justice to the profundity of the operation, it points in the right direction.

Education no doubt significantly contributes to the production of social circumstance (reality), but it reflects and produces much more than "values"; like religion or material conditions, the social practice of education produces human subjectivity. In turn, particular forms of subjectivity lend themselves to the production of particular material conditions—ways of being—and particular knowledges (education as reproduction seems too limited a concept to capture the overdetermined nature of this social practice). That is why education is so important.

Sloterdijk (1987, 72) opines in his influential *Critique of Cynical Reason*:

> From the first look we take at our experiences we believe we can say who we are. The second look will make it clear that education is behind every particular way of being. What seemed to be nature, on closer observation reveals itself as code.

This way of perceiving the educative process allows education to be conceptualized as a "cultural material" system for subjective production. Accordingly, education is the production, representation, regulation, and distribution of *codified* (explicit, formal) knowledge and the social practice based in that codified knowledge, directed toward the production of ideal types of subjectivity—the human "subject" that is itself a contingent and performative site (sight) that cannot but physically, affectively, intellectually, and cognitively embody what it has learned.[3]

The teachings of Deleuze and Guatarri and Foucault inform this definition, as does Gur-Ze'ev's (1998, n.p.) concept of "normalizing education":[4]

> Control of the legitimization, production, representation and distribution of knowledge enables the reduction of the human subject into a "subject" who will function as an object or an agent of "her" system. In this sense the control of knowledge enables much more than the possibilities of policing social behavior: it provides the means for establishing an unchallenged legitimization for a certain hegemonic version of the production of the "subject," the normalized subject, her possibilities and limitations. Such a control is usually called "education."

As well as leaving out the ancient division between manual and mental, this cultural materialist definition does not distinguish between forms of education on the basis of delivery either. For example, between formal, informal, and nonformal education is not elicited because each has become a *codified technology* for subjective development in its own right (e.g., advertising, *eLearning*). As well, differentiations such as these make less sense in the contemporary electronically induced multimodal (blended) communications environment than they did when extrapersonal social mediation (and education) was bimodal (face-to-face or bookish). Nor does this definition hold to conventional demarcations between adult and childhood education in that both are codified practices for subjective delimitation.

Conventional demarcations between education, training, religion, and propaganda (the spreading of ideas, information, or rumor for the purpose of helping or injuring an institution, a cause, or a person) are not elicited either. Indeed, hiving off one of the codified means for subjective constitution and naming it education, while other codified means are construed as propaganda or "the media" and set in binary opposition to education, perpetuates an "immaculate conception" of education (Spanos 1993). In turn, this "immaculate conception," this name—Education—remains magical and rhetorical, allowing Education to perform ideologically to maintain and at the same time hide the specific material and cultural investments that are embedded in any and all forms of education, historically and at present.

Education however has no ontological status independent of agentic factors (human beings, machines that carry systemic logic, etc.). Education is not the institutions that comprise it except in as much as they are expressive of the social relations and practices that humans create and institutionalize (e.g., schools as carriers of interested knowledge formative and expressive of class, gender, etc.). Education is not a "thing" or an ideal state, but a social process with no existence independent of its manifestation in quotidian practice. Importantly, moving beyond the material/ideal divide to a cultural materialist definition allows the historicization of education as a discourse and social practice, a common enough exercise, but as importantly for this work, this definition allows for the historicization of the educational product—subjectivity.[5]

This is not to suggest that forms of education are morally, technically, or ethically equal, that critical pedagogy for example is equivalent to warfare training, though it may be in that critical pedagogy, like soldierly pedagogy, is directed toward the production of a preferred "ideal type" of human. At the minimum, the soldier, like a student enlightened by exposure to critical pedagogy, is "empowered" in as much as each learns a *code* encapsulated by unequivocal acceptance of the rules of a language, of a symbolic universe. The student and soldier are similarly empowered in that each has been provided with specific conceptual technologies, affect, skills, and rules for access to "reality," even if the one pedagogy is based in reflectivity while the other isn't.

Education is "always already" political—who will choose what is taught, what is learned, and to what ends? Who will choose the "ideal type" that is to form the model to which the educative exercise will be directed, who will say if it is to be directed toward the production of a "consumer" or "producer" for example? At a global level, the current educative process is geared more and more to consumptive rather than productive labor, whereby subjectivization is as dependent upon learning to consume as it is on learning to produce, this accounting for the rise of advertising, public relations, and marketing as major forms of contemporary education. Education viewed this way is a zero sum game. If the educative process is directed to the formation of a certain (ideal) type of subjectivity, it cannot at the same time be directed to the formation of another type of subjectivity premised in different parameters, different language games if you will, though such could be the unintended result of this always imperfect process.

Deleuze (1995) and Deleuze and Guatarri (1983, 1987) have provided generative schematics for this *production of subjectivity model* of education. Following their work, if somewhat loosely, contemporary education is a process directed toward the installation of *codes* in order to control the *flow* of subjectivity based in the *desire* to expend energy maximally, to the point that this expenditure becomes entropic or antisystemic (Deleuze and Guatarri call this antiproduction).[6] According to Deleuze and Guatarri, capitalism is the most advanced system to create and control (regulate) the flow of desire yet developed. Education is a primary means of "flow control," of ensuring that subjectivity is formed within certain parameters that are currently determined by the capitalist system.

Capitalism is unique in that it released subjective formation from the determinate conditions of societies of sovereignty because of a formative "de-" and "re-" territorialization of the human grounded in the detachment of labor from the land. This detachment rendered the grounded servitude of the peasant archaic, replacing it with liberal freedom based in abstracted labor power, best expressed by the move from the land and its nonmonetary entitlements (the commons, etc.) to waged work in the mills, the cloth factories that signaled the arrival of industrialism. This move from the reliance on ground rent to capture surplus, often paid in kind by the peasant, to labor detached from land, abstracted as labor power, naturally enough was accompanied by the liquefying of assets (the move to money). Marx called this primitive accumulation. This fundamental systemic difference rendered subjectivity in different terms, providing both the means and ends for the reconfiguration of the human and education.

After that initial wrenching from the land, subjects in the industrializing and capitalizing European states embarked on constant de-territorialization and re-territorialization, manufacturing their own subjectivity (autopoiesis) under the auspices of this specifically capitalist process. The unconscious in this Deleuzian model is fused with the *socius* and operates to produce desire, the dissipation of energy, albeit a dissipation that occurs within the specific parameters of capitalist production that has led to spiraling cycles of de- and re-territorialization. Currently called consumerism, these tightening vectors produce shorter shelf lives for particular sets of human skills and attributes, the more rapid rendering of certain forms of subjectivity redundant.

This is why Deleuze and Guatarri call the system schizophrenic. Capitalism must continually subvert or sublate existential conditions (*ergo* Schumpeter's naming of capitalism as creative destruction). Thus the constant change to which the world has been subject since the development of capitalism in North West Europe, the "system of five hundred years" as Braudel called it. This model whereby de- and re-territorializing is ongoing is open to a range of possibility within the parameters provided by the logic of the system. The English Enclosure movement (circa 1400–1800) demonstrates how this peculiarly capitalist logic was initially imposed upon land and peoples. Deleuze and Guatarri (1987, 456) describe the process as it developed throughout Western Europe:

> The natal or the land, as we have seen elsewhere, implies a certain deterritorialization of the territories (community land, imperial provinces, seigneurial domains, etc.), and the people, a *decoding of the population*. The nation is constituted on the basis of these flows and is inseparable from the modern state that gives consistency to the corresponding land and people. It is the flow of naked [waged] labour that makes the people, just as it is the flow of capital that makes the land and its industrial base. In short, the nation is the very operation of a collective subjectivation, to which the modern State corresponds as a process of subjection.

By this account, "feudal" lands and peoples were reconstituted in terms of "property" (capitalism) and "nation," this work accomplished in the symbolic sphere by the philosophers of the Enlightenment (the making of the individual). This preindustrial capitalist reconstruction of the structure and indeed function of social and economic relations was accompanied by a corresponding reconstruction of subjectivity, the structure and function of the human, the rendering of the human in a liquid form that corresponded to the rise of money, the abstraction of wealth previously realized through land, gold, jewels, and so on.

This originary abstraction of labor and the endemic de- and reterritorialization process it inaugurated was accounted for ideologically by the originary production of the fictive liberal subject or "individual" (e.g., Luther, Locke).[7] Negri (2000, 74), speaking about the beginnings of modernity, puts it this way: "Bodies and brains were fundamentally transformed. This historical process of subjectivization was revolutionary in the sense that it determined a paradigmatic and irreversible change in the mode of life of the multitude."

This paradigmatic reconstruction was based in a new set of operating parameters whereby representation (Weber's enchanted world) was decoded altogether (Weber located the disenchantment of existence in the statist imposition of a supra-rational rationalization process; Nietzsche used the death of God to describe it). According to Deleuze and Guatarri, while all power societies deterritorialize of necessity, in despotic societies the local state is overcoded by symbolically relegating the local to "savagery" while despotism becomes the beneficiary of the overcoding (e.g., barbarous peasants as compared to loyal subjects).

Capitalism differs from despotism in that it proceeds by decoding representation altogether. This is one of capitalism's most "fundamental rhythms," as Jameson (2002, 194) puts it, "its reduction of all phenomena to the present." This reduction is currently exemplified in the decoding of education and knowledge altogether, in their reduction to commodities dependent upon the vagaries of "Market."

In this regard, capitalism is inherently unmeaningful; it can only inscribe meaning temporarily based upon the contingent and specific manifestation of the logic of the system (the system is schizophrenic; to resort to stable meaning that resides outside the system is a paranoia). Capitalism destroys the Transcendental Signified wherever it finds it, replacing the stable signification of despotic society with the irresolute signifying system demanded by the logic of the capitalist system. Under capitalism, the focus of desire moves from the *regus* (monarch) or *deus* (God)—as was the case in precapitalist societies—to abstracted wealth (money).

Deleuze and Guatarri say that instead of overcoding, as when Christianity used the celebration known as Easter to code-over (overwrite) pagan celebrations of the vernal equinox, capitalism *axiomatizes*. Eugene Holland (1991, 58), one of the major interpreters of Deleuze and Guatarri in the U.S., explains it this way:

> Capitalism differs from despotic power society in that it is an economic power society: it deterritorializes not by over-coding via representation, but by de-coding representation altogether: by substituting a calculus of abstract quantities for the codes and over-codes that defined concrete qualities under savagery and despotism. Instead of over-coding, capitalism axiomatizes: it conjoins first of all the deterritorialized and de-coded flow of pure liquid wealth henceforth invested as capital in means of production with another deterritorialized and de-coded flow: pure labor-power henceforth disciplined or "skilled" to match its pre-given object of investment on the assembly-line or some other manufacturing process. The tendency of the rate of profit to fall will then force the addition of additional axioms: production processes are continually transformed by the input of technical information flowing from the hard sciences. . . .

This systemic logic is evidenced currently in the reformation of the subjective economy in any jurisdiction where electronic information technologies are integral to production. The initial axiom stays in play, though it is appended (supplemented) by the addition of further axioms. Not surprisingly, the additional axioms are grounded in the most recent (triumphalist) realization of capitalism, the military/political/economic/cultural system termed *globalization,* which is itself grounded in the technological extension of human possibility—the "information age" or "knowledge economy"—the third great wave of capitalist technological development (Arrighi and Silver 1999; Jameson 1991, 1998; Mandel 1978; Wallerstein 1974, 1995). Modeled this way, capitalism, and what Deleuze and Guatarri (1997, 454) call its "models of realization" have passed through three stages, the preindustrial, industrial, and postindustrial, which encompass distinct forms of subjectivity as well as of the state, war, education, and technology.

In this limited sense, the technological moment, just as the educational moment, is historically determinative. For humans make their tools, including their systems of education, just as surely as those tools make them. The tools themselves, the technologies and the particular forms of subjectivity developed through them, express a systemic logic that usually remains hidden. Contemporary tools and technologies, the Internet for example, are usually *impersonal;* therefore it is difficult to determine the logic of their development and the specific interests this logic promotes and protects. Deleuze and Guatarri have provided a conceptual cornucopia to make these various "models of realization" transparent. These models of realization are evident in any area of human endeavor, in war as well as in the economy and education.

Education, war, and subjectivity conceptualized as models of realization arrived at through mutual determination allow interrelationships to be educed that usually remain foreclosed by conventional academic discourses. An overview of the connections between education, war, the economy, and knowledge production can bring to light a counternarrative wherein education is no longer granted autonomy or routine beneficence, but rather is viewed as an interested technology of subjective formation, as the primary means to realize the de- and re-territorialization process.

Education: The Primary (Post)Military/Industrial Constituent

When he was leaving office in 1961, U.S. President Eisenhower identified a "military-industrial complex" whose "total influence—economic, political, and even spiritual is felt everywhere, in every city, in every statehouse, and every office of the federal government."[8] This "military-industrial complex" was extended to the university in 1962 in the *Port Huron Statement of the Students for a Democratic Society*, a founding document of a global revolt against the military-industrial system. For a time, the "military/industrial/university complex" provided a focus for protest in every industrialized capitalist country.

However, in spite of this globalized resistance, the role of the university in maintaining and enhancing the "complex" continued to grow, even as protests against it increased exponentially. Interestingly, the military-funded university research that provided a focal point for resistance, like previous academic military research carried out by any industrial nation, proved to be of as much use to the "civil" sector as to the military sector. In this regard and others, Eisenhower's "complex," extended to the university, did not represent a break in practice, but rather a huge increase in scale and intensity.

The Cold War (1947–1990) justified this funding. That war (23–30 million died as a result of it) was fought on many fronts simultaneously, not the least of which was through knowledge production, to the point where *the research university itself proved to be the greatest war weapon ever invented.* Take the development of the hydrogen bomb and rocketry. U.S. rocketry was built on German academic knowledge expropriated when German propulsion scientists, Wernher von Braun most notably (Ph.D., University of Berlin), were shipped to the United States after World War II and interned initially. The hydrogen bomb was developed first in the United States by a group of researchers led by Edward Teller (Ph.D., University of Leipzig). While these developments did not necessarily occur on university campuses strictly speaking, they nonetheless represented the further extension of academic knowledge production (the academy) into the most lethal of war-making technologies.

The U.S. bomb was tested in 1952. Other countries soon followed: the Soviet Union in 1953, the United Kingdom in 1957,

China in 1967 and France in 1968. This exponential growth of the destructive power of war weapons (hydrogen bombs were more powerful than atom bombs by orders of magnitude) coincided with the exponential growth of codified knowledge and the unprecedented growth of every type of educational and research institution. However, most analyses of the military/industrial/university complex do not go beyond an examination of knowledge production, for example the generative knowledge, knowledge producers, and knowledge production facilities. Analysis is usually limited to the influence of military spending on material technologies, like bombs or high-stress metals, but rarely to technologies of "invisible materiality," like propaganda, political and economic theory, and educational psychology.

This applies most especially to education, that social practice/process most often conceived of as a means of countering rather than producing war, brutality, and suffering. Yet, education—the production, representation, regulation, and distribution of *codified* knowledge, and the social practice based in that codified knowledge intended to produce specific forms of subjectivity—grounded the social, scientific, and technological developments that made the Cold War possible. It is the educational product (abstracted as academic labor) that is the source of knowledge production, for example, an academic researcher whose job it is to produce novel knowledge based in new or reconfigured data, information, or knowledge, in this instance the knowledge that grounds contemporary weapons of mass destruction (WMD).

Rapid academic knowledge production has been most evident during periods of warfare, and this most definitely was the case during the Cold War period. Hacker and Hacker (1987, 744–745) identified this trend that dates to the Industrial Revolution:

> Military institutions have strongly and persistently affected other social and economic institutions, a larger reality often ignored by modern scholars of whatever political persuasion. The problem begins with an inability—or unwillingness—to understand military institutions on their own terms. Conservative and Marxist theorists alike, for example, can offer no theory to explain either the cause or effects of innovation in military technology. . . . That war often promotes technological change has become something of a truism since the Industrial Revolution allowed ideas to become

weapons swiftly enough to reshape the war in progress—when, of
course, money flows most freely.

The manifestations of Cold War military spending included the
expansion of educational systems and the development of new
knowledges to the point where education and knowledge production was restructured in every industrial nation (cf. Drucker
1957; Bell 1967; Noble 1991; Chomsky 1997; Loewen 1997; Simpson
1998). While these developments often are attributed to economic
necessity or progressive governmental policy, the funding increases most often actually were justified by appeals to military,
social and economic Cold War *preparedness* in the United States
and other nations (e.g., Canada). The well-funded overhaul of
high school science and mathematics in the United States and parts
of Canada through the installation of curriculum developed under the authority of the U.S. National Academy of Sciences (itself
set up in 1863 under U.S. President Lincoln to harness science to
the Union war effort) in the 1960s provides a paradigm instance.
The "Sputnik scare" benefited education immensely.

In effect, the post-World War II expansion of the educational
system and knowledge production was more a function of war
than of general cultural and economic development. However,
that martial intrusion into the school, university, and knowledge
formation justified by the Cold War has been combined with an
overarching corporate intrusion recently (Readings 1996; Miyoshi
2000). Although corporate influence on the university goes back
at least a century, the military and corporate factors combined—
the military-capitalist complex—currently control most high-cost
knowledge production in universities, though often in ways which
are not immediately evident. The research and development
agenda of any large university viewed longitudinally attests to
this connection as does the specific knowledge produced (cf.
Chomsky 1997; Loewen 1997; Simpson 1998).

"Hi-tech" pharmaceuticals, teaching technologies, electronics,
clothes, cars, "the weaponization of space," foreign policy, war
strategy, social research—all have been affected by military research and development, if not determined by it entirely. However, the profundity of the way in which this corporatist military
control of contemporary knowledge production pervades, and in

large part determines knowledge production, and with that quotidian existence in postindustrial jurisdictions, is far from apparent. The role of university research and of the specific university research made possible by the U.S. Department of Defense in forming and maintaining contemporary world conditions (the world-system) is vastly underappreciated.[9] The "conceptual architectures"—the "cognitive apparatuses"—that frame knowledge production and transmission by the postindustrial human were built in good part upon knowledge developed for military purposes initially.

Education makes these conceptual apparatuses; education *machines* contemporary subjectivity; neither education, nor subjectivity exist "outside history," in some space beyond the reach of material, in this instance corporatist military conditions. Quite the contrary: Education is a force that forms and in turn is formed by contemporary conditions (reality), at one time by the interests of the Church, then the State more strictly speaking, and now by (post)military/industrial capital to which the State has voluntarily and perhaps temporarily relinquished some national authority. It is shocking to understand that many supposedly peaceful industrial jurisdictions have been at war continuously, if not actually then virtually, since the early 1940s. Contemporary perpetual war does not date to 2001 as some have claimed (cf. Vidal 2002), but to 1940.

A world at war, virtually or actually, has framed contemporary existence. War and its related conditions form the dialectic of contemporary cognitive engagement. The French war theorists Paul Virilio and S. Lotringer (1998, 26) speak of global economic warfare and write, "All of us are already civilian soldiers without knowing it. And some of us know it. The great stroke of luck for the military class's terrorism is that no one recognizes it. People don't recognize the militarized part of their identity, of their consciousness." Ubiquity and pervasiveness—and seeming inevitability—conceal the existence and impact of contemporary militarism (i.e., running an economy "as if" total war was imminent).

Education however was not so central a social, economic, and military force until quite recently. The deliberate production of highly regulated subjectivity *en masse* was not so central to the world-system until the industrialization of Europe and North

America. That revolutionary change to the mode of production produced a corresponding change to the mode of education. Education, too, was industrialized, and like production generally, education expanded vastly. This same process again was evident with the establishment of postindustrial economies (circa 1940–2000). Education was postindustrialized this time, and again expanded in concert with the Cold War and the third technological stage of capitalist development.

This third period of capitalist educational and economic development became evident in the 1940s when electronics began to be integrated into industrial economies.[10] Between 1940 and 2000, as between 1840 and 1890, the quantitative technological change was of such magnitude and variety that it proved qualititative (Hegel). This mode change saw education enter the twenty-first century as the *primary* driving force in the world economy.

The émigré German business analyst Peter Drucker was one of the first to identify the dependence of advanced economies and militaries upon education. In *Landmarks of Tomorrow* (1957, 123–124), Drucker articulated what he termed "The Educated Society" and "The Educational Revolution": "The higher education of a country controls its military, its technological, and its economic potential. In an age of superpowers and absolute weapons, higher education may indeed be the only area in which a country can still be ahead, can still gain decisive advantage." As Drucker understood, in advanced industrial economies, the supply of highly educated people had become the decisive military and economic factor.

This situation, however, existed long before it became fashionable to theorize it. The strategic value of a reliable supply of highly and uniformly educated people was already evident by the mid-nineteenth century. This is the actuality of the educational landscape—for a hundred and fifty years at least, education has been the most strategically vital of contemporary social practices (a good way to conceive of contemporary education is as a global system [postindustrial process] devoted to the production of subjectivity). Education plays out Weber's (1968, 225) assertion regarding *Gesellschaft* societies: "This means fundamentally *domination through knowledge.*" Of course, the overriding importance of education and knowledge development in a postindustrial economy has become a commonplace; at the same time, however, the profound strategic importance of these operations remains underappreciated.

This lack of appreciation may be especially prevalent amongst educators themselves, especially teachers and theorists. Ramirez and Boli (1987, 2) are among the few educationists who have addressed the strategic value of education in a historical perspective. They place education into a formative relationship with warfare and national development:

> . . . most comparative studies of education entirely overlook the historical origins of state systems of schooling, thereby ignoring the sociological institutionalization of the social innovation. . . . We show that in some cases military defeat or a failure to keep pace with industrial development in rival countries stimulated the state to turn to education as a means of national revitalization to avoid losing power and prestige in the inter-state system.

Notwithstanding the avoidance of other such investigations in the Anglophone academy, *the strategic value of compelled mass elementary and select advanced education, and of continuous knowledge production and continuous operational improvement has been known and acted upon since the early nineteenth century.* Nineteenth-century German "grade" schools, polytechnics, and research universities are exemplars, as is the *Kindergarten,* another nineteenth century Prussian invention (Friedrich Fröbel). Given the generative role of Prussia in developing contemporary educational and knowledge production systems, it is not surprising that even the concept of *lifelong learning* dates to nineteenth-century Prussia. The constant subjective upgrading and continuous quality improvement that is currently considered novel and progressive was being incorporated into the Prussian educational system from the mid-nineteenth century, mostly through vocational upgrading. Prussia then already conceived of education stretching from cradle to grave, as a continuous flow process.

Prussia was the first state to turn to education as a means to redevelop the state, the military, the economy, and the people after its humiliating defeat by Napoleon in 1806 (until then Prussia had long been home to Europe's best armies) (Melton 1988; Schleunes 1989). The University of Berlin, the world's first research university, was founded by the von Humboldt brothers in 1810.

Hegel developed much of his statist war theory while in its employ; Marx and Engels attended. Alumni include 29 Nobel prize winners. Von Braun attended, as did von Neumann, the "father" of contemporary computing. Einstein and Planck attended, as did the German nationalist poets and theorists Heine and Fichte. Von Bismarck, the person responsible for the unification of Germany, attended, as did the philosophers Schopenhauer and Schelling. Perhaps the University of Chicago is the only university extant that emulates the sheer academic power of the University of Berlin before it was (understandably) split apart by the Russians after World War II ended.

The Prussian Kriegsakademie (war college) was founded by the great military thinker and leader von Scharnhorst in 1807. Shortly after, von Clausewitz, following the thinking of Hegel and von Scharnhorst, began working on the greatest work of military (and civil) strategy ever (*On War*, Berlin, 1832). Already existing German universities were modified, expanded, and provided with new missions when scientific research functions were added.

And Prussia was not alone in using education to strategic advantage, though it did so more comprehensively than other states. Napoleon had established the landmark École Polytechnique in 1794. Though it was not a war college strictly speaking, it was fully devoted to training only military engineers by the early nineteenth century. The United States Military Academy (USMA) at West Point, New York, was founded in 1802 by U.S. President Jefferson. It preceded the Prussian academization of its military education slightly. After difficulties during its start-up, the academy looked to Europe for assistance. An incoming superintendent, Colonel Sylvanus Thayer, toured Europe in 1817 on behalf of the USMA and returned to West Point with an up-to-date library and a host of new concepts. His tenure as the USMA superintendent (1817–1833) led to an educational, organizational, and technological revolution in the United States (and then globally) (Hacker and Hacker 1987; Hacker 1989). Thayer, too, might be considered a "founding father" of the republic.

The system that is so often confused today with education itself—extensive writing, grading, and examination, developed in Europe toward the end of the eighteenth century—was introduced into the United States by Thayer. These revolutionary pedagogical practices (education previously was not systemized and there were few quality control mechanisms) provided the United States with USMA graduates who proved to be of enormous influence, both in the United States and globally. Those graduating from the USMA after Thayer's reforms were largely responsible for the construction of railway lines, bridges, harbors, and roads in the United States for the better part of the nineteenth century. The modern business enterprise was invented by these same graduates, with railway companies the paradigm example in this instance. These pioneers in organizational structure, theory, and practice almost without exception graduated from the USMA following Thayer's introduction of the new educational practices of writing, grading, and examination (Hoskin 1988, 1993; Hoskin and Macve 1993).

Talking of the way West Point graduates fanned out across the U.S. landscape, Hacker (1989, 64) characterizes the influence of West Point graduates as "Thayer's direct and indirect 'pedagogical insemination of the country' through Thayer's system and West Point graduates." The influence of these graduates evidenced in the *capitalist military/industrial restructuring of time, space, subjectivity (the socius).* This existential reformation (de- and re-territorialization) was of such scope and depth that it can be compared to the Enclosure movement and the Industrial Revolution in Great Britain (the Industrial Revolution in Britain was more organic, initially proceeding within parameters that were more strictly industrial/commercial than military/industrial). However, this particular revolution in human affairs remains vastly underappreciated, academically and popularly.

From this point, the power of education to form material conditions in a direct way in industrial societies was evident. Research universities, schools, military colleges, and like institutions provided the primary influence on the development of the human and its environs throughout the twentieth century. The sciences, technologies, policies, and theories developed by those working for these institutions, at Moscow State University, Universität Jena, the University of Chicago, Stanford University, the Massachusetts Institute of Technology, Universität Leipzig, and many other institutes of research and higher learning have produced quotidian existence for the last century. These universities are complex knowledge production *machines* whose product, if not in the main, then partially anyway, is knowledge that grounds various forms of war-making.

During the nineteenth and early twentieth centuries, education, knowledge production, and knowledge delivery was *formalized, systematized, nationalized, industrialized,* and *capitalized* in the United States, Germany, and France, and then in Russia, Japan, and Britain, and in Turkey and Egypt less successfully (Stavrianos 1981). More contentiously, many forms of knowledge and education were *weaponized* simultaneously (a weapon is something that can injure, defeat, or destroy). The results of this *military-industrial education* were already evident in Europe after the Franco-Prussian War (1871) and in the United States after the Civil War (1865) (the Prussian model of state schooling and university research and training was adopted across the United States in the nineteenth century).[11]

However, it wasn't until World War I that the impact of the new educational processes, systems, and institutions became fully apparent. The immensity of that war was a function of the education and knowledge produced and disseminated by the newly militarized and industrialized school systems and research universities (e.g., high explosives; industrial transportation and communication systems; officers trained in the new educational systems; millions of industrially skilled tradesmen; the statist ability to mobilize whole nations, psychically and economically, to imbue whole populations with nationalist fervor and hatred).

After that war, and increasingly throughout the twentieth century, the science and technology produced by research universities *weaponized* most every arena of academic knowledge production. Though the particular science originally may have been located outside these parameters, as was the case with experimental psychology, a genealogical excavation of any "hard" science, of the behavioral sciences, and even mathematics will demonstrate that these arenas of knowledge development were *weaponized,* often from their earliest beginnings. Now, early in the twenty-first century, with foreigners attacking the U.S. mainland, the production and dissemination of weaponized knowledge has become even more central to the contemporary corporatist warfare economy.

The Guardian newspaper in the United Kingdom and *The Chronicle of Higher Education* in the U.S. have documented the privatization, militarization, and marketization of education for a number of years. *The Guardian* reported (Kalaftidés 2001), "Total spending on education amounts to $2 trillion, or one 20th of world GDP. As Glenn R. Jones sees it: "Education is one of the fastest-growing of all markets. Private training and the adult education industry are expected to achieve double-digit growth throughout the next decade.'"

Education reconceptualized ideally and reformed materially is the world's leading industry (at least 2 trillion $US). In 2001 (at the Qatar meeting), 144 World Trade Organization (WTO) countries signed a declaration which included the liberalization of trade in services, including higher education. The U.S. government, supported by a number of well-funded lobbying organizations, is pushing for education to be fully included under the General Agreement on Trade in Services (GATS). That country has an education export industry that is as large as the rest of the world's put together, and stands to benefit enormously if education is included in a GATS treaty. "Education" may be the only area in which the United States still holds a clear economic "competitive advantage." If educational services are fully included under the GATS, further ramifications for public education systems anywhere in the world could be enormous.

The WTO nondiscrimination clause could entail the global privatization of education by requiring signatory governments to provide equal funding to private institutions in all areas of educational endeavor and allow privately held foreign operations to take over public educational systems in signatory countries. Even without changes to the GATS, the internationalization of material and immaterial production (the new global division of labor) and of ownership (a new globalized owning class) already have changed the landscape of the knowledge production (research and development) and dissemination (education) industries quite significantly.

China and India are developing huge knowledge production and dissemination systems that are for the most part grounded in the logic of capitalism, in its axiomatic. These countries and others, like Korea, are joining Hong Kong and Singapore in a vast expansion of research and teaching universities and technical and trades training. These countries are having success in attracting

Western-based knowledge production and processing industries. Microsoft, Charles Schwab, AOL, Accenture, American Express, Infosys, British Airways, and many other corporations have large global support operations in India.

It is in this regard that education is most important—for education produces subjectivity, the most marketable contemporary commodity. It is the human being itself, human thought and attributes, not the material output occasioned by that human directly, that drives a postindustrial economy. Subjectivity itself is the primary source of wealth in the select jurisdictions that can be considered postindustrial (this process sometimes is referred to as the aestheticization of existence).[12] In luxurious postindustrial jurisdictions like Canada and Sweden, and increasingly in select regions of "underdeveloped" jurisdictions like China, Egypt, Turkey, and India, wealth development is predicated upon the development of the "late capitalist subject" (the postindustrial human being).

To deterritorialize and reterritorialize that which was reterritorialized in the first place, this is the logic of the system. There is nothing inevitable about how the logic is manifested, what will be commoditized or recommoditized and turned into a source of profit; but that human existence, however it is realized, is commoditized under capitalism cannot be doubted. On a global level, the awarding of one of the first reconstruction contracts in Iraq after the 2003 U.S. invasion to an education company called Creative Associates International Inc. speaks to this process—as did U.S. (re)educational strategies in Germany and Japan after World War II ended. The elementary schooling system in Iraq was up and running again by October 2003, before the material delivery systems for water or electricity.

This is not to suggest that the axiomatic is realized uncomplicatedly, that it does not engender resistance, that it does not endure compromise or defeat in instances, or that it cannot be superceded. Global and local resistance to the military and economic takeover of Iraq by the United States provides an obvious example. As well, this is not to suggest that there are not "essential" aspects of the human that reside outside this developmental process, albeit they too may be socially formed initially. As Deleuze and Guatarri (1987, 175) put it, "As a general rule, relative deterritorialization (transcodings) reterritorialize on a deterritorialization that is in certain respects absolute [sedimented, overcoded]." Thus, a subjective "kernel," or irreducible remainder, always retains "overcoding"—colonized once—and placed outside the de- and re-territorializing process (cf. Sloterdijk, 1987). However, that this logic, this continual re- and de-territorialization, girds contemporary education, empire, and war is certainly far from obvious. Education still is perceived as a pastoral process that cannot but be indiscriminately beneficial even though the mutually determinative relationships between knowledge production, education, empire, and war have been generally evident in every industrially developed jurisdiction for at least a century.

Most academic theory cannot account for this relationship; neither Marxism nor most Marxist theory can account for material conditions whereby no one force provides the primary driving factor; likewise for classical and neoclassical economic theory wherein the Market ostensibly provides law-like social ordering and war is technically an aberration. At the same time, capitalism may be more dependent upon state and military expenditures than it ever has been previously. A cursory look at some academic history provides substantiation for this thesis. The enabling knowledges that ground contemporary existence—and warfare—date to the nineteenth century. They were for the most part developed in the United States and Germany.

The industrial development of "propaganda," or conversely, the development of industrialized propaganda, provides an instructive instance. Though propaganda, like war, has a past that stretches back into prehistory, its initial industrial development (dependent on mass media, human psychology, etc.) occurred during World War I (1914–1918) in the United States and Great Britain initially. It was developed to control domestic populations and promote statist war efforts at home just as much as it was to demoralize the enemy. The civil (commercial) application of this military knowledge—this waging of psychic warfare—was called propaganda for some time after World War I until it was set apart under the appellation of advertising in the late 1920s (Jowett and O'Donnell 1999).

However, the ability of propaganda to create perception, a form of education in its own right, was based on education as defined traditionally. Pick (1993, 201), in *War Machine: The Rationalisation of Slaughter in the Modern Age,* points out that Einstein "insists that the susceptibilities of the educated individual and the hypnotized masses cannot be easily differentiated. Indeed, if anything the intellectual and educated were more vulnerable than the uncultured population to collective manipulation."[13] Jacques Ellul, the French theologian and technology critic, developed a thesis similar to Einstein's. In *Propaganda: The Formation of Men's Attitudes,* Ellul (1965, 110–111) observed a similar "peculiar susceptibility" of the educated:

> These facts [regarding the social implementation of literacy] leave no doubt that the development of primary education is a fundamental condition for the organization of propaganda, even though such a conclusion may run counter to many prejudices. . . . [T]he need for a certain cultural level to make people susceptible to propaganda is best understood if one looks at one of propaganda's most important devices—the manipulation of symbols. . . . [I]t is only normal that the most educated people (intellectuals) are the first to be reached by such propaganda.

For Ellul, urbanization, education, and industrialization are necessary preconditions for the development and use of "propaganda." Goebbels himself, Ellul (93) writes, "recognized that the peasants could be reached only if their structured milieu was shattered; and the difficulties that Lenin experienced in integrating the Russian peasantry into the pattern of revolution are well known."

The destruction of a "structured milieu" in order to render a society receptive to various messages is most certainly a favored military strategy. Psychological operations (psyops) have been developed for just that purpose. While Sun-Tze outlined these methods more than two thousand years ago, it wasn't until the First World War that they were scientized (academized) and turned on domestic populations. This, of course, is an active form of education. On the other hand, the formation of "credulity" is a "passive" form, whereby education itself circumscribes social possibility in specific ways, whereby education creates the conditions for a human to develop who is susceptible to constant de- and reterritorialization.

The initial development of industrial propaganda was very much a military production. U.S. President Wilson ran for a second term in office promising that he would keep the United States out of World War I, though once elected he did the opposite. However, in spite of formally declaring war, Wilson still needed to overcome domestic resistance to the U.S. war effort. About a week after war was declared, a month after his reelection, Wilson formed the Committee on Public Information (CPI) to promote the war in the United States and publicize the ostensible reasons for U.S. involvement abroad (e.g., national determination for colonized peoples that matched with the "open door" economic policy favorable to U.S. capitalist interests). His efforts were widely supported by industrialists and bankers who had themselves been attempting to raise popular support for the war against the German empire.

Also called the Creel Commission after its leader, the populist journalist George Creel, the CPI looked to business, the academy, and the arts for its membership. The CPI put human psychology and mass communication technologies to work in the quotidian environment. Edward Bernays (*Propaganda*, 1928), who went on to found the field of public relations, served on the committee.[14] Hitler admired British First World War propaganda and his Propaganda Leader, Goebbels, studied Bernays. The Nazis used propaganda techniques developed in the United Kingdom and United States to create fear and even hysteria in the domestic population of Germany. As all propagandists and advertisers do, Goebbels bombarded the population with repetitive messages. One regarded "secret weapons" that would be turned on Germany if they did not defeat the enemy quickly. It is interesting to note that industrial propaganda was invented in democratic states and adopted by totalitarian regimes. It remains highly effective after nearly a century.

However, to suggest that academic martial inventions and their mass application did not engender academic resistance would be to misstate the case. For example, the noted U.S. philosopher and educationist John Dewey spoke out against the constant peacetime use of propaganda by the state and private sector after the First World War. Though Dewey joined with U.S. ruling elites to promote World War I, after that war he became a "people's champion," warning of the dangers of propaganda and arguing that citizens should be taught the methods of propaganda so that they could defend themselves against this form of *psychic warfare* (Gary 1991, 17). An example of collective resistance is proffered by the antiwar movements that date to the 1950s. This form of resistance was manifest globally from its inception, and was most severe during the Vietnam War. Ironically, this resistance was in part a function of new telecommunications technologies (satellite communications, for example) developed for military purposes initially. The commercial application of those military technologies turned the Vietnam War into the world's first TV war; in subsequent imperial wars, the television imagery supplied to postindustrial populations was chosen more circumspectly (this too is a tactical and strategic decision despite "leakage").[15]

Experimental psychology provides another example of military knowledge that was turned to civilian usage. However, experimental psychology, like organic chemistry, was not a function of military research and development initially. Wilhelm Wundt (1832–1920) is often credited with its founding. He established the first "psychological testing laboratory" in 1875. His influence was so great that he is credited with moving the study termed "psychology" from the auspices of philosophy to those of the sciences (Wundt theorized apperception, an educational staple). Wundt's scientific work, carried out at the University of Leipzig, like Hegel's philosophy, was remarkably influential outside Germany, especially in the United States Lionni and Klass, from *The Leipzig Connection* (1993, 14), remark:

> The first of Wundt's American students to return to the United States was G. Stanley Hall. Returning from Leipzig in 1883, he joined the faculty of Baltimore's new Johns Hopkins University, which was being established after the model of the great German universities. Hall organized the psychology laboratory . . . and, in 1887, established the *American Journal of Psychology*. . . . In 1892 he played a leading role in founding the American Psychological Association. . . . Hall was also instrumental in furthering the career of a man who was to have an unusually profound effect on the course of American education: John Dewey.

However, experimental psychology entered the practice and lexicon of warfare before it entered the lexicon and practice of education. When Wilson led the United States into World War I, the army decided it needed a standardized means to sort hundreds of thousands of recruits quickly. A committee of leading psychologists was struck to develop a way to do this (similar to the committee on propaganda). The intelligence quotient (IQ) test resulted. By the end of the war, nearly 2 million American men had taken the Army intelligence tests (the alpha test for literates, the beta tests for illiterates; literacy itself a relatively new concept had entered the educational lexicon a couple of decades earlier).

Stephen J. Gould (1981) traced the postwar influence of the testing movements on educators and the public schools. He noted the key role played by Robert Gagne and Robert Glaser in promoting military technologies in public education (i.e., learning theory, instructional design). The direct connection between education and war unearthed by Gould has not entered educational studies however. Noble (1991, 25) comments: "Military influence on education has become invisible to most observers, who are content to trace educational programs and technologies to 'educational psychology.'" This sentiment is expressed as well by Jonassen (1996, 58–59):

> The influence of the behavioral theory on instructional design can be traced from writings by Dewey, Thorndike, and, of course, B.F. Skinner. In addition, during World War II, military trainers (and psychologists) stated learning outcomes in terms of "performance" and found the need to identify specific "tasks" for a specific job (Gropper, 1983). Based on training in the military during the Second World War, a commitment to achieve practice and reinforcement became major components to the behaviorist-developed instructional design model (as well as other nonbehavioristic models).

Educational technology, instructional technology (design, programming), and educational psychology are so tightly related as to make them almost inseparable. For example, programmed instruction was based in educational psychology (learning theory) and then combined with the educational technology developed during World War II by the U.S. military (e.g., the use of films in classrooms, the layout for textbooks, extensive use of graphs and charts). Again, from Jonassen's (1996, 26) brief history of the influence of war and militarism on education:

Specific military discourses entered the field at this point in time (World War II) and helped shape educational technology in the academy. Both psychological and military discourses are evident in the WWII research texts. Furthermore, we believe that the juncture of behaviorism (this time, operant conditioning, not connectionism) and military pedagogy was fortuitous (a marriage made in heaven), and together they formed a solid theoretical base for the field. The way knowledge was structured in operant conditioning and military pedagogy was quite similar.

This "solid theoretical base" has only strengthened. For example, the current revolution in military affairs (RMA) is manifest pedagogically in the feedback loops and expectation of failure that recently have been built into U.S. Air Force (USAF) training, this placing military pedagogy in line with contemporary progressive (civil) pedagogy. This pedagogical advance is credited with providing the USAF with human performance capabilities not yet attained in other jurisdictions. This example evidences that "civil" and "military" education have become even more blended since WWII ended (demarcations between civil and military knowledge and technology are losing any meaning). Addressing the "engineering of education," Noble (1991, 26) concludes:

> Training specialists, educational technologists and education psychologists have not been the only ones whose military endeavors have shaped and colored educational research. In military research on new weapons systems, psychologists and engineers are increasingly viewed as working on two complementary components of the same man machine system. Training, too, and the research and design of training systems, are also being perceived of as engineering disciplines.

Educational delivery systems have been affected as much as pedagogy by U.S. military spending. The U.S. Navy and Army recently invested more than a billion dollars in *eLearning* (*The Chronicle of Higher Education*, November 17, 2000, "Colleges and Companies Team Up to Vie for Role in Army Program," "Navy Picks Institutions for Online-Learning Effort"), much of this vast sum dedicated to systems development. However, *eLearning* and the information age itself have a more direct and long-standing military provenance. They were in effect produced by U.S. Department of Defense spending during the Cold War period (1947–1990). Scrape off most any postindustrial artifact or endeavour and a military provenance will become evident.

The Defense Advanced Research Projects Agency (DARPA), the academic research coordination agency of the U.S. Department of Defense, was established in 1958 in response to the "Sputnik emergency."[16] DARPA, which has maintained a remarkably low profile until recently, is the exemplar par excellence of the "total influence" of the "military-industrial complex" brought to light by Eisenhower in 1961 in his "Farewell Speech to the Nation." The pivotal role of DARPA in building the enabling communications and computing technologies that ground postindustrialism (the Information Age and *eLearning* for instance) is documented in some detail in the U.S. National Science Foundation Report, *Funding a Revolution: Government Support for Computing Research* (1999).

The report outlines the central role of DARPA in developing the systems theory and artificial intelligence models that allowed for research of a large scale and complexity, and in the development of the telecommunications systems and computing infrastructure that ground the "information economy" (postindustrialism). Simply, this formerly obscure U.S. military agency produced the technologies that ground contemporary postindustrial existence. Life as we know it is an *offshoot* of post-WWII U.S. weapons research and development.

From a 1997 DARPA report titled *Technology Transition:*[17]

DARPA began to invest in information technology nearly thirty-five years ago. The period since then has seen significant changes in the field unlike any in the history of technology. In 1962 computers were scarce and expensive. Mainframes, the only available computers, were accessible to a few individuals who had direct access to a computation center. There was no field of computer science nor any computer science departments in our universities. There were no computer networks . . . Today, only thirty-five years later, the Internet links tens of millions of users across the world. Real-time digital communications systems link individual war fighters and weapon systems on the battlefield to their commanders and on to the National Command Authority. Nearly every office worker has a computer on his or her desk, usually linked to a network. . . . DARPA, more than any other government agency or any single corporation, has been responsible for this revolution.

Yet, that statement, as the full report attests, is much too modest—for not only was DARPA "more than any other agency governmental agency . . . responsible" for the "computer revolution," DARPA's role in fueling the information revolution in its entirety has been pervasive and enduring. DARPA has been credited with "between a third and a half of all the major innovations in computer science and technology" (*What Will Be*, by Michael Dertouzos, HarperCollins, 1997). The innovations it did not develop no doubt were funded by the U.S. government as well, or at the least not developed independently of work DARPA had funded (perhaps even if the work was performed in the U.S.S.R.).

DARPA's influence is solely a function of U.S. government funding of university research (Hughes 1998, 3; U.S. National Science Foundation Report 1999). In Hughes's phrase, "DARPA is the military-industrial-university complex." While these reports document the reach of U.S. Department of Defense spending, their address of the implications of the spending is limited to a discussion of various technologies and weapons systems. Understandably, the qualitative impact of this spending—for example the social implications of a "permanent arms economy"—are not examined.

Research programs that DARPA has initiated since September 2001 may have an even greater effect on existence.[18] Much current research concerns weapons systems (e.g., surveillance systems) that are being designed to function in the quotidian environment rather than in a traditional war theatre, *in the everyday lives that are the theatre of war in the "age of terrorism."* Consider a current project with potentially vast implications. DARPA recently awarded contracts to the Carnegie Mellon University's School of Computer Science (Pittsburgh, Pa.) and SRI International (Menlo Park, Calif.) that may influence the development of education so profoundly as to render aspects of the "great Western project" functionally redundant, of much less use economically, socially and militarily.

The contracts were awarded for the purpose of developing the Perceptive Assistant that Learns (PAL), which is "software that could significantly advance the science of cognitive systems and revolutionize how computers interact with humans":

> The program, called Perceptive Assistant that Learns (PAL), is expected to yield new technology of significant value to the military, business, and academic sectors. It will spur pioneering research in cognitive information processing, including areas of artificial intelligence, machine learning, knowledge representation and reasoning, machine perception, natural language processing, and human-computer interaction.

The PAL program is managed by DARPA's Information Processing Technology Office (IPTO). That office is responsible for developing the ARPANet, the Internet, large-scale parallel processing, and many other computer technologies. A portion of its current work concerns the creation of artificial intelligence, what are called cognitive computing systems. If successful, these systems will have the ability to reason, learn from experience, explain themselves, and respond intelligently to situations the systems are not familiar with. The advantages of such machines for waging contemporary warfare whether military, ideological, or economic are immediately obvious.

These systems (dead labor) could do work now done by the highly educated research analysts (living labor) employed by the thousands in every area of the private and public sectors, in banking, industry, education, government, and the military. These thinking systems could technologically displace that last redoubt of humanism, the educated human being. This would amount to another capitalist technological displacement and social devaluation of education, defined functionally or liberally, another downgrading of the "great Western project" that in many respects reached its acme in North America during the Cold War period.

Again what is evident is the strategic value of compelled mass elementary and select advanced education, combined with continuous knowledge production and continuous operational improvement. It is ironic indeed that the educational successes evidenced by the third great wave of capitalist technological development are putting the education system that produced these successes out of business. Such is the logic of the system.

References

Arrighi, G., and Silver, B. (1999). *Chaos and governance in the modern world-system*. Minneapolis: University of Minnesota Press.

Bell, D. (1967). "The Post-industrial Society: A Speculative View." In E. Hutchings (ed.), *Scientific progress and human values*. New York: American Elsevier.

———. (1973). *The coming of postindustrial society: A venture in social forecasting*. New York: Basic Books.

Boli J., Ramirez, F., and Meyer, J. (1987). "Explaining the Origins and Expansion of Mass Education." *Comparative Education Review*, 29(2), 145–170.

Braudel, F. (1967). *Capitalism and material life, 1400–1800*. New York: Harper & Row.

Brown, W. (1995). *States of injury: Power and freedom in late modernity*. Princeton, NJ: Princeton University Press.

Chomsky, N. (1997). *The cold war & the university: Toward an intellectual history of the postwar years*. New York: New Press.

Coombs, P., et al. (1973). *New paths to learning*. New York: UNICEF.

"Colleges and Companies Team Up to Vie for Role in Army Program." (2000, November 17). *The Chronicle of Higher Education*.

DARPA Over the Years (n.d). Retrieved April 21, 2003, from http://www.darpa.mil/body/overtheyears.html

DARPA *Technology Transition* (1997). Retrieved April 21, 2003 from http://www.darpa.mil/body/pdf/transition.pdf

Deleuze, G. (1995). *Negotiations*. New York: Columbia University Press.

Deleuze, G., and Guatarri, F. (1983). *Anti-Oedipus: Capitalism and schizophrenia*. Minneapolis: University of Minnesota Press.

———. (1987). *A thousand plateaus: Capitalism and schizophrenia*. Minneapolis: University of Minnesota Press.

Derrida, J. (2003). *Philosophy in a time of terror*. Chicago: University of Chicago Press.

Drucker, P. (1957). *Landmarks of tomorrow*. New York: Harper.

Eisenhower, D. (1961). *Farewell Address to the Nation*. January 17, 1961. Retrieved April 19, 2003, from http://mcadams.posc.mu.edu/ike.htm

Falk, C. (2003). *Education is war: The constitution of postindustrial learning*. Burnaby, British Columbia: Simon Fraser University.

Gary, B. (1999). *The nervous liberals: Propaganda anxieties from World War I to the cold war*. New York: Columbia University Press.

Gould, Stephen J. (1981). *The mismeasure of man*. New York: Norton.

Guattari, F. (1995). *Chaosmosis: An ethico-aesthetic paradigm*. Bloomington: Indiana University Press.

Gur-Ze'ev, I. (1998). "Toward a Nonrepressive Critical Pedagogy." *Educational Theory*, (48)4, 463–486.

———. (1999). "Knowledge and Violence." *Encyclopedia of Philosophy of Education*. Retrieved April 19, 2003, from http://construct.haifa.ac.il/~ilangz/new/.

Hacker, S. (1989). *Pleasure, power and technology.* Boston: Unwin Hyman.

Hacker, B., and Hacker, S. (1987). "Military Institutions and the Labour Process: Noneconomic Sources of Technological Change, Women's Subordination, and the Organization of Work." *Technology and Culture*, 28(4), 743–775.

Holland, E. (1991). "Deterritorializing 'Deterritorialization'—From the *Anti-Oedipus* to *A Thousand Plateaus.*" *SubStance*, 66.

Hoskin, K. (1993). "Education and the Genesis of Disciplinarity: The Unexpected Reversal." In E. Messer-Davidow, D. Shumway, and D. Sylvan (eds.), *Knowledges: historical and critical studies in disciplinarity.* Charlottesville: University Press of Virginia, pp. 271–304.

———. (1988). "The Genesis of Accountability: The West Point Connections." *Accounting, Organization and Society*, 13(1), 37–73.

Hoskin, K., and Macve, R. (1993). "Accounting as Discipline: The Overlooked Supplement." In E. Messer-Davidow, D. Shumway & D. Sylvan (eds.), *Knowledges: historical and critical studies in disciplinarity.* Charlottesville: University Press of Virginia, pp. 25–53.

Jameson, F. (1991). *Postmodernism, or, the cultural logic of late capitalism.* Durham, NC: Duke University Press.

———. (1998). *The cultural turn: selected writings on the postmodern 1983–1998.* London: Verso.

Jonassen, D. (ed.). (1996). *Handbook of research for educational communications and technology.* Macmillan Library Reference USA. New York: Simon & Schuster Macmillian.

Jonathan, R. (1997). *Illusory freedoms: liberalism, education and the market.* Oxford: Blackwell Publishers.

Jowett, G., and O'Donnell, V. (1999). *Propaganda and persuasion.* Thousand Oaks, CA: Sage Publications.

Kalaftidés, L. (2001). "Education: On the ropes." *EducationGuardian.co.uk.* Retrieved April 14, 2003, from http://education.guardian.co.uk/higher/education/partner/story/0,9887,596045,00.html

Lionni, P., and Klass, L. (1993). *The Leipzig connection.* Portland, OR: Heron Books.

Loewen, R. (1997). *Creating the cold war university: The transformation of Stanford.* Berkeley: University of California Press.

Mandel, E. (1978). *Late Capitalism.* London: Verso, 1978.

McLuhan, M., and Fiore, Q. (1968). *War and peace in the global village: An inventory of some of the current spastic situations that could be eliminated by more feedforward.* New York: McGraw-Hill.

Melton, J.V.H. (1988). *Absolutism and the eighteenth-century origins of compulsory schooling in Prussia and Austria.* New York: Cambridge University Press.

Meyer, J., Ramirez, F., and Soysal, Y. (1992). "World Expansion of Mass Education, 1870–1980." *Sociology of Education,* 65(2), 128–149.

Miyoshi. M. (2000). "Ivory Tower in Escrow." *boundary 2,* 27(1), 7–50.

"Navy Picks Institutions for Online-Learning Effort." (2000, November 17). *The Chronicle of Higher Education.*

Negri, A. (1998). *Back to the Future: A Portable Document,* Retrieved April 14, 2003, from http://www.sozialistische-klassiker.org/Negri/negri03.pdf.

Noble, D. (1991). *The classroom arsenal: Military research, information technology, and public education.* London: The Falmer Press.

Pick, D. (1993). *War machine: The rationalisation of slaughter in the modern age.* Yale University Press.

Polenburg, R. (1972). *War and society: The United States, 1941–1945.* Philadelphia: Lippincott.

Porter, B. (1994). *War and the rise of the state: The military foundations of modern politics.* New York: Free Press.

Readings, W. (1996). *The university in ruins.* Cambridge: Harvard University Press.

Schleunes, K. (1989). *Schooling and society: The politics of education in Prussia and Bavaria, 1750–1900.* Oxford: Berg Publishers.

Simpson, C. (1998). *Universities and empire: Money and politics in the social sciences during the cold war.* New York: New Press.

Sloterdijk, P. (1987). *Critique of cynical reason.* Minneapolis: University of Minnesota Press.

Spanos, W. (1993). *The end of education: Toward posthumanism.* Minneapolis: University of Minnesota Press.

Stavrianos, P. (1981). *Global rift: the Third World comes of age.* New York: Morrow.

Toraine, A. (1970). *The post-industrial society: Tomorrow's social history: classes, conflicts and culture in the programmed society.* New York: Random House.

U.S. National Science Foundation Report (1999). *Funding a Revolution: Government Support for Computing Research.* Retrieved April 19, 2003, from http://www.nap.edu/readingroom/books/far/contents.html.

Vidal, G. (2002). *Perpetual war for perpetual peace: How we got to be so hated.* New York: Thunder's Mouth Press/Nation Books.

Virilio, P. (1994). *The vision machine.* Bloomington: Indiana University Press.

Virilio, P., and Lotringer, S. (1998). *Pure war.* Brooklyn, NY: Semiotext (e).

Wallerstein, I. (1974). *The modern world-system.* New York: Academic Press.

———. (1995). *Historical capitalism; with capitalist civilization.* London: Verso.

Weber, M. (1968). *Economy and society,* edited by G. Roth and C. Wittich. Berkeley: University of California Press.

Notes

1. For a more lengthy exploration of the themes developed in this article, see Falk, C. (2003) *Education is war: the constitution of postindustrial learning.*

2. Athusser (1969, 101) defines overdetermination: ". . . the 'contradiction' is inseparable from the total structure of the social body in which it is found, inseparable from its formal conditions of existence, and even from the instances it governs; it is radically affected by them, determining, but also determined in one and the same movement, and determined by the various levels and instances of the social formations it animates; it might be called overdetermined in its principle."

3. Weber's (1978, 21) "ideal type" is an abstraction. He explains:

> The more sharply and precisely the ideal type has been constructed, thus the more abstract and unrealistic in this it is, the better able it is to perform its functions in formulating terminology, classifications and hypotheses.

This Weberian concept underlies the author's use of "ideal type" in relation to subjectivity.

4. Gur-Ze'ev (1999) in *Knowledge and Violence* writes:

> Normalized education constitutes and commands the "subject" in four levels: 1. Control of the psychic construction of the "subject," her psychological possibilities and strivings, as well as the limits of controlling and changing their borders. 2. Control of the conceptual apparatus, associations and their integration with the psychic level and its presence in the conceptual level. 3. Control of collective and private self-conscious. 4. Control of the function of the "subject" in "her" reality and the minimization of the possibilities for change in the representation of reality that normalizing education reflects and serves.

5. Guatarri (1995, 1–2) writes:

> At least three types of problem prompt us to enlarge the definition of subjectivity beyond the classical opposition between

individual subject and society, and in doing so, revise the models of the unconscious currently in circulation: the irruption of subjective factors at the forefront of current events, the massive development of machinic productions of subjectivity and, finally, the recent prominence of ethological and ecological perspectives on human subjectivity.

6. Deleuze and Guatarri (1987, 399) elaborate on the relationship between desire and its effectuations, which differ in time/space depending upon the particular assemblage:

But if it is true that all assemblages [an assemblage establishes connections between multiplicities drawn from different orders, for example a certain field of reality, of representation and subjectivity] are assemblages of desire, the question is whether the assemblages of war and work, considered in themselves, do not fundamentally mobilize passions of different orders. Passions are effectuations of desire that differ according to the assemblage: it is not the same justice or the same cruelty, the same pity, etc. The work regime is inseparable from an organization and a development of Form, corresponding to which is the formation of the subject. This is the passional regime of feeling as "the form of the worker."

7. Wendy Brown (1995, 106) writes:

In Marx's account, the ruse of power peculiar to liberal constitutionalism centers upon granting freedom, equality and representation to abstract rather than concrete subjects. The substitution of abstract political subjects for actual ones not only forfeits the project of emancipation but resubjugates us precisely by emancipating substitutes for it—by emancipating our abstracted representatives in the state and naming this process "freedom." The subject is thus ideally emancipated [in original] through its anointing as an abstract person, a formally free and equal human being [as free as anyone else to sleep under the bridge], and is practically resubordinated through this idealist disavowal of the material constituents of personhood, which contain and constrain our freedom. Thus, because we are in this way subjugated by the very discourse of our freedom, liberal freedom is structurally, not merely definitionally, ambiguous.

8. From Eisenhower's *Farewell Address to the Nation* (1961):

The conjunction of an immense military establishment and huge arms industry is new in the American experience. The total influence—economic, political, and even spiritual—is felt in every city, every statehouse, and every office of the federal government. . . . In the councils of government, we must guard against unwarranted influence, whether sought or unsought, by the military-industrial complex.

9. The concept of "world-system" as it is used here is based in the work of Immanuel Wallerstein and Fernand Braudel. World-system refers to the world as one large ecological and social system organized through a global division of wealth/labour produced within an inter-statist system of governance. In line with Wallerstein, world-system theory grounds this work methodologically as well. It inverts the prevailing Anglophone paradigm for knowledge production, namely structuralist-functionalism whereby social analysis proceeds from an ascertainable complex reality (in theory anyway) to "lawful" generalizations (nomothetic); this work begins with the abstract (e.g., education, world-system, empire, systemic logic) and moves to a presentation of complex reality (idiographic).

10. Mandel provided the technological periodization for this work. He (1978, 18) writes:

Fundamental revolutions in power technology—the technology of the production of motive machines by machines—thus appears as the determinant moment in revolutions of technology as a whole. Machine production of steam-driven motors since 1848; machine production of electric and combustion motors since the end of the 19th century; machine production of electronic and nuclear-powered apparatuses since the '40s of the 20th century—these are the three general revolutions in technology engendered by the capitalist mode of production since the "original" industrial revolution of the later 18th century.

11. The formation of U.S. Land Grant Colleges offers an exemplar. The United States during that country's Civil War (the North) established a federal system for education/training in three mandated areas, agricultural, mechanical, and military (the Morrill Agricultural College Act of 1862). It is credited by some theorists with allowing the United States to transition to a "knowledge economy." It has proven adaptable in adjusting to various forms of agriculture, industry, and warfare.

Porter (1994, 261–62) outlines the way in which war imperatives in the early 1860s proved formative of the national institutional fabric of the United States:

In addition to the Bureau of Internal Revenue, the war saw the founding of the Department of Agriculture, the Bureau of

Immigration, and the National Academy of Sciences, founded in 1863 in the hope of harnessing science to the war effort. An activist Congress passed the Homestead Act of 1862, and the Immigration Act of 1864; it also established the Union Pacific and Central Pacific Railroad companies as federally chartered corporations. All these measures had some link to the war effort.

12. Negri (1998), in *Back to the Future: A Portable Document,* states that the production of wealth through the production of subjectivity is, "one of the most central aspects of this revolution we are living through. Really it is no longer possible to imagine the production of wealth and knowledge except through the production of subjectivity, and thus through the general reproduction of vital processes." The revitalization of human capital theory can be read as symptomatic of this systemic logic.

13. Virilio (1994, 23) explains that this "peculiar susceptibility" that may not have been quite so straightforward—that it took some to instill "learned ignorance."

> The retreat from the mathematically derived mechanical explanation took time. Max Planck postulated quantum theory in 1900, "quanta" being mathematical facts that cannot be accounted for. After that, as Sir Arthur Eddington remarked, "every genuine law of nature stood a good chance of seeming irrational to the rational man." These facts were difficult to accept, for they not only went against cumulative scientific prejudice, they went equally against the dominant philosophies and ideologies.

14. This book is long out of print and a full reference is not available. *Visiting Edward Bernays* by Stuart Ewen documents Bernays' profound understanding of the implications of the work of the CPI. See http://www.adbusters.org/oldwebsite/Articles/bernay.html

15. Postindustrial society is totally-blended, rhetorical demarcations between war and peace, education and training, civil and military notwithstanding. Speaking of the Vietnam war (1964–1975) Marshall McLuhan and Quentin Fiore (1968, 134) provided a glimpse of "total blending" in *War and Peace in the Global Village*: "The television war has meant the end of the dichotomy between civilian and military. The public is now participant in every phase of the war, and the main actions of the war are now being fought in the American home itself." The "playing fields of Eton," symbolic of high British imperialism, have been displaced by the "living rooms of the nation," an image more suitable for the age of democratic imperialism.

16. *DARPA Over the Years* http://www.darpa.mil/body/overthe years.html

17. See DARPA (1997) *Technology Transition.* http://www.darpa.mil/body/pdf/transition.pdf

18. Visit the DARPA home site http://www.darpa.mil/ for links to sites outlining DARPA's operations.

Chapter Eight

War as Globalization

The "Education" of the Iraqi People

Michael A. Peters

War is the continuation of policy by other means.
—*Carl von Clausewitz*

A people, starved and sickened by sanctions, then pulver-ized by war, is going to emerge from this trauma to find that their country has been sold out from under them. They will also discover that their newfound *freedom*—for which so many of their loved ones perished—comes pre-shackled with irreversible economic decisions that were made in board-rooms while the bombs were still falling. They will then be told to vote for their new leaders, and welcomed to the won-derful world of democracy.

—*Naomi Klein*

1. Introduction

This chapter investigates the following assertions: that war and globalization go hand in hand; that contemporary globalization *is* a form of war (and war may be a form of globalization); that militarization and war are integral parts of the neoliberal agenda; and that there are inextricable links between the U.S. military-industrial complex, the free market, and world order. The chapter investigates these claims within the context of the war against Iraq and provides some background to questions concerning a civilizational analysis of globalization that contextualizes the U.S. National Security Strategy and the neoconservative influence in the White House. It concludes by making some remarks concerning the role of education in understanding the relationship between war and globalization. The chapter, strictly speaking, is not a philosophical one, although it raises philosophical questions. It is rather an essay in traditional political economy that relates the question of war and globalization to contemporary events with the aim of marking out a role for education in their philosophical and political understanding. Educationally speaking, we need to understand this specific event—the war against Iraq—in terms of an emerging global politics.[1]

In the remainder of this introduction, first, and in general terms, I establish a presumption in favor of the assertion that war is a form of globalization. In the emerging economic and sociological discourse of globalization, the tendency has been to distinguish the dimensions of globalization. For instance, Christopher Chase-Dunn remarks:

> During the late 1980s a new term entered popular discourse: *globalization*. Instead of clarifying issues of world development the buzzword rather seemed to add confusion and misunderstandings. There are at least five different dimensions of globalization that need to be distinguished:
>
> - economic globalization
> - political globalization
> - common ecological constraints
> - cultural values and institutions, and
> - globalization of communication (Fred W. Riggs, "Globalization: Key Concepts," http://www2.hawaii.edu/~fredr/glocon.htm).

It is clear that these dimensions or elements overlap considerably. In this well-developed analysis of globalization, Riggs identifies some twelve dimensions articulated in terms of world systems theory. None of these dimensions explicitly mentions or profiles war as an aspect of globalization. Indeed, war as an aspect of globalization has been a consistently neglected feature in the literature until the recent war against Iraq.

Yet war is not only an ancient means of globalization, perhaps among the earliest forms along with trade and travel, but also arguably a form of globalization that encompasses many of the other dimensions. In its neoliberal form we might take the Anglo-American war against Iraq as a current example.

The war is being prosecuted in the name of the liberation of the Iraqi people against a "brutal dictator." It simultaneously involves the huge organized movement of troops (over 250,000), war machines, goods, and "humanitarian aid." The war can be studied in terms of its economic rationale and effects—not only the story of the fate of Middle East oil, but also the neoliberal postwar reconstruction based on principles worked out in the so-called Washington Consensus and implemented by the World Bank and IMF. It can be studied from the perspective of political globalization—in particular, the history of the Iraqi state by the British under a mandate from the League of Nations in 1921, the rise of the Baath party, and the formation of the modern Iraqi state. This conception of the development of the modern Iraqi state raises questions concerning postcoloniality—whether the present can be understood as a break with the past—and it also raises questions about the breakdown of the international rule of law, the diminished role of the U.N., the split in EU politics, and the divergence in "strategic culture" between Europe and the U.S.

Clearly, also, and still following Chase-Dunn's dimensions of globalization, the relationship between globalization and war might be studied from the perspective of ecological globalization. Here one would need to consider not only the ecological effects of war on the region but also the grand narrative of oil and its role in U.S. ecological politics. The category termed "cultural values and institutions" is especially relevant in that students of globalization and of global citizenship need to understand the kinds of argument that have recently been advanced by the likes of Samuel

Huntington (1996) in his influential book *The Clash of Civilizations and the Remaking of World Order*, a book that Henry Kissinger described as "one of the most important books to have emerged since the end of the cold war." Huntington proposes an interpretation of the evolution of global politics after the Cold War and provides a paradigm for viewing global politics. He discusses the theme of "universal civilization," the shifting balance of power among civilizations, Muslim militancy, and conflicts generated by Western universalism. He also suggests that "clashes of civilizations are the greatest threat to world peace, and an international order based on civilizations is the surest safeguard against world war." Huntington's work has been heavily criticized by postcolonial theorists like Edward Said who argue that Huntington's thesis is based upon a series of binary oppositions and historic "we-they" constructions that ignore the hybridization that has gone on with peoples since the great diasporas of the modern era. Certainly, the binary oppositions and historic "we-they" prejudices came to play a pivotal role in the speeches of George W. Bush increasingly after September 11, and tended to dichotomize the Christian West against the Islamic world.

Globalization of communication makes a vital and interesting case-study in the context of war, and especially in the war against Iraq, with the war of propaganda on both sides, the fight for the airwaves and frequencies, the global presence of Islamic TV and radio, the depiction of "on-the-spot" reports from news agencies, and the potential for the media to shape national consciousness and identity on a daily basis.

Education has a crucial role to play in examining *war as globalization* and in relation to each of the dimensions outlined above. It is the means by which schools and universities can provide the necessary depth in subject matter and in theory to understand unfolding events that are shaping the post-Cold War global order. It is the means by which the traditional disciplines can study globalization and the prospect of global citizenship in all its political, economic, and cultural complexity. It is also the means by which the construction of the nation-state and national identity through war can be studied. Finally, it is the means through which students can understand war as a catastrophic means of globalization and learn to empathize with the suffering of the Iraqi people.

2. Globalization: A Civilizational Analysis[2]

The West has failed. It shall all go up in a great fire, and all
shall be ended. . . . All the East is moving. . . . It is time for all
to depart who would not be slaves.
—The Return of the King; *vol. 3 of* The Lord of the Rings
*by J.R.R. Tolkien, 1995. Spoken by the Steward Denethor as he
contemplates what he assumes will be the impending triumph
of Sauron.*[3]

Samuel Huntington published his article "The Clash of Civilizations?" in *Foreign Affairs* in 1993, causing more discussion and
debate than any other article in that journal, which has been published since the 1940s. *The Clash of Civilizations and the Remaking of
World Order* was published some four years later. (I shall refer to
the 2002 edition.) In the book, the question mark disappears and
Huntington, more assured now of his thesis and direction, maintains that the book is "an interpretation of the evolution of global
politics after the Cold War"—"a framework, a paradigm, for viewing global politics that will be meaningful to scholars and useful
to policymakers" (13).

Huntington argues that a "clash of civilizations" is occurring
as Western, Islamic, and Asian cultural systems collide. This
civilizational or cultural clash, rather than ideology, will determine future world order. His argument is actually a lot subtler
than most critics make out. Certainly, one of his main contentions
is that cultural consciousness is growing and that it is getting stronger, not weaker. States and peoples may now band together because of cultural and religious similarities rather than ideological
ones, as in the past. This creates a multipolar world based loosely
on civilizations rather than on ideologies, and in this situation
Americans must reaffirm their Western identity. Asia and Islam
are exploding demographically. Asia, in addition, is expanding
militarily and economically. The West, by comparison, may be
declining in relative influence. The fact that the world is modernizing does not mean that it is Westernizing. The impact of urbanization and mass communications, coupled with poverty and ethnic divisions, will not necessarily lead to peoples elsewhere in the
world adopting Western values and institutions as their own. The

Western belief that parliamentary democracy and free markets are universal institutions suitable for everyone will increasingly bring the West into conflict with civilizations—notably, Islam and the Chinese—that operate on the basis of different values and will not willingly or slavishly adopt Western values and institutions.

Huntington provides a brief summary of the book in the following terms: "The central theme of this book is that culture and cultural identities, which at the broadest level are civilizational identities, are shaping the patterns of cohesion, disintegration, and conflict in the post-Cold War world" and elaborates this main proposition in terms of five corollaries that correspond to the book's structure:

1. For the first time in history global politics is both multipolar and multicivilizational; modernization is distinct from Westernization and is producing neither a universal civilization in any meaningful sense nor the Westernization of non-Western societies

2. The balance of power among civilizations is shifting: the West is declining in relative influence; Asian civilizations are expanding their economic, military, and political strength; Islam is exploding demographically with destabilizing consequences for Muslim countries and their neighbors; and non-Western civilizations generally are reaffirming the value of their own cultures.

3. A civilization-based world order is emerging: societies sharing cultural affinities cooperate with each other; efforts to shift societies from one civilization to another are unsuccessful; and countries group themselves around the lead or core states of their civilization.

4. The West's universalist pretensions increasingly bring it into conflict with other civilizations, most seriously with Islam and China; at the local level fault line wars, largely between Muslims and non-Muslims, generate "kin-country rallying," the threat of broader escalation, and hence efforts by core states to halt these wars.

5. The survival of the West depends on Americans reaffirming their Western identity and Westerners accepting their civilization as unique, not universal, and uniting to renew and preserve it against challenges from non-Western societies. Avoidance of a global war of civilizations depends on world leaders accepting and cooperating to maintain the multicivilizational character of global politics (Huntington 2002, 20–21).

The concept of "the West" underlies Huntington's analysis, and even though he pays some attention to the historical development of the concept, he does not question its unity or coherence or, indeed, its historical origins. His main point is to drive a wedge between notions of Western civilization and modernization. As he argues: "Western civilization emerged in the eighth and ninth centuries and developed its distinctive characteristics in the following centuries. It did not begin to modernize until the seventeenth and eighteenth centuries. The West was the West long before it was modern" (69). Drawing on the huge literature that has focused on the distinctiveness of the West—from Weber through Toynbee and Spengler to Braudel, Wallerstein, and Fernández-Arnesto—Huntington marks out the following core essential characteristics of Western civilization: the classical legacy, Catholicism and Protestanism, European languages, separation of spiritual and temporal authority, rule of law, social pluralism, representative bodies, individualism. Huntington does not discuss the extant literature; he merely acknowledges it. He provides no explanation of why he asserts that Western civilization emerges in the eighth and ninth centuries. Elsewhere he maintains "Western civilization is usually dated as emerging about AD 700 or 800" (46) and he recognizes three major components—Europe, North America, and Latin America. While he identifies the West with what used to be called Western Christendom and, in the modern era, Euroamerica—North Atlantic civilization—he also recognizes both the white settler societies of Australia and New Zealand and the historical differences between America and Europe. He writes:

> The relation between the two major components of the West has, however, changed over time. For much of their history, Americans defined their society in opposition to Europe. America was the land of freedom, equality, opportunity, the future; Europe represented oppression, class conflict, hierarchy, and backwardness. American, it has been argued, was a distinct civilization. This positing of an opposition between America and Europe was, in considerable measure, a result of the fact that at least until the end of the nineteenth century America had only limited contacts with non-Western civilizations. Once the United States moved out on the world scene, however, the sense of a broader identity with Europe developed (46).[4]

Huntington's analysis is at once prophetic and in parts factual and also infuriatingly overly simplistic. Even if we accept his analysis, it does not follow that we should accept his prescription. Certainly, there is reason to think that President Bush or those in his administration have taken to heart his analysis and their security and defense plans might be interpreted in part as a response to "the decline of the West" with the promotion of a single sustainable world model of political and economic development based on "freedom, democracy, and free enterprise."

3. Neoliberalism and War: Post-Iraq Reconstruction and the Imposition of American Democracy

The great struggles of the twentieth century between liberty and totalitarianism ended with a decisive victory for the forces of freedom—and a single sustainable model for national success: freedom, democracy, and free enterprise. In the twenty-first century, only nations that share a commitment to protecting basic human rights and guaranteeing political and economic freedom will be able to unleash the potential of their people and assure their future prosperity. People everywhere want to be able to speak freely; choose who will govern them; worship as they please; educate their children—male and female; own property; and enjoy the benefits of their labor. These values of freedom are right and true for every person, in every society—and the duty of protecting these values against their enemies is the common calling of freedom-loving people across the globe and across the ages.
—*George W. Bush, The White House, September 17, 2002. The National Security Strategy of the United States of America. (http://www.whitehouse.gov/nsc/nss.html).*

As George W Bush makes manifestly clear in this document written before the Iraq War, his administration considers there is "a single sustainable model for national success: freedom, democracy, and free enterprise." The document articulates the doctrine of pre-emptive strike—of "identifying and destroying the threat before it reaches our borders" (5). What is of relevance to the argument I am advancing is the close fit between security at home and military intervention based on preemptive strike against rogue states, on the one hand, and the export of democracy and the commitment to economic globalization, on the other. Thus, of the eight pillars of American security, the National Security Strategy document lists, alongside the defeat of global terror and a strategy to combat "WMD," "ignit[ing] a new era of global economic growth through free markets and free trade" and "expand[ing] the circle of development by opening societies and building the infrastructure for democracy" (3). The emphasis on economic growth, free trade, and free markets is at the heart of American security strategy. In particular this means: "pro-growth legal and regulatory policies," lower tax rates to encourage investment, rule of law, "strong financial systems that allow capital to be put to its most efficient use," "sound fiscal policies to support business activity," free trade," and investment in health and education. Throughout the document, reference is made to the roles of the IMF, WB, and WTO. As President Bush indicates, "the United States will use this moment of opportunity to extend the benefits of freedom across the globe. We will actively work to bring the hope of democracy, development, free markets, and free trade to every corner of the world" (2).

The model for the National Security Strategy, a blueprint for U.S. global domination, was written well before President Bush even took power in January 2001. The document, entitled *Rebuilding America's Defenses: Strategies, Forces and Resources for a New Century*, was written in September 2000 by the neoconservative think-tank Project for the New American Century (PNAC), and it reveals that President Bush and his cabinet were planning a premeditated attack on Iraq to secure "regime change" well before he was elected. The blueprint for the creation of a "global Pax Americana," posted on the PNAC website (http://www.newamericancentury.org), was drawn up by Dick Cheney (now Vice-President), Donald Rumsfeld (Secretary of Defense), Paul Wolfowitz (Rumsfeld's deputy), George W Bush's younger brother Jeb, and Lewis Libby (Cheney's chief of staff). The document clearly indicates that Bush's cabinet intended to take military control of the Gulf region, whether or not Saddam Hussein was in power.

The Project for the New American Century was established in 1997 as part of the New Citizenship Project by William Kristol (chairman) and Gary Schmitt (president). Its stated goal is to promote American global leadership, and it originated as a set of conservative criticisms of American foreign and defense policy under the Clinton Administration. Its aims to provide a vision for post-Cold War global politics:

> As the 20th century draws to a close, the United States stands as the world's preeminent power. Having led the West to victory in the Cold War, America faces an opportunity and a challenge: Does the United States have the vision to build upon the achievements of past decades? Does the United States have the resolve to shape a new century favorable to American principles and interests? (http://www.newamericancentury.org/statementofprinciples.htm).

The statement of principles then articulates what is required in a way that clearly ties increased militarism to neoliberal economic principles:

- [W]e need to increase defense spending significantly if we are to carry out our global responsibilities today and modernize our armed forces for the future;
- we need to strengthen our ties to democratic allies and to challenge regimes hostile to our interests and values;
- we need to promote the cause of political and economic freedom abroad;
- we need to accept responsibility for America's unique role in preserving and extending an international order friendly to our security, our prosperity, and our principles. (http://www.new americancentury.org/statementofprinciples.htm)

The document is signed by a group of neoconservatives that later came to play a central role in the Bush administration, including William J. Bennett, Jeb Bush, Dick Cheney, I. Lewis Libby, Donald Rumsfeld, and Paul Wolfowitz.[5]

The PNAC website contains the document *Rebuilding America's Defenses: Strategies, Forces and Resources for a New Century.*[6] In essence the report seeks to establish four core missions for the U.S. military, viz, defend the American homeland; fight and decisively win multiple, simultaneous major theater wars; perform "constabulary" duties; and "transform U.S. forces to exploit the 'revolution in military affairs.'" In order to carry out these core missions, the United States must: maintain nuclear strategic superiority; restore personnel strength in active-duty staff; reposition U.S. forces to shift permanent forces to S.E. Europe and S.E. Asia; modernize current U.S. forces selectively (proceed with the F-22 program); cancel "roadblock" programs (e.g., Joint Strike Fighter); develop and deploy global missile defenses; control the new "international commons of space and cyberspace; increase military spending (to 3.8% of GDP); and exploit the "revolution in military affairs to insure long-term superiority" (e.g., application of advanced technologies).

In other words, in the post–Cold War period, when many other nations, especially in Europe, were reducing defense spending, PNAC argued that America faced new military imperatives and must prepare "for a future that promises to be very different and potentially much more dangerous" (4). The document sets out a strategy for repositioning American forces in respect of Europe, the Persian Gulf, and East Asia, with a greater naval presence in the Pacific. It makes the case for security and defense strategy that prefigures that adopted by the Bush administration, including the war against Iraq.

Judging from the PNAC site, there is an inextricable link between U.S. militarism and the promotion of so-called "free markets, free trade, and democracy," with an emphasis on global capital markets, the role of the IMF, WB, and NATO in post-Cold War world architecture and a growing reluctance to become part of European world institutions such as the International Criminal Court.[7]

The Iraq War—probably an illegal war if we are to judge by the Nuremberg Principles adopted by the International Law Commission of the U.N.[8]—is clearly an extension of the neoliberal/neoconservative[9] project of globalization. The post-war reconstruction is driven by the same principles that underwrote the "Washington Consensus," in particular, the privatization of public services, which is entirely unsuitable for a country that has such a poorly developed public sector.[10] Moreover, Halliburton, one of the world's largest oil and gas companies, of which Cheney was

CEO from 1995–2000, has been granted contracts to resurrect Iraqi oilfields, along with other U.S. companies (including Bechtel, the Fluor Corporation, and the Louis Berger Group, which also have strong links to the present U.S. administration).

Between January 31st and March 4th, 2003, the United States Agency for International Development (USAID) issued nine procurement actions—eight Requests for Proposals (RFPs) and one Request for Applications (RFA)—for reconstruction work in war-torn Iraq in compliance with the Federal Acquisition Regulations (FAR). These included proposals for: personnel support (International Resources Group, $7.1m); seaport development (Stevedoring Services of America, $4.8m); primary and secondary education (Creative Associates International, $1m initially, up to $62.6m over 12 months);[11] local governance (Research Triangle Institute, $7.9m initially, up to $167.9m over 12 months); capital reconstruction (Bechtel, $34.6m initially, up to $680m over 18 months); with further requests for proposals in theater logistical support, public health and airport administration. All these contracts have been let to American companies linked to the present administration.

The economic and political reconstruction of Iraq is in the control of the U.S.-U.K. military partnership, and the United States has resisted a central and determining role for the U.N.

In a U.S.-led congress of Iraqi opposition forces held in London, in December 2002, "the work group on Iraq"—composed of 32 Iraqis from different political, ethnic, and religious backgrounds—prepared a paper based on four assumptions: the United States will lead a military coalition to change the regime in Iraq; the aim of the war is, not only to change the regime, but also to establish democratic rule and successful civil society; the United States and the international community commit to rebuilding state and economic institutions and the infrastructure in Iraq; the Iraqi people must be a partner with the international community in all phases of reconstruction. It also proposed a democratic political system based on the following principles: a constitutional democracy; accountability of the government and all officials; supremacy of law and respect of human rights; a federal system of government and a reduction in the centralization of power; guaranteed political representation of all Iraqis on an equal basis on all levels of government, irrespective of religion, ethnicity, or political beliefs.

Yet the export and transplant of American democracy is a project likely to fail in the sense that, it could be argued, democracy is not something that can be imposed or easily transplanted at will but requires generations of development as well as a commitment to the public sphere and public institutions to sustain it—to a local sense of identity. There are a number of factors internal to Iraq that militate against this easy imposition, including the sectarian nature of Iraqi political organizations, a long history of change through violence, the dubious nature of some of the Iraqi opposition, and weak representation of the Sunnis.[12]

While sources in the present U.S. administration point to the success of transplanting American-style democracy in Germany and Japan after WWII, the success with democracy in Russia since the collapse of the Soviet system does not augur well. There is no way that the present U.S. administration will allow an Iran-style religious government, even if the people freely elect it. The question of citizenship and democracy cannot ignore local history and local identity. For Iraq, as for other states where democracy has been imposed, the issue of culture and of local identity is paramount. A pressing question for the coming years is whether Iraq (and other Islamic states) can embrace modernity and democracy in a way that reflects its own values, culture, and sense of identity. For many if not the majority of Iraqi people, modernization does not mean Westernization, and democratization need not mean the adoption of American-style democracy.[13]

4. Globalization, Education, and Just War: The Six Tests

I began this chapter by emphasizing war as a form of globalization, especially when it is carried out in the era of empire (see Hardt and Negri 2000). I have attempted to demonstrate this in terms of the U.S.-U.K. war against Iraq and by reference to dimensions of globalization that from an empirical point of view may provide a basis for such a claim.

I also outlined a role of education in the process of coming to understand war as a form of globalization. Clearly, in the imperial project of post-war reconstruction, education also figures centrally in the battle for heart and minds.

As I write this conclusion at the end of 2003, the war against Iraq has concluded and a U.S.-U.K. effort at reconstruction has begun, with Poland and Spain being the only other powers involved in sending substantial numbers of troops to police the situation. While the "war" is over, the debate concerning its justification is not. Both in the United Kingdom and the United States, doubts are growing over the legitimacy of declaring war and, in particular, the robustness and veracity of the evidence or "intelligence" presented to the British people by Tony Blair. No weapons of mass destruction have yet been found. Now various high-ranking officials are playing down WMD, suggesting that they may never be found, even that perhaps they no longer exist. At the same time these same officials, including Rumsfeld, have suggested that the existence of WMD was never the single justification for going to war. Perhaps never before has there been such prolonged debate on the justification for war. In just war theory,[14] dating from St Thomas Aquinas,[15] there are six tests that must be satisfied[16]:

Just cause? There is no evidence of WMD yet, which was a major reason advanced by both the United States and United Kingdom. To the contrary, there was evidence that inspectors were making excellent progress and Hans Blix's own assessment indicated this. While Saddam Hussein did attack Kuwait, there has been no evidence that he was preparing to attack another state. The extent to which the United States and United Kingdom supported Iraq in weapons development during the long war between Iraq and Iran is also a historical factor worthy of note in this connection.

Legitimate authority? The U.S.-U.K. war on Iraq failed on at least two occasions over draft resolutions to secure a mandate from the United Nations Security Council, and while a draft second resolution was discussed, it was never put to the vote. This seriously impugns the case for the legitimacy of the United States and United Kingdom going to war. Other U.N. members complained that debate was stifled outside the Security Council and that huge pressure was exerted by the United States and United Kingdom and Council members to agree with the U.S.-U.K. position, but all to no avail. Historically, France indicated it would exercise its power of veto.

Right intentions? It is unclear exactly what the intentions of the United States and United Kingdom were. At the official level, both disarmament and liberation of the Iraqi people have been advanced as intentions; sometimes, in addition, wider political objectives concerning "regime change" in the Middle East have also been advanced. Disarmament may be an acceptable reason although wider political objectives are most certainly not. In relation to the criterion of right intentions, there must also be questions concerning hidden motives, especially concerning the long-term securing of Iraq's oil reserves and the achievement of American foreign policy objectives.

Likelihood of success? This is a very difficult one to make a judgment about, especially when the criteria for success are not easy to articulate. As Emerson and Tocci (2003) point out: "Winning the war, even with the stiffer than expected Iraqi resistance, is highly likely, winning the peace is much more uncertain."

Last resort? The argument concerning last resort is entirely equivocal, for as Hans Blix himself has indicated containment was working and the inspection process was yielding some results.

Proportionality? Cost estimates of mounting the war range from $95 billion to ten times that figure. The costs of reconstruction are judged to be higher, especially over the long term. How do we cost out the loss of civilian lives and destruction of infrastructure and property? What are the ecological costs? The lack of answers to these questions makes it very difficult indeed to make a judgment about proportionality.

All in all, the case looks highly dubious. This is, perhaps, why in the United Kingdom the demand for accountability together with charges of manipulation of Cabinet colleagues and the British public will not go away. Some doubt whether a case for just war (*justum bellum*) can be made at all, whether morality can or should exist in war. Michael Walzer (1977) argued that the invention of nuclear weapons altered our understanding of morality, and hence war, so much that just war theory becomes irrelevant. And yet it does not mean that war ought not be conducted within some kind of moral framework. In the era of international terrorism and the "war against terrorism," some might argue that we face a new set of conditions for war—a kind of postmodern terror in a globalized world where the normal *modern* criteria no longer apply, including the fact that war is normally construed as an activity of states against states—and that these new conditions also invalidate just war theory.

There is strong evidence emerging that the shift from the historic doctrine of containment that characterized American foreign and defense policy during the Cold War to the doctrine of "regime change" and "preemptive strike" has been accompanied in the Bush administration by a change of attitude that departs from the centuries-old discourse on just war. Ellen Meiksins Wood (2003) in *Empire of Capital* clearly documents the way in which the "war against terrorism" violates the first two criteria or principles and how the new doctrine departs from the principle of achievable goals.[17] Wood is skeptical whether the "war against terrorism" has any chance of ending terror (it may, indeed, spawn it), and she is doubtful whether military action can reorder the world in the sense outlined by Blair. Yet, even more significantly and in line with the thesis advanced in this chapter, Wood advances the argument that there is a new principle that dominates U.S. policy and contravenes both just war theory and also past American foreign and defense policy: "the new principle of war *without end*, either in purpose or in time" (Wood 2003, 149; emphasis in original). The new principle, as she documents it, was formulated by Donald Rumsfeld, Paul Wolfowitz, and Dick Cheney, with help from Richard Perle, as "Operation Infinite War"—an open war with no limits, total and infinite war (though not necessarily continuous), "indefinite in its duration, means and spatial reach" (151). Crucially, she maintains "this new ideology of war without end answers to the particular needs of the new imperialism" (151). This endless state of war is the new principle that characterizes the new imperialism we call globalization. Globalization as "surplus" imperialism does not require colonies or territories; it can control rival economies without going to war. Yet "perpetual war" is a natural concomitant and integral part of the neoliberal economic agenda, not only for the "war against terrorism" and for dealing with "rogue states," but also for sustaining the "military-research-industrial complex" and the continued militarization of communications and the aerospace industries. Perpetual war gives American enterprise a competitive edge in the global economy; it secures strategic assets, particularly nonrenewable forms like oil; it buttresses domestic rule, especially in a new "home security" environment, with emergency powers and restricted citizen rights; and, most importantly, it shapes the emerging political global system: in short, globalization as a form of war (and war as global-ization).

Acknowledgments

An early version of this paper was presented at *Global Citizenship: The Big Day,* The Global Citizenship Project, St. Andrews Build-ing, the University of Glasgow, 9 June 2003. I would like to thank, in particular, Harry Blee for the invitation and Bob Davis and Mark Olssen for helpful remarks on this paper. A version closer to this was presented under the title "Globalisation, Education and War" at the Philosophy of Education Conference, Gregynog, Univer-sity of Wales, 27–29 June 2003.

References

Bush, George W. (2002). The White House, September 17, 2002 *The National Security Strategy of the United States of America (http:// www.whitehouse.gov/nsc/nss.html).*

Chossudovsky, M. (2001). "How War and Globalization Support Ameri-can Business . . . Billions Flow to Oil and Defense Companies, Bomb-ing of Baghdad Staves Off Financial Uncertainty," February 19, 2001 (http://www.ratical.org/co-globalize/WarBiz.html).

Custers, P. (2002). "The political economy of the planned U.S. War against Iraq," Lecture held at the European Conference of People's Global Action (PGA), September 3, 2002 (http://www.nadir.org/nadir/ initiativ/agp/free/9–11/indexauthorc.htm).

Fisk, R. (2003). "This Looming War Isn't About Chemical Warheads or Human Rights: It's About Oil," *The Independent;* January 18, 2003 (http://www.nadir.org/nadir/initiativ/agp/free/iraq/ chemicalwarheads.htm).

Huntington, S. (2000). *The Clash of Civilizations and the Remaking of World Order.* New York: Simon & Schuster.

Klein, N. (2003). "Privatization in Disguise," *The Nation,* April 10, 2003 (http://www.thenation.com/doc.mhtml?i=20030428&s=klein).

Mattera, P. (2003). "Postwar Iraq: A Showcase for Privatization?" *Corpo-rate Research E-Letter EXTRA,* April 3, 2003 (http://www.corp-research.org/extra_040303.htm).

Peters, M.A. (2003). "Reconstructing the West: Compelling Visions of New World Order." Unpublished paper.

Riggs, F. (2000). "Globalization: Key Concepts," (http://www2.hawaii.edu/
~fredr/glocon.htm).

Waltzer, M. (1977). *Just and unjust wars : a moral argument with historical
illustrations.* New York: Basic Books.

Wood, E.M. (2003). *Empire of Capital.* London & New York: Verso.

Notes

1. We might also talk of the *philosophy of war* in relation to this example: how can war be defined? What are its causes? Is there a relationship between human nature and war? Is there such a thing as a just war? In what sense can we talk of responsibility for war? What acts should be deemed war crimes or crimes against humanity? What is the individual's moral and political responsibility to her fellow citizens in an unjust and illegal war? These kinds of questions achieved some prominence in the case of Iraq in the United Kingdom with the antiwar movement, the rebellion of Labour backbenchers, and the resignation of high-ranking Labour Party officials including Robin Cook and Clare Short. These questions particularly focusing on whether Tony Blair was justified in taking Britain to war—the ethics of just war—have received even more attention after the war and still remain to be satisfactorily resolved. The philosophy of war is a neglected topic in contemporary philosophy but see, for instance, the entry for "philosophy of war" and "just war theory" in the *Internet Encyclopaedia of Philosophy* (http://www.utm.edu/research/iep/w/war.htm), and the entry for "war" in *The Stanford Encyclopedia of Philosophy* (http://plato.stanford.edu/entries/war/).

2. This section draws on Peters (2003) "Deconstructing the West? Competing Vision of World Order."

3. I owe this reference to my colleague Dr. Bob Davis.

4. There is strong reason to doubt this unity and American identification with Europe given the divergences in "strategic culture" that have emerged over the Iraqi war (see Kagan 2003).

5. The full list of signatories are: Elliott Abrams, Gary Bauer, William J. Bennett, Jeb Bush, Dick Cheney, Eliot A. Cohen, Midge Decter, Paula Dobriansky, Steve Forbes, Aaron Friedberg, Francis Fukuyama, Frank Gaffney, Fred C. Ikle, Donald Kagan, Zalmay Khalilzad, I. Lewis Libby, Norman Podhoretz, Dan Quayle, Peter W. Rodman, Stephen P. Rosen, Henry S. Rowen, Donald Rumsfeld, Vin Weber, George Weigel, Paul Wolfowitz

6. See http://www.newamericancentury.org/RebuildingAmericas Defenses.pdf.

7. See, for instance, memoranda from Gary Schmitt to opinion leaders on the "IMF, Congress and American Economic Leadership" and "International criminal Court."

8. "Under General Assembly Resolution 177 (II), paragraph (a), the International Law Commission was directed to 'formulate the principles of international law recognized in the Charter of the Nuremberg Tribunal and in the judgment of the Tribunal.' In the course of the consideration of this subject, the question arose as to whether or not the Commission should ascertain to what extent the principles contained in the Charter and judgment constituted principles of international law. The conclusion was that since the Nuremberg Principles had been affirmed by the General Assembly, the task entrusted to the Commission was not to express any appreciation of these principles as principles of international law but merely to formulate them. The text below was adopted by the Commission at its second session. The Report of the Commission also contains commentaries on the principles (see *Yearbook of the International Law Commission*, 1950, Vol. II, pp. 374–378)" (taken from the Introductory Note).

9. The Washington Consensus is often referred to by the term *neoliberal* to refer to a set of policies driven by fiscal discipline, reordering of public expenditure, tax reform, liberalising interest rates, exchange rate mechanism, trade liberalisation, liberalisation of foreign direct investment, privatisation, deregulation, and property rights (Willliamson's description). I combine the term with "neoconservative" in this context because I want to emphasise the way in which the White House and American foreign policy have been captured by a group of neoconservatives including Paul Wolfowitz, Steve Cambone, Doug Feith, Scooter Libby, John Bolton, and Richard Perle, who are backed by Dick Cheney. It is important to see this second generation of neoconservatives as different both from first generation epitomised by Irving Kristol, who emerged as critics of the liberal establishment, and traditional conservatives such as Rumsfeld and Cheney.

10. See Moses Naim's "Fads and Fashion in Economic reforms: Washington Consensus or Washington Confusion?" at (http://www.imf.org/external/pubs/ft/seminar/1999/reforms/Naim.htm) and John Williamson's "What should the World Bank Think About the Washington Consensus?" available at (http://www.worldbank.org/research/journals/wbro/obsaug00/pdf/(6)Williamson.pdf) and "Did the Washington Consensus Fail?" at http://www.iie.com/publications/papers/williamson1102.htm.

11. The U.S. Agency for International Development (USAID) today announced an initial $1 million, 12–month contract granted to Creative

Associates International (CAII) "to address immediate educational needs and promote participation of the Iraqi people in a sustainable, decentralized educational system." CAII is an international consulting firm with its headquarters in Washington, D.C., and it will implement a USAID education assistance program, "Revitalization of Iraqi Schools and Stabilization of Education" (RISE). The program is said to be "a rapid response effort to increase enrollment and improve the quality of primary and secondary education through short-term immediate impact activities that will lay the foundation for more sustainable reform." The contract includes "development of baseline indicators to measure educational progress, and procuring and distributing essential school materials, equipment, and supplies." And UNAID reports, "Child-centered, participatory teaching methods will be introduced to lay the foundations for democratic practices and attitudes among students, parents and teachers" including the production of textbooks on certain school subjects (see: http://www.usaid.gov/press/releases/2003/pr030411_2.html).

12. See Ibrahim Nawar's "The Political and Institutional Reconstruction of Iraq" at http://www.siyassa.org.eg/esiyassa/ahram/2003/4/1/FILE6.HTM.

13. The United States announced recently that postwar Iraq will be divided into three parts that will come under British, Polish, and United States command, with six European countries among the 10 nations contributing troops for the "international stability force." Already reconstruction has experienced difficulties: the UN's position has been sidelined and indeed, Richard Perle has predicted its downfall; Paul Bremer has replaced Jay Garner; and Shia-led political groups have attempted to shore up power, especially in Baghdad.

14. For Just War Theory see http://www.utm.edu/research/iep/j/justwar.htm.

15. See Aquinas, "Of War," *The Summa Theologica,* (http://ethics.acusd.edu/Books/Texts/Aquinas/JustWar.html).

16. I based my account on Emerson and Tocci in "The Rubik Cube of the Wider Middle East" (http://www.ceps.be/Commentary/Apr03/EmersonTocci.php).

17. For a conventional account of just war theory considered in relation to U.S. air strikes against Iraq in 1996, see Mark Edward DeForest's article (http://law.gonzaga.edu/borders/documents/deforres.htm).

Postscript

Human Costs and the Moral Aftermath

Michael A. Peters

Events since completing this collection of essays have not invali-
dated its working premises or its joint analysis and conclusions.
If anything the combined stance, for all its differences, have been
now vindicated by subsequent events after this book went into
production in early July, 2004. First, the U.S. made an early
handover of power two days before the June 30 deadline to an
interim Iraqi government headed by Iyad Allawi. The Iraqi Governing Council, chosen by the U.S. administration in Iraq, is comprised of twenty-five people allegedly representing the country's
diverse religious and ethnic groupings, including Sunni, Turkmen,
Kurd and Shia elements. Saddam Hussein appeared before an
Iraqi judge to hear the list of charges against him, including war
crimes and genocide, although it will be some time before Saddam
finally comes to trial. He refused to sign court documents and he
has denied the legitimacy of the court's jurisdiction over him.

L. Paul Bremer, who has overseen the Coalition Provisional Authority and appointed the Governing Council, scooted out of Iraq even before the new U.S. ambassador John Negroponte presented his credentials. It remains to be seen how the handover and new interim government will fare and whether genuine sovereignty can be achieved. Already since Iraq regained sovereignty the governor of Mosul has been assassinated and there has been a massive attack in Baghdad killing and wounding dozens of people. Local resistance has not diminished and many critics question the restoration of 'sovereignty' especially in view of the new emergency powers the interim government has immediately given itself to cope with increasing insurgency and the threat to security.

There has been strong criticism of the way in which the Bush administration handed over power and its motivations for doing so, especially given Bush's unilateral stance in going to war and his lowest personal rating in the polls since the war began. The Bush administration tried to bully members of the U.N. to get its endorsement for the war and build a world coalition. Having failed in both endeavours the U.S. was determined to wage war on its own, if need be. Now, some critics argue, with mounting costs of the war and the prospect of an electoral defeat over the war, Bush sought to hand over power quickly and with the backing of the U.N. Naturally, the U.S.'s European allies have not been impressed and President Chirac, in particular, has put pressure on the U.S. demand for NATO to train Iraqi forces.

Meanwhile, at home both Bush and Blair and their national intelligence agencies have been consistently under public scrutiny and pressure for flawed, false and unsupported information that was the basis for going to war in the first place. The U.S. senate intelligence committee report was scathing about the basis of false and overstated intelligence, clearly stating that Congress would not have authorized that war if they knew what they know now. On both sides of the Atlantic the intelligence community mischaracterized and exaggerated the intelligence on Iraq's weapons of mass destruction capabilities indicating at the very least deep failure of a culture of group-think, too intimately associated with politics and with ruling ideologies. The suspicion is that the 'selling' of the Iraq war has subverted democratic processes and intelligence has been manipulated to effect decisions in foreign policy taken purely on ideological grounds. The startling fact is that no weapons of mass destruction have been found and investigations after the invasion provide no indication that Saddam had a nuclear weapons program or biological weapons. Phoney intelligence reveals the way also in which joint intelligence between the U.S. and the U.K. was responsible for rationalizing going to war against Saddam Hussein. In Britain, the Butler report (after Lord Butler) reveals a litany of failure and systemic problems, including gross omissions, inaccuracies and a too-intimate relationship between intelligence agencies and the government that did not permit necessary reality-checks. The intelligence available was "insufficiently robust" to prove Iraq was in breach of the United Nations' resolutions; a statement which questions the legality of the war. Strangely, the report does not hold anyone responsible and indeed, it specifically indicates that John Scarlet, the head of the Joint Intelligence Committee in the run up to the Iraq war, should not resign. There are early signs at the time of writing (mid July, 2004) that these intelligence failures will recoil on the re-election chances of both Bush and Blair.

In terms of the mounting costs of the Iraq war, a new report by the Institute for Policy Studies and Foreign Policy in Focus, *Paying the Price: The Mounting Costs of the Iraq War*[1] indicate human costs to the U.S. of 952 deaths of coalition forces (not counting deaths of contractors and journalists), growing terrorist recruitment and action (al-Qaeda's membership is now estimated at 18,000), low U.S. credibility and low troop morale. Economic costs have soared at over $151 billion approved by Congress for 2004 alone, not counting the increase in petrol prices, the economic impacts on military families and the social opportunity costs. Most importantly, the human costs to Iraq have been staggering: as of June 16 between 9,436 and 11,317 Iraqi civilians have been killed as a result of the U.S. invasion and ensuing occupation, while an estimated 40,000 Iraqis have been injured. The rising security costs of crime, including murder, rape and kidnapping, have skyrocketed. The economic costs in terms of unemployment, corporate war profiteering, Iraq's oil economy, the health and education

---

1. The Full report is available at http://www.ips-dc.org/iraq/costsofwar/costsofwar.pdf

infrastructure, environmental, security and sovereignty are almost beyond calculation. The report also details "costs to the world": human costs; costs in terms of international law and the violation of the U.N. Charter; damage to the legitimacy and credibility of the U.N. and its capacity to act as a world institution promoting global disarmament and conflict resolution; damage to world coalitions, to the global economy, to global security; and, above all, the damage to human rights, especially the U.S. Justice Department's reassurance to the White House that torture was legal and the mistreatment of Iraqi prisoners.

It is clear that the costs of the war—its human, economic, environment and social costs—all pale before the moral costs to the U.S. and the U.K., and to its perceived loss of world moral leadership and legitimacy not only in the eyes of the Iraqi people and other people of the world but also its own citizens, who as a consequence have experienced a loss of faith in its own institutions and values.

Glasgow, Scotland
15 July, 2004.

Index

multiculturalism, 7; and citizenship education, 86–88; and computers, 55; and cosmopolitanism, 47, 52, 163–165; and democracy, 163–167; and nationalism, 82
multiple literacies, 53–54, 59–61. *See also* literacy

NAFTA, 38, 125, 151
Napoleon Bonaparte, 215, 216
National Academy of Sciences, 212
nationalism, 73, 80–84
National Security Strategy, 24, 90–91, 246–247
NATO, 125, 156
Nazism, 4, 43–44, 83, 223
Negri, A., 36–37, 46–47, 63n5, 84, 88–89, 92, 93, 207
neoliberalism, 42–43, 61; and free trade, 26n7, 153–154; and third way, 146–150; and war, 246–251
Neumann, John von, 216
New Citizenship Project, 248
New Economics Foundation, 147–148
New Labour Party, 147–148, 171n3
New Local Government Network, 148
New Zealand, 245
NGOs. *See* non-governmental organizations
Nietzsche, Friedrich, 127, 165; and death of God, 207; and Foucault, 113, 172n16
Noble, D., 225–226
Noddings, Nel, 158–159
non-governmental organizations (NGOs), 37, 89, 92, 98, 125
"normcentricity," 158
Norquist, Grover, 189
North American Free Trade Agreement (NAFTA), 38, 125, 151
North Atlantic Treaty Organization (NATO), 125, 156
Nozick, R., 168
nuclear weapons, 138, 210–211, 249, 253
Nuremberg Principles, 249, 256n8
Nussbaum, Martha, 72, 84–88, 167, 172n16

Ohmae, Kenichi, 150
Olssen, Mark, 22, 145–171
Omar, Mullah, 12
Operation Enduring Freedom, 10–13. *See also* Iraq war
Organization for Economic Cooperation and Development (OECD), 151

Pakistan, 16, 45, 136
Palestine, 16, 26n8, 44–45, 93, 138
parrhesia, 22, 116–120, 169–170
patriarchalism, 21–22, 47, 99–101, 104–106
Patriot Act. *See* USA Patriot Act
patriotism, 185; moral panics and, 188; and tolerance, 52; and totalitarianism, 181–182
Peace Corps, 10
pedagogy, 202; for communication technologies, 50–52, 125–126, 133–139; critical, 50–51; for globalization, 122–126; for postmodernity, 60–61, 121
Perceptive Assistant that Learns (PAL), 228–229
Perle, Richard, 193, 254, 257n13
permanent war, 23, 179–181, 191–196, 213, 254–255
Peters, Michael A., 1–24, 36, 127, 146, 239–255
Petrarch, Francesco, 75
Pettit, Philip, 171
Pick, D., 222
Pilger, Zoe, 127
Plamenatz, J., 161
Planck, Max, 216
Plato, 21, 115, 119
Polanyi, Karl, 149
police brutality, 184
Popper, Karl, 158, 159, 161
pornography, 1–2, 56–57, 60, 84
Positivism, 4–5
postmodernity, 54, 64n10, 126; pedagogy for, 60–61, 121; and terrorism, 8–10. *See also* modernity
poststructuralism, 37

About the Contributors

Tina Besley, research fellow in the Department of Educational Studies at the University of Glasgow, UK, is a New Zealander with degrees in counseling and education and has been a secondary-school teacher, a LifeLine counselor, and a school counselor. Her research interests include youth issues, particularly notions of self and identity and contemporary problems; school counseling; educational policy; educational philosophy; and the work of Michel Foucault and poststructuralism. In 2002, she published *Counseling Youth: Foucault, Power and the Ethics of Subjectivity* (Praeger).

Cliff Falk holds a PhD in curriculum theory and implementation from Simon Fraser University, Burnaby, Canada. His academic work concerns the interrelationships among subjectivity, technology, capitalism, war, the state, and education.

Henry A. Giroux holds the Global Television Network Chair in Communications at McMaster University, Canada. His most recent books include *Breaking into the Movies: Film and the Culture of Politics* (Basil Blackwell, 2002), *Public Spaces/Private Lives: Democracy Beyond 9/11*(Rowman and Littlefield, 2002), and *The Abandoned Generation: Democracy Beyond the Culture of Fear* (Palgrave 2003); his forthcoming books include *The Terror of Neoliberalism* (Paradigm) and, co-authored with Susan Searls Giroux, *Take Back Higher Education: Race, Youth, and the Crisis of Democracy in the Post–Civil Rights Era* (Palgrave). His primary research areas are cultural studies, youth studies, critical pedagogy, popular culture, social theory, and the politics of higher education.

Rhonda Hammer is a research scholar with the UCLA Center for the Study of Women and a lecturer at UCLA in women's studies, communications, and education. She is co-author of *Rethinking Media Literacy,* and her book *Anti-Feminism and Family Terrorism: A Critical Feminist Perspective* was published in 2003 by Rowman and Littlefield.

Douglas Kellner holds the George Kneller Chair in the Philosophy of Education at UCLA and is author of many books on social theory, politics, history, and culture, including *Camera Politica: The Politics and Ideology of Contemporary Hollywood Film,* co-authored with Michael Ryan; *Critical Theory, Marxism, and Modernity; Jean Baudrillard: From Marxism to Postmodernism and Beyond; Postmodern Theory: Critical Interrogations,* co-authored with Steven Best; *Television and the Crisis of Democracy; The Persian Gulf TV War; Media Culture;* and *The Postmodern Turn,* co-authored with Steven Best. Recent books include a study of the 2000 U.S. presidential election, *Grand Theft 2000: Media Spectacle and the Theft of an Election,* and *The Postmodern Adventure. Science, Technology, and Cultural Studies at the Third Millennium,* co-authored with Steven Best. He has just published two books: *Media Spectacle* and *From 9/11 to Terror War: The Dangers of the Bush Legacy.*

Mark Olssen is reader and director of doctoral programs in educational studies at the University of Surrey, UK. His recent books include *Michel Foucault: Materialism and Education, Critical Theory and the Human Condition,* coauthored with Michael Peters and Colin Lankshear; *Futures of Critical Theory: Dreams of Difference,* also co-authored with Michael Peters and Colin Lankshear; and *Educational Policy: Globalization, Citizenship, Democracy,* co-authored with John Codd and Anne-Marie O'Neill. His areas of research interest include general and higher-education policy and political philosophy and education.

Michael A. Peters is research professor of education at the University of Glasgow and holds posts as adjunct professor of education at the University of Auckland and adjunct professor of communication studies at the Auckland University of Technology, NZ. He is co-director of the (online) doctoral programme in Education at the University of Glasgow. He is executive editor of *Educa-*

tional Philosophy and Theory (Blackwell) and co-editor of two in-ternational online-only journals, *Policy Futures in Education* and *E-Learning* (Triangle). He has research interests in educational theory and policy as well as in contemporary philosophy. He has published more than twenty books and edited collections in these fields, including *Critical Theory and the Human Condition* (2003); *Futures of Critical Theory* (2003); *Poststructuralism, Marxism and Neoliberalism: Between Theory and Politics* (2001); *Nietzsche's Legacy for Education: Past and Present Values* (2001); *Wittgenstein: Philoso-phy, Postmodernism, Pedagogy* (1999), co-edited with James Marshall; and *Poststructuralism, Politics and Education* (1996).

Tom Steele is senior honorary fellow at the University of Glasgow (formerly reader in adult education) and previously (in 1973–1987) was WEA organising tutor for Leeds (Swarthmore) and lecturer in adult education at the University of Leeds. His previous books include *Alfred Orage and the Leeds Arts Club,* Scholar Press (1990); *The Emergence of Cultural Studies,* Lawrence and Wishart (1997); and, co-authored with Richard Taylor and Jean Barr, *For a Radical Higher Education, After Postmodernism,* Open University/SRHE Press (2002). He is currently working on a major study of public educators and popular social movements in Europe, 1850–1940.

Richard Taylor has worked at the University of Leeds, for many years. He has been head of the School of Continuing (Adult) Edu-cation and, more recently, dean of the Faculty of Business, Law, Education and Social Studies. He has long been involved in com-munity and workers' education and in development of adult learn-ing with ethnic minority groups. He was secretary of the Univer-sities Association for Continuing Education (UACE) in the 1990s and is currently chair of the National Institute of Adult Continu-ing Education (NIACE). His doctoral study was on the British Peace Movement, and in 1988 he published a book on this theme: *Against the Bomb: The British Peace Movement 1958–1965* (Oxford University Press). He has published a total of twelve books, the most recent being (with David Watson) *Lifelong Learning and the University: A Post Dearing Agenda,* co-authored with David Watson (Falmer Press), and *For a Radical Higher Education: After Postmodernism,* co-authored with Jean Barr and Tom Steele (Open University Press and SRHE).